COASTAL COMMAND PILOT

Third Edition published 2001

First published in 1994 by
WOODFIELD PUBLISHING
Woodfield House, Babsham Lane,
Bognor Regis, West Sussex PO215EL England.

A catalogue record of this book
is available from the British Library

ISBN 1 873203 26 8

Printed and bound in Great Britain

COASTAL COMMAND PILOT

1939 – 1945

TED RAYNER

Woodfield Publishing

~WEST SUSSEX • ENGLAND ~

For Johnnie Lane & Harry Ramsey and their crews
lost without trace flying from Greenland
in an attempt to provide air escort to
an Atlantic convoy, 1st March, 1943

CONTENTS

ACKNOWLEDGEMENTS

I acknowledge with gratitude the assistance given by the following in the compilation of this book: **MRS IRENE BACON** for permission to use the poster 'England Expects' designed by her late husband Cecil Bacon; **WILLIAM BERGE**, of Kristinsand, Norway, for his account of 220 Squadron's action on the day Norway was invaded, 9th April 1940; **LT CDR DAVID HOWARTH, R.N.V.R.,** for the extract from his book "The Shetland Bus" (Thos Nelson & Sons) concerning the Alesund raid on 29th October 1941; **JACK ("HENRY") HALL** for his account of being shot down by German flak on 23rd December 1941, and of his long journey to Prisoner of War camp; **AIR CHIEF MARSHAL SIR DEREK HODGKINSON, KCB CBE DFC AFC,** for his account of being shot down by night-fighter after bombing Bremen in 'Millennium II' on 25th June 1942; **DENIS RICHARDS and HILARY ST G. SAUNDERS** for extracts from their books "Royal Air Force 1939-45", Vols I-III (H.M.S.O.); **THE PUBLIC RECORD OFFICE, KEW,** for Crown Copyright extracts from files – 220 Squadron Operational Record Book (AIR 27/1366); 269 Squadron Operational Record Book (AIR 27/1565); and Coastal Command file AIR 15, with permission of the Controller, H.M. Stationery Office; **LOCKHEED AIRCRAFT CORPORATION** for Hudson aircraft development details and photograph; **THE AIR MINISTRY** for references to war-time Air Publications A.P. 1525A and 1690E – Pilot's Notes – and photographs of cockpit layouts; **IMPERIAL WAR MUSEUM, LONDON,** for 'still' photographs taken from the film "Coastal Command"; **DAVID BROWN**, Author of 'Thornaby Aerodrome & Wartime Memories' for photographs 'Reconnaissance of Sylt', 'Luftwaffe map of Thornaby', 'Tees-side Landmarks', and 'Christmas 1940 Menu'; **ROYAL AIR FORCE MUSEUM, HENDON,** for Hudson cockpit information. **FLT LIEUTENANT BERNARD DORRINGTON**, RAF(Ret'd), who used his 35 years as RAF pilot on many types and many places to ensure that, in proof-reading, "not a phrase, quotation, route, station, footpath, town, village, aircraft type, flying routine, was passed without it being soundly researched"; **AND NOT LEAST MY WIFE**, for her certainty that someone will buy the book.

FOREWORD

Air Chief Marshal Sir Derek Hodgkinson
KCB, CBE, DFC, AFC, *(Retd).*

TED RAYNER captures well the spirit of the thousands of young men who joined the Royal Air Force as Volunteer Reservists at the outbreak of the 1939–45 war. I must admit that as a Regular I was a bit apprehensive at their advent, but they settled down to Service life remarkably quickly and played their part in front line squadrons so gallantly that we were soon filled with admiration and respect. Certainly, in No. 220 Squadron, where Rayner and I were together, they pulled more than their weight and became an invaluable part of the Unit.

Operating the Hudson, a converted airliner, at long range under the noses of the Luftwaffe fighter bases in Denmark and Norway was quite often a daunting experience. The aircraft was no match for the ME109 and ME110 which it came up against, and many were shot down. Nevertheless, morale was high and the Squadrons gave a good account of themselves and caused the enemy considerable damage.

Operating from Iceland and Greenland was no joke either, due to the atrocious weather conditions the crews had to contend with on most of their patrols. It says a lot for their training and their guts that they managed so well.

The story of all this, and much else, is well told in this book with perception and humour. I recommend it, not only to those who took part in these or similar operations, but to all who might be interested in the part the Royal Air Force played in a largely unsung and forgotten aspect of the 1939-45 war.

England expects

NATIONAL SERVICE

CHAPTER 1

NOT ONE OF THE FEW....
BUT ONE OF THE SEVERAL....
BEFORE THE MANY

The Manchester Ship Canal, seen from the air, is a landmark no one can miss. Even from an aircraft flying upside down, there is no doubt that the wide, clearly-defined channel was made by man to be traversed by ocean-going vessels. It was a waterway of great importance to the city and its hinterland, and by 1939, as for several years before, Manchester Liners were operating ships of up to 10,000 tons.

During the afternoon of Sunday, 29th July 1939, a casual observer would have noticed such a vessel making its slow and stately way outward bound, a wisp of smoke drifting upwards from its broad funnel towards the low clouds which encircled small pockets of sunshine. Caught in one of these, directly over the ship, was an inverted aircraft, held as if by an invisible thread from above, like an angler's bait through a hole in the ice.

It was my first flight in a Tiger Moth.

In May of that fateful year, in response to the ever-encroaching demands of Nazi Germany, the British Government had introduced conscription for 18-year-old youths. Even more shattering to the inhabitants of the small town in which I had grown up, nestling in the valleys of Rossendale in Lancashire, had been the consequences of Prime Minister Chamberlain's return from Munich on 30th September 1938, holding the paper which he claimed would "ensure peace for our time". His opinion of those with whom he had been negotiating was revealed by the engineer on the flight, who said that on the way out they carried a hamper of food prepared by the Savoy Hotel. It was restocked by a Munich hotel for the return flight. The Prime Minister asked where the food was from, and when he was told he said it would give him great satisfaction if the food remained untouched. It was digestive biscuits all the way home.

The impact of those anxious days had been that the green sward of the small park in front of the Parish Church had been dug up to make Air Raid Shelters: the well-patronised garden seats put aside, the turves used as protective cover for the damp, dark trenches below. The events of the intervening winter emphasized the fact that peace was transient, war was likely, and young men would be leaving.

Being just 19 at the time, I was a certain candidate. A career with Martins Bank was unfolding and I had just taken Part One of the Institute of Bankers' Exam, which did little to persuade me that I was in the right job. My voluntary reading matter during the previous 'formative' years had progressed from the flying adventures of 'Biggles' to a well-balanced mixture of 'Men Only', 'The Aeroplane' and 'Flight'. Occasionally, as an acknowledgement of a possible future need, I attempted a cursory dip into the financial pages of 'The Manchester Guardian'. Evidence enough that flying would have been preferred as a career had it been a matter of choice; however, peacetime family circumstances decreed instead that it was a matter of obligation.

Sounds and sights of war – on radio and cinema screen, and the changing political map of Europe brought about by alien military might, made the acceptance of conscription a matter of relief rather than regret. The poster designed by Cecil Bacon for the Ministry of Labour provided suitable exhortation. To a background of Britannia with a Union Jack shield, and silhouettes of battleships on the horizon, the clarion call of 'England Expects' was displayed in large letters at the top, with groups of uniformed figures in front, representing all the Services into which the men and women would be called. Agree with it or not, the nation felt that this was a positive reminder to aggressors. In millions of homes, however, it was a reminder of an early departure and a very different life for son, brother, grandson, nephew.

I was in that Tiger Moth upside down over the Manchester Ship Canal because of the introduction of conscription. Now that a lengthy absence from home had become unavoidable, it had been agreed that I should apply to join the RAF Volunteer Reserve as a pilot. This was a scheme based upon RAFVR 'Town Centres' in cities such as London, Manchester, Newcastle etc., where lectures and ground instruction would be given, with an associated nearby airfield for flying training. Evenings at the Town Centres, weekends at the airfield, and a commitment to a fortnight's continuous training.

Acceptance depended upon passing a written test and a stringent medical examination. I was less concerned about the latter than the former. I lived halfway up a steep hill and we used to make a pastime of running up alongside the local 'bus. Some of the drivers seemed to enjoy showing their distaste of these antics; perhaps speed was limited by the surface of the road – even in the late 1930s only the middle was of tarmac, and about a yard of each outer side was of compacted stones to provide a better foothold for the diminishing horse-drawn traffic. There was a 'bus stop halfway up the hill, when, for anything longer than a sharp halt, the conductor would dismount to place a chock under each rear wheel. This was where we caught our breath. Later, we matched the improved performance of the 'buses by following them up the hill on bicycles.

There was the benefit of our home-made gymnasium – four of us had lain concrete on the earthen floor of the arched cellar and whitewashed the rough stone walls. We set bolts in the concrete to take the base of the punch-ball, one of only two pieces of fixed equipment we could afford. The other was a horizontal bar suspended from the ceiling. When we read of the organised fitness programme of the Hitler Youth, it seemed we were merely dabbling. In that June of 1939, however, my chosen form of Service seemed eminently attainable; even the mile-long walk to the train after seeing my girlfriend home became a training opportunity, and being obliged as a junior bank-clerk to take my holiday at a time of the manager's choosing fitted my grand strategy.

My holiday was to be the first week in June, and my RAF medical had been arranged for the middle of the month. To Jersey I would go, returning fit as a fiddle after early morning runs along the beach at Portelet Bay, amid other Spartan activities. My return would encompass my first experience of flying – to Southampton in a de Havilland Rapide Air Liner. So, on a beautifully clear day, speeding over the sea at about 4,000 feet, my belief that I too could be an aviator was amply confirmed. I felt at one with the aircraft.

That was not how I felt upside down in a Tiger Moth a month later.

The RAFVR Town Centre in Manchester was in a rather ugly commercial building near the city centre. My home was twenty miles to the north, on a LMS railway branch line from Manchester Victoria station. There was an hourly service, so the problem was not in getting to the VR Town Centre, but in getting to Barton aerodrome, about six miles to the west. Obvious answer: a motor car. If I could add to my meagre finances the savings which had accrued over the years from gift and thrift, and which had been cared for on my behalf, I would have enough to buy one. There could be no carefree credit for a bank clerk on £70 per annum.

Funding requests approved, I became the proud owner of a presentable 1937 Morris 8 saloon, BTD 686, and gladly accepted the offer of driving lessons from the chauffeur to a doctor whose practice was near the bank, and as my tutor lived a little further up the hill from my home, for a couple of months we travelled to work by car instead of by 'bus. The Driving Test Examiner was a lady, and in the course of conversation I was encouraged to explain my good fortune in becoming a youthful car owner. She revealed that she was the widow of an RAF pilot, and after pointing out a few minor driving transgressions, she told me I had passed, and added with a smile: "Be careful in the air as well as on the roads. Good luck!" As I watched her walk across the market square to her own car, I vaguely felt the implications of her parting message. It became clear in its wartime context: There are old pilots and there are bold pilots, but few old bold pilots.

About twenty sports jacket-and-flannelled young men were at the first Town Centre lecture I attended in July, 1939. Throughout the brief period until mobilisation six weeks later, the instructors had our sympathy, which could be seen in the genial, light-hearted response to a chaotic situation. They had been given a syllabus to follow on the assumption that the classes would be sufficiently homogeneous in educational attainment, attitude and social background, to enable them to be treated as in the Service proper. In fact, there were some whose working day meant they arrived in the middle of a lecture; some who had to miss several sessions; others dependent on public transport who had to leave early. It was soon obvious that there was a possibility of failure for some who were finding the application of Maths and Physics even more difficult than I was. Yet, in the underlying turmoil, the staff responded to the fact that, disparate though we may be, here was a rapidly increasing group of young men eager to fly as part of the RAF, and in that way to carry out the National Service required of them.

It was during the break of an unusual Saturday afternoon lecture that a fellow novice, Simon, and I crossed the street to a small tea-shop round the corner. We had just ordered when a very attractive blonde girl entered, and took a seat at a table next but one to ours. In the middle of a sentence intended as a preference for Austin cars rather than Morris, he stopped and gaped. Our tea-tray came, I poured, but he was unaware of it. Her tea-tray arrived, she poured, and Simon was very much aware of it. The magazine she had been reading dropped to the floor.

In a flash, he was up, hand already outstretched, but in moving across his foot caught against the leg of the intervening chair, and he arrived with a crash on the young lady's table. Both hands had gone out to parry his arrival, one of which caught the saucer containing the teacup, and this contrived a merry somersault on its way to the floor, shedding its contents meanwhile on the open pages of the magazine. Simon stood aghast, looking from the young lady to the sponge-like quality of the pages, which he then picked up and shook, as if a terrier with a rabbit. The slight sprinkling which the locality received cooled any hint of a charitable acceptance of this performance, but seemed to make him realise there was only one thing to do.

"I'm terribly sorry," he mumbled, "I'll get another copy for you!" and he escaped from the shop, taking the dripping magazine with him.

As he disappeared, a faint smile played about the lips of the charming young lady, and with the aid of a dip in her handbag, she resumed her composure. The fracas had fortunately left her untouched, and as a replacement tea-tray arrived, our eyes met. I raised my eyebrows in a quizzical grimace; she responded with the mere suggestion of a smile and a shake of the head. We then both looked down and laughed, as the waitress mopped up the remains of the spilt tea, most of which had gone out of the door with Simon and the magazine.

He returned, panting, but holding aloft his prize. He considered that this gave him the right to take his chair from our table to hers, and sit upon it whilst laying the magazine before her, caressing its cover with his hand. Apologies again, then seeing an opportunity for advancement:

"I really would like to make this up to you. How about...."

"But you certainly have done!" she intervened, "Look, you've bought me this month's issue! The one I had was last month's!"

Whilst he was looking at the cover, dumbfounded, I suddenly realised it was time to reassemble for the concluding part of the lecture. I went across and tapped him on the shoulder, and, as I was almost as speechless as he was, but for a very different reason, I pointed to the door. As I was leaving, I vaguely heard his parting conversation, and, clear as a sweet-sounding bell, her lilting reply:

"That's all right, I have time to kill. I shall be here for some time yet."

At the end of the lecture, after a restless half-hour for Simon, he was up and away before others had closed their notebooks. By a series of whispered instructions I had been requested, nay ordered, also to leave in haste to bring my Morris 8 to the door of the tearooms. This I almost achieved, but was thwarted by a red M.G. coming round a corner from behind the Town Centre to cut across in front of me. It drew up precisely in front of the shop door. Intent on claiming at least second place and not yet accustomed to small-space parking, when next I looked at the M.G. it was empty. The door of the tea-shop was opening, and out stepped the young lady, followed by our lecturer. Chatting merrily together, they boarded the M.G. We were parked bonnet to bonnet, and as they pulled out to drive off, charming as ever she gave me a wave of the hand. Then Simon emerged.

"There's always tomorrow," I said. I don't think he heard.

Our tomorrow became my first visit to Barton aerodrome. The previous weekend had been one of incessant rain and low cloud, but the blue skies of this one held the promise of a first flight in a Tiger Moth. Driving through the north-west suburbs of Manchester I was surprised when, quite abruptly, the buildings merged into a smaller-than-expected grass field dotted with the odd hangar and workshop, and a few wooden buildings. And of course, a wind-sock just past the entrance, with its twin across the field. Then came Chat Moss and George Stephenson's line from Manchester to Liverpool – the world's first passenger railway. Four or five yellow-hued Tiger Moths fluttered around joyously in the air, or settled on the ground, as if they relished the name and took it to heart. Or so it seemed, in my expectancy, for I had come here to join them.

As I approached a group of similar hopefuls sitting on the ground in front of the Control Tower, one of them, sensing a newcomer, jabbed a finger in the direction of the open door in the side of the building. I entered, and was greeted by a sergeant who asked for my name and number.

"Rayner 754466" I replied with some pride on this, the first occasion on which I had given official verbal expression to actually belonging.

Pride, however, usually comes before a fall.

"We'll fit you in today if we can," he said without conviction.

I joined the others sitting, lying, or sleeping on the grass outside. It was apparent from the conversation that one or two had flown as much as three hours, a few had been up once, and several were waiting for a first flight as I was. We were unsure about the number of aircraft and instructors available, but whatever the number it was apparent that it was inadequate. However, the time spent sitting around wasn't completely wasted – one might almost call it familiarisation time, fraternally and tutorially, discussing the basic elements of flying and the pearls of wisdom from those who had actually left the ground.

Lunchtime came – some had brought sandwiches to make sure they would be readily available should there be a chance to fly – and the small clubroom filled with a jostling crowd. Basically, the 'Mess' was a wooden hut, manfully exploited, heaving with VR types at the weekend but recovering in fitful occupation during the rest of the week. We were vaguely aware of the existence of a flying club, but were left in no doubt that the airfield was shared by a group known as the Civil Air Guard, flying small blue monoplanes from the other side of the field.

"They're Swallows using Pobjoy Niagaras" someone said, which was ambiguous to me as I didn't know which referred to the aircraft and which to the engine. I checked and found some irony in the fact that the company producing the Swallow owned the manufacturing rights for the German Klemm monoplane, and a Mr Hordern had flown the British Klemm Swallow's maiden flight.

The report of it in "The Aeroplane" stated that 'he had persuaded the machine to fly so slowly that it was overtaken by a galloping horse. In his hands the BK

Swallow seemed like a well-behaved bird. It flew fast or crawled and landed with a lightness and precision of which any bird would be proud.'

None of the pilots flying them at Barton seemed to have Mr Hordern's attributes, and as they were said to dislike military flying but hoped to be useful in other ways if the clouds of war had no silver lining, they remained distant participants.

Afternoon faded into evening, and for most of us our hopes of flying that day declined with the setting sun.

The following Sunday, the morning yielded nothing more than similar frustration. Admittedly, there were one or two meaningful interludes: a visit to the parachute packing section; an explanation of the symbols in the square in front of the Control Tower which had to be checked from the air before landing an aircraft; and even a change in luncheon menu in the Mess.

It was approaching four o'clock when Mr Hill, one of the instructors, passed by the small group to which I had attached myself, just as I was adding a few choice words to a dialogue expressing our mutual frustration and boredom. He stopped, turned, looked at me and said:

"What's your name, son?" – this seemed quite incongruous, as he was about fifteen inches shorter and didn't appear to be much older.

I replied, casting a glance around in what I hoped was an inference that I had merely voiced a common theme.

"Well, Rayner, you may think of yourself as today's Mick Mannock, darting off to live your life in the heavens instead of being glad to be on terra firma, but you'll find there's a lot of waiting to be done, whether you're in the air or on the ground. Come with me!" – and he walked off towards the Control Tower.

I followed, but not before I had received one or two knowing, perhaps sympathetic, glances from the others. At the door the instructor called over his shoulder "Get yourself a parachute and a helmet and wait by Tiger A for 'orses." Is he in a joking mood, I thought, and am I actually going to fly? As I walked across to the aircraft with the parachute slung across my back, my helmet swinging in the other hand, I gave a nonchalant but slightly superior wave to the disbelieving onlookers.

He came out, followed by a mechanic, whose job it was to swing the propeller in the engine-starting procedure.

"You get in the rear cockpit, plug in your intercom down there and put the safety-straps on," and he closed the small flap on the side of the fuselage which in the down position allowed a little more room when squeezing into the small open cockpit. I could just see his head as he settled himself into the front seat, then as I looked around this new environment of dials, joystick and rudder pedals, I heard the mechanic call:

"Petrol on, switches off, throttle closed, suck in", which my pilot repeated. The mechanic turned the propeller by hand a few times,

"Petrol on, switches on, throttle closed, contact!" – another swing and the engine fired enthusiastically. I saw the instruments fluctuate with equal enthusiasm, and when they had settled down I noticed the throttle control slide forward, and heard the engine respond. We couldn't be taking off from here! No, be rational in your excitement, just testing the engine at full power. As the revs dropped came the call and response "Chocks away!" and we moved forward, to taxi bumpily to the edge of the airfield, coming to a halt across the line of flight for take-offs and landings. I watched the helmeted head in front lean forward for the final check, then sweep from side to side to make sure it was clear for take-off.

We turned into wind, the engine reached a smooth crescendo and with a caressing bounce or two we were up, up, up! Hardly had the buildings below diminished to the size of a town model before, in a turn to the left, the upper wing seemed to be brushing the clouds. Here and there, shafts of sunlight pierced the grey expanse, and in one of these I could see a large ship in a glistening stretch of water. The Manchester Ship Canal!

Mr Hill spoke not a word, but flew the Tiger Moth towards the Canal. My pleasure in recognising it was enhanced by the fact that we appeared to be heading for the majestic vessel sailing on it. Would we give the crew a jaunty wave or two, I wondered? Suddenly, the aircraft made a corkscrew turn to the right, my feet came off the floor, and I felt the weight of my body on the safety straps. As my head flopped back I could see the ship and the Canal, whether best described as above or below the Tiger Moth was a finer point which hardly concerned me at the time. For we – gulp – were upside down!

I suddenly became very hot, and would ridiculously prefer to think it was heat from the funnel of the ship over which we seemed to be poised, instead of the panic which had gripped me. For the safety strap had almost slipped off my left shoulder, and, against the weight of my body, I was desperately trying to keep it in place with my right arm straining across my chest. With my left arm outstretched I tried to reach the tube through which I could speak to the pilot – if only to say "Good Bye!" but to no avail. The more I inched towards it, the more the strap half-inched down my shoulder. I could see that my left hand would very shortly be needed to keep the right shoulder strap in place if the opposite strap reached the point of no return. Having by this time come to a vacant stretch of canal, I wondered how deep the water might be and whether, being an Aquarian, this had been foretold in the stars. Still in this condition of suspended animation, I was suddenly thrown against the side of the cockpit, and the horizon went into a rapid flick to the right. We had half-rolled to the left to regain normal flight, and as the fear diminished the nausea increased. As a precaution against further manoeuvres, I tightened the straps to the extent that normal breathing was somewhat impaired, but if the choice was between a lack of O_2 and a surfeit of H_2O, I was very much aware of which I preferred at that moment. However, my instructor evidently considered that the lesson he intended to teach me was over, and after the experience it seemed to me we floated light as a feather down to the airfield. So I managed to keep my nausea to myself, although my colleagues obviously recognised signs of distress as I passed by on my way to the locker room. I understood from Mr Hill's brief remarks that discipline in the RAF could be maintained in a variety of ways, but I doubt if he had been aware of the full implications of his method.

The addition of a further one and a half hour's flying time which I logged during the month of August seemed tame by comparison, being mostly familiarisation of the controls, gentle turns, and a look around the circuit. By the end of that month, both the airfield and the Town Centre were beginning to clear the decks for what was to come, the T.C. in particular being very concerned with the problems of mobilisation.

By the end of August 1939 most people in Britain believed there could be but one outcome to the situation now facing Poland, next in line for German occupation following Austria and Czechoslovakia. There were by that time about 5,000 embryo pilots in the RAF Volunteer Reserve, and we who served largely by waiting would have been surprised if the average flying time of each member was more than two hours. This supposition and a growing realisation of our military weakness led to an imagined dialogue between a member of our Diplomatic Corps and his German counterpart: *German*: Our Luftwaffe is much bigger than your Air Force. *Brit Dip*: Ah! but have you counted the brave 5,000 sports jacket-and-flannelled Volunteer Reserve pilots who have achieved 10,000 flying hours? *German*: Each pilot? *Brit Dip*: Ah no! In total!

Mobilisation papers were sent out on 1st September 1939, with orders to report to the VR Town Centre as soon as possible after the declaration of war, should the ultimatum requiring the withdrawal of German troops from Poland not be met. The radio broadcast at 11.15 a.m. on Sunday, 3rd September, ended with the words "....and therefore this country is at war with Germany."

Although recent events had been leading inexorably to this conclusion, we heard it with some disbelief – a mere twenty years since the end of the First World

War in which my father had suffered grievously. I looked at my mother, tight-lipped with calm resignation, and for the first time, I think, there came a better understanding of her stoicism against the unkind circumstances of her life – a youngest daughter caring for her aged mother until she died, then married in 1912, still almost a newly-wed when Kitchener's finger pointed at her husband in the 'War to end Wars', leading eventually to his untimely death in 1924. Now her son was called for the kind of service in which, from what she knew of that earlier conflict, the chances of survival were slight.

Brenda, the girl of the moment, had joined us in our small living room that morning, and she and I stood opposite the radio, whilst mother was sitting close enough to it to suggest she might want to put her hand across the speaker to stop the tragic news. As my eyes moved to and fro between her and the radio, I was aware of Brenda looking at me, forcing a smile, and as our hands met I felt an encouraging squeeze. Had it happened on the cinema screen, I would have thought it too sentimental.

Speed of thought is quite surprising in such moments of silence. Once these feelings had registered in genuine empathy, I felt some elation at the prospects ahead. I had little idea of what was likely to follow, but at last I had my preferred career ahead, and I was anxious to prove that I, too, could fly a 'Dawn Patrol'. That was indeed good fortune, as I thought of pals who at that fateful moment could only surmise, hope, or fear, how they were to serve, or indeed survive. I doubt if, as call-up papers arrived, the Guards, the Navy, the infantry, Signals, Marines or Fire Service were to offer them the same satisfaction as I was sure the RAF was to give to me.

On Monday, 4th September, it was obvious that the Town Centre staff had either been working much overtime or were led by an organising genius – or both – for within minutes we had each received precise instructions and a week's pay. Sergeant's pay! The terms of enlistment were that, as pilot u/t (under training) we were Leading Aircraftmen, but upon mobilization became Sergeants, with reversion to LAC if the coveted 'wings' were not awarded. With more cash in our pockets than many of us had been used to, we were told to await further orders, failing which to report back the following Monday. When I arrived home I spread the notes on the kitchen table and insisted mother should have them, but I doubt she even bothered to put them in her purse, knowing her son too well to believe he could avoid one or two extravagances in the charged atmosphere of delayed but inevitable departure. She was right! I was offered a smiling refund almost before the excuses – petrol, gifts, a meal out – had left my lips.

Brenda was an apprentice hairdresser in Madam's Salon in Bank Street, and, like many such assistants at the time, she worked until 8p.m. every weekday, except Tuesday, early closing. For me, the arrival of the postman determined whether I had another day's reprieve from immediate departure, and if so I would visit family and friends during the day, then at 7.55p.m. park my little car outside the Salon, cheerfully knowing that Madam thought it quite outrageous that her virtual slave should be going home in such style. When the moon is full, however, such style plays second fiddle to romance, and on the last Saturday night, after dancing to the swinging seven-piece band at the local Astoria Ballroom and being primed by the soft-drinks-only on offer there, we strolled, with adequate recuperative pauses, along by the river for the two and a half miles to her home, then I caught the 11.05 train back for the last time.

Kit bags were issued when we reported to the T.C. the following Monday. Movement afoot! To many onlookers it must have appeared strange to see young men in sports jacket livery carrying empty Service kit-bags, emerging from a commonplace building in Manchester's commercial centre. However, the foresight was amply rewarded, for later in the week the postman delivered the call to arms and the kit-bag was subjected to three days of gradual expansion. Fortunately the only additions to it which awaited at the Town Centre were a hairbrush and a button stick, the sum of equipment available for issue. There was no indication of when the uniform and tunic buttons to be polished might become available.

My cousin Ruth had caused quite a stir among our contemporaries by becoming one of the few lady drivers in the village, and she volunteered to accompany me to the Town Centre in my Morris 8, so that she could drive the car back home. So, following Sunday's multiple farewells from many aunts, uncles, cousins and friends, with that morning's expressively silent hug from mother, I now stood, literally, on the threshold that led to a changed world, as the car began its return journey amid prolonged waving which would have done justice to an expert in semaphore.

No sooner into the building than out again, we assembled in two ranks on the pavement, and were marched through the streets to the station, the uniformed sergeant in charge and the blue circle on the kitbags being the only evidence that we were R.A.F NCO's on the way to – somewhere. The fact that the station was Manchester London Road (later Piccadilly) started speculation, since most trains from there went to the southern part of the country, and the guessing continued for about an hour, after which we were resigned to wait and see. There were half-a-dozen compartments reserved for us on the train, and I sat opposite Tom, from Prestwich, a ginger-haired lad with a small trim moustache, who had the enviable experience of having flown in an Avro Tutor, and taking part in shooting parties on the sands of

Morecambe Bay. A likely fighter pilot we thought; a great friend until we parted company at the end of flying training.

It became evident that we were on the old Midland line to St Pancras, and would surely have been on the more direct route if we were to go as far as London. We arrived at Bedford and were ordered to disembark to a motor coach which was waiting. We passed through Bedfordshire St Neots to go along the A45 in an easterly direction, and conjecture became certainty when the skyline suggested an attractive collection of historic buildings.

Cambridge! As we approached the city, through the coach window I saw the level expanse of farming landscape which had been home to my paternal grandparents until the economic consequences of imported wheat caused them to migrate to the new industries of the north.

The coach turned into the long leafy glades of Queens Road and as we approached the Backs we went through a gateway opposite, then stopped in front of a modern building which was hardly in accord with the mind's eye view of an ancient University. We were lined up in two rows, kitbags at our sides, for a peremptory welcome: "This is the Memorial Court of Clare College. You will be billeted here about three to a room. When the first three reach that doorway, the second three follow, and so on. Dump kitbags, then collect straw palliasses and blankets." Through the window we could look across Queens Road to the verdant Backs beyond. The day had seen a transformation scene the equal of any pantomime.

CHAPTER 2

BEST FOOT FORWARD

The designation 'Initial Training Wing' given by the RAF to this motley collection of would-be pilots, civilian instructors, administrative officers and Warrant Officer drill instructors, offered inadequate recognition of the delights of being in such a place at such a time – the emerging autumn colours, the beauty of the buildings, and the growing pride with which we marched through the streets. "Licking 'em into shape!" in the words of Warrant Officer Tynant, our drill instructor.

"There's an 'undred of you lot over there, and there's me over 'ere, but if you think you can slack off with me, think again! You will drill like sergeants, you will be'ave like sergeants, and you will look like sergeants!" This encouraged some disbelieving and mischievous glances, as the nearest approach to uniform among us was the odd pair of RAF trousers here and the odd blue shirt and black tie there, with not a sign of sergeants' chevrons. We were still the sports jacket-and-flannels brigade, and were to remain so for at least another two weeks.

The Establishment had other problems. We could only be considered guests, or even visitors, and from the end of September we shared accommodation, meals, the Backs, and the city itself with the remaining undergraduates who had not as yet been called up. Some seemed to regard their gowns as an essential uniform, but most adopted a friendly attitude, found wanting as far as the dons were concerned, and never more so than in the Dining Hall, Refectory, or Nosh Hall – typical RAF slang to cover unexpected embarrassment of taking meals in the splendour of a great panelled room with all the accoutrement of gracious living.

Three times a day we crossed Queens Road from Clare Memorial Court to meals at Trinity Hall, unless we happened to end a drill session close by, appetites sharpened by the keen autumn air, when we would enter with more noise than was considered appropriate, eat the meal quickly, then happily saunter across to our rooms to recover from the morning's exertions. The usual programme was half-a-day on drill, the other half on lectures, a hotch-potch of subjects and lecturers which was, in those early days, as much as could be provided for this No 1 War Course, No 1 I.T.W.

During the first two weeks, the instructor who worked hardest, suffered most frustration, and had least recognition for his efforts was undoubtedly the Warrant Officer. Perhaps it was fortunate that his name – Tynant – was easily corrupted to 'The Tyrant' for with such a reference we knew what to expect when failing to meet the standards he set. He knew he had little enough time to teach us the rudiments of drill; he realised – and we never gave it a thought – that although we were primarily aircrew, we would occasionally have other NCO, and later perhaps officer, duties to perform. As an experienced psychological tactician, the Tyrant was obviously aware of the demeaning use of enforced haircuts: it wasn't that we found barbers objectionable, merely that pride was cut to the quick along with the trimmings, for most of us were members of the 'Brylcreem Brigade' which emulated heroes such as Denis Compton, swashbuckling England batsman. To suffer "Get yer 'air cut, young sir!" within the first few days, when I had visited my local barber before leaving home, was unexpected but not surprising. To be given the same order the very next day, after the necessary visit to a Cambridge barber who was no tonsorial artist, was both surprising and unexpected! It evoked a response which quickly faded as a reminder of the consequences came with an elbow in the ribs from the colleague standing next to me, who had just escaped similar treatment.

"Sir" I began, "you told me...."

The Warrant Officer, usually a study in perpetual motion when going down the ranks, halted in disbelief, turned about smartly, and took one very effective pace towards me.

"Did I hear your lilting voice, sergeant?"

Caution had replaced courage as I replied:

"Sir" – the inflection and the tone made it an innocent question – "you told me to have my hair cut?"

He glanced at my half-shaven head and obviously saw good reason for a repeat performance.

"Yes sergeant, I did! Do it!"

"Very good, Sir!" with equally strong emphasis on each of the three words.

He looked me in the eye, as I gazed past him to a more attractive setting, then with another smart turn he passed down the ranks, selecting other customers for the thriving barbers of the city. However, I decided I would not be amongst them, and appeared on parade the next day with my hair intact, waiting for inevitable retribution. He approached, he stopped, he looked, he passed, and our strictly personal relationship was over. I was just one of the mob thereafter, although on one occasion I did earn a silent eye-brow-lifting commendation for my handling of the squad during drill.

Hair certainly seemed to be of unwarranted importance during that first week, as if the style of the pre-war RAF had been determined by the lengths to which it could be subdued on the heads of other ranks, and the extent to which it could be encouraged to grow on the upper lips of officer pilots. Its importance was not accepted in either sense by No 1 War Course, and a colleague who had thespian interests attempted to ensure that the Warrant Officer was aware of this. On parade one morning, underneath the forage cap recently issued, he wore a wig which blended remarkably well with his own hair, which had perforce been somewhat emasculated. The wig, however, although short at the sides, was long at the back. It nestled in tight, neat waves.

Burdened on such parades with too many bodies and a shortage of time, instead of the meticulous perusal of each individual which he originally thought necessary, the Warrant Officer now carried out his orders 'to expedite matters' by passing along the front of the ranks accompanied by one of his chosen few. This underling was instructed to note the name and number of anyone thought likely to need more than a cursory glance along the rear in achieving the 'short back' to complement the 'short sides'. He had almost passed the wig-wearer when, out of the corner of his eye, he saw the long hair at the back. With mouth agape, and mind confused at apparently having missed this culprit before, he pointed an accusing finger at the offending tresses whilst the assistant noted the wearer's name and number, and passed on, no doubt working up a head of steam to be released on his return journey down the rear. With a quickening of pace and little interest in anyone else on parade, he turned – but still very smartly – at the end of the rank, and strode past the twenty or so bodies to the place where he expected to find the defaulter. But of long wavy hair there was none!

"Where is he?" he yelled, "Where is that Amami boy?" His notary had found the pace too much for him and was only now approaching the spot. Unable to help visually, he called the name and number as required. The erstwhile wig-wearer answered with a loud "Sir!" and even had the gall to mutter, as he went to 'at ease' then 'attention', the chanting by which the Tyrant taught his charges: "Right foot smartly out, hands behind the back; right foot smartly in – lift that knee – hands smartly by the sides, stretch those fingers!"

The W.O. looked again at the shaven back of the accused's head, took a step back, glanced at others on each side, then grabbed the notebook from his aide. As if the hoax had been written on the page, we knew he knew, and he knew we knew that nothing could be done directly. The result was not unexpected. Dispassionately he faced the parade and announced that as our drill was not yet satisfactory, after supper he would be pleased to take us on one of his five-mile route marches. Perhaps he didn't realize we were beginning to enjoy them.

"And" he added, naming and numbering the apparent miscreant "will report to my office".

Although we were told of a strip-search, the disappearance of the wig remained a mystery to us, and a secret to the magicians.

Before long, our feelings towards Mr Tynant mellowed considerably. We knew that we would not have suffered gladly an instructor any less strict but fair, any less professional, and any less determined that we should reach the standards he set. Pride was making an obvious appearance.

As if to test our adaptability, High Command – indeed it must have been the highest Command as it applied to all the Forces – decreed that henceforth marching would be in columns of three, not four, which had been the old-established rule and to which we had just become accustomed. However, we had become proficient enough to make the change without too many false moves. In my case, it made little difference; being tall, at the order "On parade – tallest on the right, shortest on the left!" I knew where I had to go, and what I had to do. "Marker attention!" – and I stood thus, whilst on my left the rest sized, changed places as necessary, and awaited the command "Right dress!" when with outstretched right arm and head so inclined, adequate spacing appeared followed by the command "Eyes front!" Then I would call "One", the next man "Two", then "Three" and so on, "One, two, three; One, two, three".... in Con Brio waltz time, or even occasionally Con Delicatezza! Before the change to three ranks, it had been "One, two, three, four; One, two, three, four".... more a Foxtrot tempo, and often rather Burlesco!

One reason for the delay in the appearance of our uniform was that few of the measurements of our bodies seemed to coincide with those of the tunics, and, in particular, the trousers. We quickly acquired shirts, ties, sweaters, socks, boots; and, thanks no doubt to the efforts of local seamstresses, we were virtually all in uniform by the middle of October. "Oh joy!" was the likely cry of Cambridge photographers, who had seen most of their bread-and-butter poseurs from the Colleges disappear in the clouds of war.

For most of us, this was a first visit to Cambridge, and the fine autumn weather enhanced the pastoral beauty of the Backs, where we perfected our drill, and the grandeur of the buildings, frequently tinted with the pink glow of twilight by the time we were off-duty, able to join the throng on King's Parade and Trinity Street. Recently introduced wartime restrictions on places of entertainment and social activity had closed a surprising number, but who needed more relaxation than a stroll by the river, a pint of ale in the hand, where the willows touch the water – or idly watching rowing practice from Jesus Green? Boats were still available for hire at the Mill Pond by Silver Street bridge, and an hour on the shimmering water drifting casually between bowers of early autumn colours was transport to Elysium.

We became familiar with several college lecture rooms during the last month of our stay, when the authorities had responded to our needs. Whether the result of an offer by dons in psychology-related subjects, or at the behest of the RAF, some of us were required to take part in tests which were intended to help in the selection of aircrew. We picked up large pepper-pots, one in each hand, decided which was very slightly the heavier, then put them down again, whereupon they were haphazardly moved around, and we repeated the exercise. This was followed by an assessment of their relative weights using one hand only, placing them in correct sequence, then doing the same with the other hand.

Whilst moving along a thin line on the floor as if on a tightrope with one arm held out, we had to hold various weights on the outstretched hand. This was then repeated, blindfold. One of the leading pranksters told how he started to juggle with four of the pots, which greatly impressed the supervisor. So far as I know, it was not used to determine who should fly and who should not!

There were several non-verbal tests which were strange to most of us, having had an education based on the three R's and the linguistic application of pen to paper. We were told that the results of these tests were likely to follow our flying careers, so that at some stage there may be a correlation which could be useful in selection. Whether this in fact occurred is doubtful, as in a further six years' service I never met any pilots whose selection procedure had included juggling with large pepper-pots. Suspicion has it that we were the raw material of a thesis.

On one memorable occasion, what seemed to be the whole of the RAF establishment in the city was summoned to one of those lecture-theatres with long bench seats arranged one above the other in ten or a dozen rows – a veritable cockpit. Someone remarked that the title of the expected discourse was "Health Education – Hygiene", so it was no surprise when a Flight Lieutenant Medical Officer walked in, picked up a piece of chalk, threw it in the air and neatly caught it. Applause burst forth. He responded by writing the word ' Hygiene' on the blackboard, and, putting down the chalk, dusted off his hands as if to signify that the necessary visual aid was now in place. After a brief preliminary discourse on the advantages of keeping clean, avoiding lice and crabs, and keeping one's hair short (more than one smile was turned towards Warrant Officer Tynant), he pointed to his visual aid.

"Girls!" he said, "Of couse, it may be Hi! Jessica, or Hi! Joan in your case, and not Hi! Jean!" – guffaws at the pun – "but you're all strapping young men" –

flexing of muscles – "and it's to be expected that the fair sex will have a hold on you!" – wolf whistles!

"What happens though when you go overseas and you embrace the entente cordiale in France, you visit the Harem Scarem in Cairo, or the place your mother wouldn't want you to be found dead in, in India? You forget home cookies, you want a bit of crumpet there and then, and you meet Syph and Gon!" Then, sparing no blushes, he launched into a vivid description of venereal diseases so that by the time we were released from the details of depravity we were beginning to believe that the main effort in any sexual activity should be, as Hillaire Belloc would have put it 'to avoid the dreadful state I now relate'.

In this short period of transition from the freedom of civilian life to the stereotyping of the Service, different attitudes emerged from time to time. Here were a hundred .young men who were motivated by their flights of fancy, for whom every situation had potential for fun; and providing those situations were men with the serious mission of inducing a realisation of what was to come. Perhaps this was the most important part of our training.

By the end of October, the time spent on drilling and marching had converted us into a cohesive unit which, I would guess, gave a certain pride even to Warrant Officer Tynant when we marched through the streets of Cambridge as if we had been given the freedom of the city. We lacked a military band to head the column, but there was adequate compensation in our spirited rendering of the several verses and choruses of 'Rolling Home', 'There's a Tavern in the Town', and 'It's a long way to Tipperary'. Needless to say, such enthusiastic outbursts were not allowed in the cloistered parts of the city.

The marching manoeuvre which caused lasting difficulty to those endowed with the syndrome acknowledged by drill-masters as 'two left feet', was in changing step – a simple matter when solo, but always with a certain ragged effect when performed by two hundred marching feet. To perform this manoeuvre in unison was the purpose behind our arrival one morning at the head of the long length of Trumpington Road. The march began with our customary smart swinging of the arms and picking up of the feet, the rhythm just about to encourage us to burst into song, when the Warrant Officer (no longer 'the tyrant') gave the command "Change step!" In the next pace or two the result would have made any onlooker – and mercifully there were few – believe we must have been marching in bare feet on red hot coals.

We knew we could expect a lengthy procedural analysis – a 'bawling out' in our drillmaster's terms. This was immediately followed by another attempt.

"By the left, qui-ick march!" came the command, and the W.O. picked up the tempo: "Left, right, left, right! Cha-ange step! Right-left-right!" (The latter three into two time). Not yet perfect, off we went again. The W.O.'s practised eye quickly spotted that one sergeant in the middle rank was now out of step with the rest, already settling down again into an easy, swinging gait. Allowing a step or two for self-correction which did not occur, he gave the command:

"Sergeant Hall, change step!"

Immediately, Sgt Hall did so, but so, equally without hesitation, did most of the rest, and those who did not, recovered very quickly so that the recovery was hardly noticeable. Sgt Hall was still out of step.

The W.O. tried again, with an emphasis which must surely have made very clear what was expected! This repeat allowed those who had not seen the possibilities of the situation the first time, to take the hint, so that on this second command, Sgt Hall changed step, and, with equal precision, so did the rest. Sgt Hall was still out of step!

The Warrant Officer called a halt, then gave unique expression to his thoughts on the matter. The facetious explanation offered by the ringleader now seemed to be a cruel reflection on a drill-instructor's mode of speech.

"Sir," he said "we thought your command was 'Sergeants all, change step!'"

Mr Tynant looked at us as if to say 'I expected better of you lot!' and ordered Sgt Hall out of line so that he could have personal attention in this manoeuvre, suffering for our misdemeanour. We then continued the march, and on each occasion when the command "Change step!" was given, it was carried out with exemplary precision throughout the ranks. By the time we turned for the march back, a rapport had been established between the erstwhile tyrant and the squad, which was to last for the rest of the course, and those marching close by heard him joining in the songs – when away from the public gaze.

We felt we had earned the long-weekend leave we were given at the end of October. Londoners had no problem in getting home quickly, and even those who came from midland cities would not lose too much time in travel. But it was galling to find that the Newcastle lads would be home before our Manchester group because of the time taken to reach a main-line to the north-west. However, we found that by taking a taxi to Bedford we could reach Manchester by the early evening – two whole days before returning by the same means. We were released after the midday meal on Friday, and within minutes a convoy of three taxis was on its way, each somehow confining seven bodies within it.

It was a dark, gloomy evening when I left Manchester London Road station to walk across to Victoria, and I saw for the first time the depressing effect of preparations for war on a great city. Along the route I had known well as bustling thoroughfares – Piccadilly, Market Street, Corporation Street – there were no lights apart from the dim hooded headlamps of two or three subdued vehicles and the occasional flash of a torch. Most of the few people I passed seemed to be either in uniform or wearing armbands which signified some official duty, and nowhere could one see the carefree loitering of a few weeks before. Sandbags protecting some entrances were a frequent hazard, and windows were criss-crossed with tape against the shattering which would come with the expected bombs.

There was little additional sign of life as I travelled in the reverse direction at about five o'clock on the Sunday evening, this time on one of the large red and cream trams, quite superfluous to the needs of the four passengers. As I walked along the station platform, one of my colleagues beckoned through a carriage window, and I saw the local contingent had arrived early to secure places in the Dining Car. A porter knocked on the window to remind us it was time to pull down the black-out blinds, and the interior, dimly lit from wall-lights with red lampshades which turned the table-cloths pale pink and made the cutlery glow, gave unseemly emphasis to what had already become romantic memories of the weekend.

"Pity it's you across the table, and not the girl I've left behind!" someone muttered.

However, a good meal, some horse-play with the soup – "You sound like a nag at a trough!" – an assessment of the wine-waiter's chances of joining the Navy – "Hope he handles the rum better than this wine!" – and alcohol which exceeded medicinal measures, contrived to set us slumbering, so that the train was about to leave Bedford before the guard realised there twenty RAF types about to leave the train. As midnight approached we fell into the taxis – had the windows been open it would have been easier to pass some of us through in a prone position – and moved through the Cambridgeshire country- side in such a way that familiarisation with 'g', the force of gravity in an aircraft, would seem as nought compared with the experience.

Recovery the next day was not helped by the order to report to the Medical Section which was based in St. John's College. Vaccination! We had already been inoculated against most of the germs the rest of the world was likely to throw at us, but vaccination against pox evidently warranted a special parade. I was a lucky number five for the needle, so I managed to avoid seeing what happened as arm after arm was squeezed and injected. We were granted twenty-four hours off strenuous duty, but there was considerable restlessness even so, to the annoyance of one or two of the 'borrowed' academic lecturers.

It was said that there would be some pus around the injected area if the vaccine had 'taken', and a swelling if it had 'taken well'. In my case, only a superlative 'take' could describe the large painful swelling which appeared. I was taken off all duties, and ordered to report to the medical section for hot poultices twice a day. With the arm in a sling, I strolled from Clare, lingering on the bridge over the river in Garret Hostel Lane, round Caius College, along Trinity Street and through the gateway of St John's to the medical dressing room, whence I could see the lawn and the river beyond. Waiting in that setting was very pleasant and the surroundings helped to mitigate the effect of hot poultices on the tender spot. Retracing my steps, I usually had time to read up some of my lecture notes, join the others for the midday meal, then repeat the visit. After three days of this, it was back to the normal routine, keeping well clear of swinging arms which may come into contact with the tender spot.

The fact that there had been no discernible pattern to the course, apart from drill and the usual Service inspections, was readily excused by the problems and interruptions of supplying uniform and kit, of finding lecturers and accommodation, and of developing a common syllabus suitable for the differing lengths of pre-war training undertaken by members of the course. It was hardly the introduction to wartime aviation we had expected, but it was undoubtedly pleasant in the glorious autumn weather which so enhanced the beauty of tree-canopy and stone edifice. That our smart bearing of the last month had impressed at least some of the citizens of Cambridge was evident at our departure. Posted in mid-November to flying training, and now all in full uniform, we marched along Station Road to the accompaniment of waving hands and calls of "Good luck!" We gave a startled Army officer walking in the opposite direction a smart "Eyes right!" and felt we were ready for anything.

Tiger Moth

Approach to Fair Oaks aerodrome November 1939

CHAPTER 3

PER TIGER MOTH AD ASTRA

I t was well known that elementary flying training would be carried out on
one of two types of aircraft – the de Havilland Tiger Moth, or the Miles
Magister. Tales had been told about the latter, and we had been well informed,
as they were used at a training school nearby. Some members of our I.T.W. course
had met u/t pilots being trained on them. Recovery from a spin was said to be one
of the problems, and one or two aircraft had apparently 'spun in' to the ground. As
we journeyed south, the conversation on the train centred on a strong preference
for the Tiger Moth, whilst rumour rumbled on about the supposed faults of the
Magister. We knew that we had been posted to No 18 Elementary Flying Training
School, but where was it and what did they fly?

Secrecy of movement being much overdone at that stage of the war, we would
have to wait until we reached the Rail Transport Officer in London for an answer
to the first part of the question, and until we reached our destination for the
answer to the second part. At Liverpool Street station, the R.T.O's order that we
should proceed to Waterloo brought a cheer from those who recalled that the
EFTS near Maidenhead, White Waltham, had Magisters, and the appropriate
London terminus would have been Paddington. Reaching Waterloo, all was
revealed: we were to leave the train at Woking, where transport would be waiting,
and less than an hour later we were turning off the A319 through the gates of Fair
Oaks aerodrome. And there, as if in welcome, facing us outside the nearest hangar,
was a pristine Tiger Moth looking as newly- arrived as we were.

There were 30 of us on that Number One War Course and again the problem
of accommodation faced the resident staff. Since 1937 the airfield had been a
Reserve Flying School under the command of Sq/Ldr Cyril Arthur, who continued
as CO when it was designated No 18 EFTS. He was to be responsible for the
training of more than 6,000 pilots during the war, having first flown with the
RFC in 1917. For the reservists there had been little need for anything more than
overnight accommodation. But the influx of pupil pilots and instructors led to the
requisitioning of two large country houses at nearby Stanners Hill.

Daylight was fading into a typical November dusk as we trudged with heavy
kitbags up the pot-holed lane to the ornate front door of the mansion. "You will

---

be using the tradesmen's entrance!" a disembodied voice announced. Entering thus, and mounting two flights of back stairs, three colleagues and I found we were to share a bedroom in the servants' quarters on the second floor, but this was luxury because there were camp beds in support of the familiar straw mattresses! There was also a kettle, and though it took a day or two to organise, early morning and late evening beverages were soon available.

After minimum unpacking, we had to return to the airfield for the evening meal. By this time, it was dark and the muddy pot-holes in the quarter-mile long lane evoked suitable curses from those outside the beam of the only two torches we could muster. On return, such trivialities were soon forgotten in a real bed at the end of a long day.

The following morning, the airfield reminded me of Manchester V.R's Barton, except that the industrial environs of the latter were absent from this pleasant countryside. There were buildings on the north side of the grass landing-ground and rolling countryside to the south, with the graceful spire of a church in Woking just visible in the distance. A twin-gabled brick-built farmhouse was a reminder of the days before the airfield was opened in the mid-30's. The control tower, long low hangar, workshops and hutted lecture rooms represented the working side; the square-built camouflage-painted 'Club' block, the social side. This was to be known as the Mess, although it was little more than a buffet bar and tables, with an anteroom adjoining. Thus began the routine – rise at 6.30 a.m., down to the Mess to finish breakfast by eight, then half-day alternating sessions of flying/lectures, lectures/flying, supper at 6.30, and occasionally time to enjoy a pint, and join in whilst someone thumped out a popular tune on the piano.

At 8.30 on that first morning, when the instructors had appeared from their out-of-camp accommodation, it seemed strange that most of them were not in uniform, apart from the C.O., two attached sergeant pilots, and the RAF Flying Test Officer, Pilot Officer Dale. Following the introductory session and general briefing the aim was to get everyone up in the air for a short period during the day. This was encouraging; perhaps the waiting days were over!

Even during the busiest weekend in flying club days, Fair Oaks could not have been busier! To me, the flight was more a lesson in airmanship than familiarisation of the airfield and surroundings. Perhaps the intention was that the first impression should be of the need to be watchful of other aircraft, for one could look to the left during the flight and see two or three almost in haphazard formation, then look to the right and see the same. What a sight! Sturdy yet graceful, with yellow underside, black and brown fuselage with RAF roundels on the side, and two brown spheres of leather helmets behind tiny windscreens on top, the Tiger Moth soon replaced concern with confidence. Every pilot's favourite training aircraft!

The sub-group to which I was allocated was the first to fly on the morning of Day Two. Until we became familiar with the palaver, the preparations for a flight took longer than the flight itself. This was not the time of year to indulge in open-cockpit flying in lightweight overalls or shirt and slacks; as this was meant to be a three-months' course through the winter, we would not have that pleasant experience. Even before the colder conditions of the worst winter days, it was sometimes freezing at low altitudes, and we were glad of the kit provided: fur-lined inner flying suit, canvas-based outer with useful map- pockets, fur-lined flying boots – best to get a size too big then one could add another pair of socks – and inner silk, median woollen, and outer leather gauntlet gloves, with a cosy leather helmet, goggles, and perhaps a silk scarf to complete the ensemble. On the ground, all this was cumbersome, particularly after collecting a parachute and walking somewhat less than jauntily to the aircraft, where one could reduce the load a little by placing the parachute, but not yet oneself, in the cockpit. Before that could be done, there was the very important matter of the external inspection.

"Enough fuel?" – check the fuel gauge by the tank on the upper wing;

"Undercarriage O.K.?" – see that the wheels and legs are serviceable and the tyres properly inflated;

"Fabric undamaged?" – no tears or slackening of the surface;

"Controls fully manoeuvrable?" – inspect the ailerons, elevator and rudder for movement, and to ensure any external ties removed;

"Pitot head cover off?" – has to be open to the airflow for the airspeed indicator in the cockpit to work, as it depends on air pressure.

After the check, one would open the side-flap into the cockpit, step up on to the wing and into the seat. After my experience over the Manchester Ship Canal, I needed no bidding to tighten the safety belts.

Introduction to flying training consisted of familiarisation of the airfield area, and the effect of the controls – centrally placed control column or 'joystick', left and right rudder pedals, and engine throttle control mounted on the left side of the cockpit. First came taxying the aircraft to a suitable position for take-off, and to have long legs was an advantage, as with stick held back to keep the tail on the ground, forceful use of the rudder was needed. The autumn chill and wet weather had thinned and softened the grass cover on the airfield, and the indentations of wheel-marks and the ruts of tail-skids felt like ripples as the Tiger moved.

A complete grass surface always allows take-off and landing into wind so these marks of many landings were more numerous in the direction of the south- westerly prevailing wind, and to have to cross them into, for example, a north-westerly take-off gave the sensation of moving over a rough corrugated surface.

Most pilots found that certain sequences were best learnt by rote, since time spent in the aircraft had to be limited. We evolved our own simulation of circuit flying – take-off, climb, downwind leg, descent and landing – known to all as 'circuits and bumps'. Stan, who shared the room at Stanners Hill with Tom, Geoff and me, lived in London, and returning from an overnight visit during the second weekend, he brought back a model of a Tiger Moth which had moveable controls. Fortunately for the safety of the model during his journey, he had been able to detach the wings.

After supper the next night, we retired to our room, and prepared the model for 'take-off'. The patter between us was meant as a check on the understanding of the procedure we each had gained so far.

"Taxi towards the take-off point, keeping a close watch on other aircraft, particularly any approaching for a landing. Use just enough throttle to keep the aircraft moving at a gentle pace, and hold the stick back to keep the tail-skid on the ground. Stop at right-angles to your intended take-off path."

"Remember you don't have any brakes!"

"Right! .... and carry out your pre-take-off check. When the sky is clear of aircraft approaching, turn ninety degrees into wind, check its direction again by the wind sock, steadily open the throttle and away we go!"

"What are you doing with the stick now, Tom?"

"By this time you will have eased it forward to bring the tail off the ground, getting the fuselage parallel to it, and with sufficient forward pressure on the stick to keep the wheels on the deck until the air speed indicator shows you've reached flying speed. Then ease the stick gently back."

"Rudder?"

"Obviously, you've been using the pedals to keep straight."

"Not so much of the obviously. You forget a major item and you'll soon be off this course!"

"Well, we're in the air now! Immediately after take-off, the important thing is to get a hundred feet of height between you and the ground in case of emergency, then throttle back slightly to best climbing speed. To achieve a climbing attitude by moving the stick back, the elevators which are hinged to the tailplane move up, to increase downward pressure on the tail."

"The opposite in descent, with of course more lift for the tailplane."

"Clever lad! At five hundred feet for the cross-wind leg, we make a climbing turn to the left, by pressure on the left rudder pedal, also moving the stick left and back a little."

"Why?"

"It's either that or increasing the engine power, or both, because otherwise total lift is reduced in a turn. When the stick is moved to the left, the aileron – the hinged part at the back of a wing – comes up, and the one on the right goes down. This reduces the lift on the left wing, and relatively increases the lift on the right, which persuades the aircraft it's got to tilt to the left."

"And?"

"What? .... please carry on!"

"Once you're in the turn, the outer wing will be moving through the air faster than the inner, so it will have more lift, i.e. you'll need a light touch on the stick, one eye on the turn and bank indicator, and the other on the rate of climb indicator. You come out of the turn when you're ninety degrees to your take-off path, continue climbing to 1,000 feet, level out, and turn another ninety degrees on to the downwind leg. You now see the airfield down on your left; check the position of other aircraft."

"Don't forget to check the signal square in front of the Control Tower," Tom reminded us, "the large white T-shaped board which shows the direction of landing, and...."

"That's not likely to change during the five minutes you've been in the air!"

"Nevertheless, it's the first thing you have to check if you're going to land at a strange airfield, and we're supposed to be learning a routine! We're now sufficiently past the edge of our airfield to allow the necessary final approach distance, so we make another ninety degree left turn and start descending crosswind to 500 feet."

"Pray tell us how that is achieved!"

"Even you, my son, might think of throttling back the engine and moving the stick forward, although you may need to adjust in a descending turn – for the same reason, I hasten to add, as Stan succinctly stated."

"Suppose there's a strong wind blowing?"

"Ah, then you'll need to make your turn earlier from the downwind leg, because all the time you're crosswind, you are being blown further away from the airfield. At 500 feet, just short of your chosen boundary crossing-point, turn into wind and line up for your final approach. You'll now have to adjust your rate of descent and use of engine power so that you cross the boundary at a height of about thirty feet. Your speed during this descent should have been about 10 m.p.h. above stalling speed, and...."

"What is stalling speed?"

"The speed of the airflow over the wing at or below which there is insufficient lift to keep the aircraft airborne, and your speed should have almost dropped to that as you skim over the grass just inside the airfield. You'll be easing the joystick back as you almost close the throttle, and the fuselage will be parallel to the ground, the nose will be coming up, the tail down...."

"Why?"

"Because as you ease the stick back, the elevators on the tailplane will be hinged up, against the airflow, reducing the lift on the tail and depressing it. So that as you feel she is ready to settle, you are tail down at stalling speed, and if you're lucky the wheels will touch just before the tail-skid."

"You haven't mentioned the rudder," said Geoff, who in the air had found legs less willing to co-operate with the brain than had arms and hands.

"Obviously you do what's necessary to keep the aircraft pointing in the right direction, but you'll certainly need a bit of nifty footwork after you've landed to offset any swing, or shall we say diversion from the appointed path as a result of imperfections of the landing surface."

"You've forgotten to mention an important point! Left hand on the throttle during final descent and landing, in case you need power for more control, or in emergency action such as a baulked landing."

"Thank you, 'Wing Commander'; one thing I haven't forgotten is to turn across wind as soon as I reach the end of the landing run, so that I can check the position of other aircraft before taxying."

And the model aircraft then rose majestically from the end of the space between the beds to land on the flat top of Stan's locker. Determined to have the last word, Geoff pointed out that it hadn't made a circuit, whereupon Stan immediately 'shot him down'.

He seemed anxious to give some realism to these deliberations the following morning. There had been a light fall of snow and a ground frost during the night, and large parts of the ground were slippery. We were sitting in flying kit on the gentle slope at the north side of the airfield, waiting for the snow-ice to melt and the low clouds to lift. A discussion arose about some detail we had omitted from our account of circuit flying routine, when Stan jumped up and crossed to one of the Tiger Moths parked about twenty yards away. He stood by the tail and lifted it until the fuselage was parallel to the ground. Then with one hand hooked under the tailplane, he moved the elevator up and down with the other.

"Look'" he yelled, "I told you the stick would be almost between your legs if you wanted maximum movement of the elevator" then...."What the....Hey!"

Subconsciously, he had been pushing forward. He had failed to notice that there were no chocks under the wheels, and with the tail-skid off the ground, the slope and the push were just sufficient for the 'plane to start to trundle forward. As he tried to stop this movement, his feet slipped on the ice and he began a rapid movement as if treading water, but reaction to this only caused more forward pressure on the aircraft. Our response to this absurd situation was a burst of laughter, until we realised that he appeared unable to put the tail down, being fearful of the consequences if, in his present state of unbalance, he unhooked his fingers from underneath the tailplane. After all, the 'skin' of a Tiger Moth was only stretched and doped canvas – easily damaged, even if easily repaired.

Like a line-astern waddle of ducks in our cumbersome flying kit, we scrambled across to his aid, and grabbed the rear fuselage as he spreadeagled himself across the tailplane, then slipped slowly into a heap on the ground. An instructor came over, and looking down at Stan, said

"You're coming up on a weather test with me," and with appropriate sarcasm "thank you for getting the kite ready for me! Do you think a couple of chocks would be a good idea?"

Stan gave the rear of the aeroplane a very close inspection before clambering aboard.

Although the weather in December 1939 was unkind, most of us managed to go solo before Christmas, the average time taken being about eight hours. Most of this was spent on take-offs and landings, but a reasonable proficiency also had to be achieved in recovery from unusual flying circumstances.

One of these was spinning, when the aircraft would go round and round in a vertical dive as if trying to bore a way through the air, and, it sometimes seemed, possibly through the ground as well! Few stomachs remained undisturbed. A really vicious incipient spin is not easily achieved in a Tiger Moth; if left to its own devices it prefers to be gentle. You climb up to 3,000 feet or more, look around – and below! – hold the nose way up, close the throttle, and feel invisibly attached to the blue sky or billowy cloud beyond the idling propeller. Then comes the sinking feeling as the air speed indicator needle makes its slow, anti-clockwise move around the dial. You begin to float on air, with the odd little shudder as if the Moth is shaking the dust off her wings, and you can feel her preparing to dip a wing and go into a gently gyrating fall towards earth. That was the impression you got when the instructor explained it on the ground. But up here his interpretation is different: you feel a sudden kick on the rudder, then the aircraft flicks over viciously. In a split second you are no longer looking up at the blue sky, but directly down on a rapidly revolving mixture of greens and browns which seem to be coming up to meet you. "Do something!" says a voice in your earphones.

You think 'Surely we weren't rotating like this when he demonstrated it'. You don't do the obvious thing which, if you wanted to come out of an ordinary dive, would be to pull the stick back. No! First, stop this wretched revolving. You momentarily ignore the stick as if you are determined the earth shall have you and quickly apply full opposite rudder to the direction of the spin. As the spinning stops ease the stick forward, and centralise the rudder. You are in trouble if you are not now responding to the normal procedure for recovery from a dive, and when the Moth is again 'straight and level', you find your enthusiasm for flying returns!

The answer to the question 'How are you feeling?' might vary, but most instructors saw to it that after an introduction to spinning, the aircraft landed quickly and stopped as near as possible to the toilet block.

Another essential item before going solo was the procedure in case of engine failure in the air, or more likely, what you hoped to do in that event. If a rapid check of instruments and switches meant that engine power really had deserted the aircraft, the pilot had to decide over what sort of distance he could keep the aircraft in the air at the appropriate gliding speed.

Obviously, height would help, and whereas failure at 10,000 feet on a clear day could be met with some equanimity, the result of failure just after take-off seldom left even an engine suitable for analytical dissection! Having decided the best spot for an emergency landing – a space free of obstacles on and around the chosen area – one would then look for indications of wind direction and speed, perhaps smoke from a nearby chimney, movement of clouds, swaying of trees, and make the necessary gliding turns to approach and land into wind. Although we had not yet reached the stage of leaving Mother Airfield for another, this was also the procedure to adopt if we were hopelessly lost on a cross-country flight, except that then we would still have engine power to help in the search for a suitable spot for landing.

After the sporadic ground-instruction at I.T.W., it came as no surprise when a fresh start was made at Fair Oaks: Airmanship, Rules of the Air, Basic Navigation, Armaments. A welcome break from sitting at tables, listening and writing, was the practical way in which we learnt the Morse Code. Tapping keys were set up on tables, and, once accustomed to the difference between a 'dit' (short tap) and a 'dah' (long tap) and their differing combinations to represent letters, it was possible to communicate with a colleague similarly employed. In the general hubbub, many words were passed and comments made on instructors which would have upset them and us had they been passed in open language. Spoken emphasis in certain words was correlated to a Morse letter as an aid to learning: dit dah dit dit (1) 'librarian'; dit dit dah dit (f) 'effervescent'; dah dit dah dit (c) 'cream in coffee', and so on. Most of us knew, and many were later to need 'dit dit dit, dah dah dah, dit dit dit' (S.O.S.)

The Armaments Instructor was a civilian, Mr Bishop, a forthright man who would have embellished the phrase 'a spade is a spade' with at least three unprintable words. He had been an air-gunner and, with an imagined well-worn helmet in place, one could see him behind a machine gun in an open cockpit in the 1914–18 conflict. Even sensible clay-pigeons would stay in their hides if he appeared with a shotgun! When he stripped a .303 Browning or a Lewis machine-gun, it seemed to disintegrate rapidly of its own accord. Few of us relished the command "Now you do it!" If the purpose was to give us confidence in the Browning, he fitted the role perfectly, and any potential fighter pilot must have been heartened by a demonstration on the firing range.

"Multiply that by eight, and you'll see how your Hurricane can cut through a Jerry kite!" he exclaimed, with suitable profanities in emphasis.

We only paraded once for the benefit of some important visitor, and the fortnightly pay parades were carried out with the minimum of fuss. It would indeed have seemed strange for a civilian staff to be commenting on the shine on our buttons; nevertheless we were proud enough in what we were doing to make sure that they shone. The situation also allowed imaginative and highly decorative variations in the flying clothing we wore.

It was in December, with the prospect of a weekend leave ahead, that I arranged to travel north to spend it with Brenda. However, the newly-appointed P.E. instructor considered my inclusion in a game of soccer more important than a romantic interlude, and would not yield to my pleas. Resolving that my determination should match his, I took a hammer from the coal-shed at the billet and applied it with some force to my big toe. The toe responded favourably, and he had to agree that an unfortunate mishap precluded my participation in that form of sport. Which enabled me, I thought, to participate in my chosen form of sport.

However, the beginning of a severe winter intervened: with snow on the pitch the match was cancelled, as was the weekend leave for fear of delay in returning, and within a week of very little flying, we were sent on indefinite leave. In my case, with a toe in the early stages of recovery!

That Christmas of 1939 was the last for several years when the table would be heavy with food readily available. On the 28th December, meat rationing was introduced, and on the following 8th January, bacon, butter, and sugar rationing, and each Friday was to be a meatless day. Mother's revising of her list of recipes was an appropriate reminder that there was at least one advantage in canteen feeding!

Conditions remained unfit for flying into the second week of January, and when the recall from leave eventually came, there was still snow on the hills of Lancashire. My leave ended as I was staying at Brenda's home, which was along a lane a mile from the nearest main road, by the railway line to Bury and Manchester. Heavy snow had fallen during the night, the lane was blocked and the railway line covered, but news from the village three miles lower down the valley was that transport there might soon be moving. With sheets of brown paper tied round the lower half of my trousers I set off down the railway line. There was no sign of the tracks, just a level expanse of snow, glittering white, spread as if by a mighty trowel between the sides of the cutting. The fingers of snow hanging from the trees had just begun an occasional drip as the frosts of the night yielded to the hazy sunshine. Where the cutting became an embankment I turned for some perspective of the distance my plodding feet had brought me. Feeling that my dragging footsteps had vandalized the ephemeral beauty of the scene, I turned, and looked only ahead at the panorama as yet unspoilt. Thomas Hardy's lines from 'Snow in the Suburbs' came to mind:

> A sparrow enters the tree,
> Whereupon immediately
> A snow-lump his own slight size
> Descends on him and showers his head and eyes,
> And overturns him,
> And near inurns him,
> And lights on another twig, when its brush
> Starts off a volley of other lodging lumps with a rush !

When the next village came into view the magic was lost, and I was back in a world where snow was nothing more than a nuisance. As I slithered up the slope at the end of the railway station platform, a face in the booking office window left me in no doubt that the railway was not yet ready to cater for passengers that day, but the driver of the 'bus squelching its way along the road viewed me with more charity. Until, that is, he saw the condition of my trousers and boots! As I eventually travelled south, leaving the greying remnants of snow behind, I was full of hope that the remainder of January 1940 would yield more flying than had December 1939.

A surprise greeted our recall to Fair Oaks. All the flying instructors were now in uniform, most of them in the rank of Flying Officer. My instructor was probably in his early forties, and I had little contact with him other than through the speaking tube of a Tiger Moth.

I assumed he was married, as were most of the others; they all disappeared quite quickly when flying ceased for the day. Mine seemed to enjoy spinning even less than I, and neither did aerobatics appear to be his favourite pastime in an aircraft. Whereas he could be reasonably analytical about mistakes in other aspects of flying, I seldom felt satisfied with his brief explanations of why my slow rolls lacked some finesse. I was happier doing loops when flying solo rather than dual, as there always seemed to be a 'guiding hand' on the controls during such manoeuvres when he was with me.

There were times when a navigator's guiding hand would have been appreciated. As proficiency grew, so the distance we might stray from the airfield increased, with map-reading assuming greater importance as we prepared for the eventual Cross-country Test. From the air, I was beguiled by the beauty of the rolling countryside, gentle even in the depths of winter, the brown criss-cross canopy of trees blending with the dark earth of newly-ploughed pasture, or the yellow stubble not yet cultivated. So different to the stark hand of winter on the Pennines. Here, over the Hog's Back, with the ribbon of the A 31 along its spine, or watching the mild activity around Virginia Water to the south of Windsor Great Park, or on Ascot Heath, it was too easy for the eye to wander from the cockpit instruments, for such places were now within familiar territory. But as we left these places further behind and the weather became more capricious, the number of forced-landings increased.

On one occasion a colleague who had lost his bearings after carrying out an exercise in misty weather, had to make an emergency landing. He found a large field and made a perfect landing, being immediately accosted by a farm worker brandishing a pitchfork, who, doubting the attempted identification, demanded that the pilot should "coom 'dahn 'ere".

"I've 'eard tell o' these 'ere fifth clumnist Nazis!" was the apparent reason for this demand, and suave words in reply would obviously naught avail. Certainly an explanation that this aircraft could not have flown from enemy territory would be a waste of time, so he felt round his neck for his identity tag, but it wasn't there. Thinking he might find it in his tunic pocket, he thrust in a hand, and found a round flat object about three inches in diameter. He pulled it out and discovered that it was a beer mat advertising the local beer. Offering it to the farm worker with a "join me in a pint of the best next time I'm your way!" he was greatly relieved to see the menacing scowl replaced by an expansive smile.

"Why din 'e tell us?" offered his erstwhile assailant, whose help in placing the field's location enabled Phil to find it on the map. He welcomed the offer to assist his take-off by holding the wing-tip, whilst the Moth was swung round ready to taxi down-wind for his take-off run. As his assistant released his hold the wheels faltered in a shallow pool of water. The aircraft began to tip forward, so Phil held the stick back and opened the throttle to jockey her through, sending a spray of muddy water behind. As he took off he could see his helper shaking himself down and realised he must have been immediately behind the aircraft, taking the full force of the spray. Nevertheless, Phil got a cheery wave as he flew low over his saviour.

"I thought the slipstream might help to dry him off!"

It was whilst thumbing through magazines in the Mess after an hour's perfect solo flying on a rare sunlit winter's day, that I found my thoughts in words on the printed page. Written by a cadet at Cranwell who later became an Air Vice Marshal, it captured the euphoria of a score of solo flying hours:

> *How can they know the joy to be alive*
> *Who have not flown?*
> *To loop and spin, and roll and climb and dive,*
> *The very sky one's own!*
> *The surge of power as engines race,*
> *The sting of speed,*
> *The rude wind – buffet in one's face –*
> *To live indeed!*

Elation was subdued and different thoughts attended when taking off with the Flying Test Officer in the accompanying cockpit. Progress rather than perfection was his watchword, and one or two colleagues on the course were told that they would need, and would have, a second chance to show it, but no more. Thankfully, I got through it without too many mistakes: take-off, climbing turns, loop, roll-off-the-top, spin, steep turns, gliding and precautionary approaches, climb at full power, approach and overshoot, then two landings.

"Not impressive, but satisfactory" was the verdict. Then: "Were you nervous? A little! Just as well – you've got to know what fear in the air is and what it does to you before you can overcome it." I and others had from time to time already recognised a benign introduction to it, even in reaching this stage!

Being within easy distance of London, which still had most of its peacetime attractions to offer, there was no great enthusiasm for organised activities at weekends, and as petrol was still available, I resolved to go home and return in my Morris 8, a distance of about 240 miles. Most of the Saturday was spent in preparing the car for this unusual test of stamina, and in order to demonstrate to Brenda that I cared as much for her as I did for the Morris, I devoted to her an equivalent time on the Sunday. My departure time was therefore about 9 p.m. on the Sunday evening and, with very little traffic on the roads and in an area I knew well, the first part of the journey passed quickly. From then on, however, the problems of the blackout emerged in the gloom. With the standard masks on the headlamps reducing the beam to below horizontal, it was impossible to read directions on signposts, and where there was uncertainty at a junction about which road to take, it was necessary to stop and shine a torchlight on the board.

As I drove on, the luminous hands of the large pocket-watch fixed to the dashboard reminded me that my journey was behind schedule, but a glimmer of moon- light on the far horizon gave some hope that soon I may be able to increase speed. An hour later, by slowing at each junction to 10 m.p.h., the moonlight helped me identify names on the signposts. As dawn was breaking over the western outskirts of London, I was on a long straight stretch of road between Slough and Windsor, and I noticed distant traffic lights at the far end. When next I was aware of them I was almost upon them and I had no recollection of the intervening distance. I had succumbed and snatched forty or so winks; fortunately there was no other traffic – and the lights were accommodatingly green! I arrived in time to have a hurried breakfast, then to the Flight Detail. I was due to fly with my instructor at 8.30, and the exercise was spinning. Why had I bothered to eat!

Afternoon lectures that day were concerned with final preparations for the two Cross-country Tests, the first a continuous triangular flight, and the ultimate Test which involved a landing at a distant (in Tiger Moth terms) airfield. I was dozing off for lack of sleep the night before, in the middle of a discourse on magnetic variation, when a dig in the ribs reminded me we were going out to 'swing' a compass, the colloquial term for moving an aircraft through compass headings to verify the readings externally. After supper I was glad I had the car to take me up to Stanners Hill, and I was asleep on my bed still in uniform when the others came in three hours later.

Stubborn mists and heavy showers in early March again interrupted flying; it was obvious that the disadvantages of an overall grass surface were now greater than the advantage of always being able to take- off/land into wind. Many pre-war

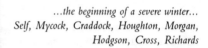

*Fair Oaks "All the trimmings" with Tiger
Moth in background*

*...the beginning of a severe winter...
Self, Mycock, Craddock, Houghton, Morgan,
Hodgson, Cross, Richards*

*All the flying
instructors were
now in uniform...
C.O. S/Ldr
Arthur 2nd row,
7th from left. Most
pilots u/t went to
Little Rissington.*

airfields were located on relatively free-draining substrata such as chalk, but now airfields would have to be built precisely where they were needed rather than seeking to use a benign geology. So, at six months into the war and in a bad winter, 'Weather unfit for flying' referred to conditions on the ground as well as in the air at aerodromes lacking a concrete runway. This was so at Fair Oaks, particularly when snow showers left patches of ice by night, which by day thawed into puddles hidden among the grass.

Taking off for local flying on a day when fingers of mist in the valley merged with sombre hanging clouds, I felt a sudden drag on the wheels as they splashed through one of these puddles, and the nose of the Moth dipped alarmingly. I made sure the throttle lever was fully forward, and yanked the stick back so that she took off like a startled hen, but, equally like a hen, she could remain airborne for a short distance only. In testimony to the rugged undercarriage, she flopped, sagged, seemed to squat momentarily, then gathered speed as if making up for fruitless effort and soared from earth like a bird migrating to drier, warmer climes. If that was her intention she was soon disappointed, for the mist thickened and the clouds threatened, until, after a few steep turns, I had lost my bearings. I found a railway line but couldn't place it on the map, so I decided to fly along it to the nearest station, where I might find the name clearly displayed on a large sign at the end of an open platform. I could see as I approached the station at a height of about fifty feet that I was out of luck.

A canopy appeared to cover the whole length of the platform, so I would have to go as low as possible over it, hoping to glimpse the name under the other side. I failed to see it – but standing in splendid isolation in the open at the far end of the platform was the sign 'BROOKWOOD'. I climbed, turned, and continued down the line to Woking, and back at the airfield I made sure I avoided the wet patch as I landed.

By the end of March we were venturing further afield not only in the air but also on the ground, and one evening Tom and I were in a pub near Camberley, having arranged to meet a pal of mine from pre-war days who had recently joined the Marines. He was stationed nearby, so we decided to give him a demonstration of Tiger Moth virtuosity, as in recent days Tom and I had been detailed for solo flying at the same time. Two days later, a little late for a Dawn Patrol, we approached the appointed spot south of Bisley Common, in line astern, to be greeted by a group of Marines drawn up ready to spring to a smart salute as we flew by.

Without the benefit of any instruction in formation flying, we had nevertheless decided that I would break to the left in a climbing turn and Tom would similarly break to the right, then we would both swoop across our original track at right angles. That was as much as we had planned, but the wild gesticulations of our audience had an hypnotic effect on both of us, and we continued to climb, turn, and swoop another four or five times before I pointed towards Fair Oaks and we re-formed into a side-by-side pair, waggling our wings vigorously as we passed them on our homeward track.

The month of April approached, and I had to get my car back home before the course ended. On the first available Friday afternoon when flying was cancelled because of the weather, Tom and I set off for Lancashire. The few fog patches we encountered around the Midlands multiplied in number and intensity as we approached Manchester. Without his intimate knowledge of the city streets we would have been baulked, but worse was to come going north to his home in the suburb of Prestwich. Even with the hinged windscreen locked open, it was impossible to see forward, so Tom held the passenger door open with one hand and shone a torch on the kerb with the other, calling "One foot", "Two feet", "Six inches", according to the distance of the car from the kerb. When it disappeared at a junction, he got out and was lost in the night, returning with instructions such as "Forty five degrees left", upon which we inched forward until we picked up the kerb again. I stayed at Tom's overnight, took the car the further fifteen miles home the next morning, and we returned by train to prepare for final Tests.

'Plane: Anson I

COASTAL COMMAND PILOT

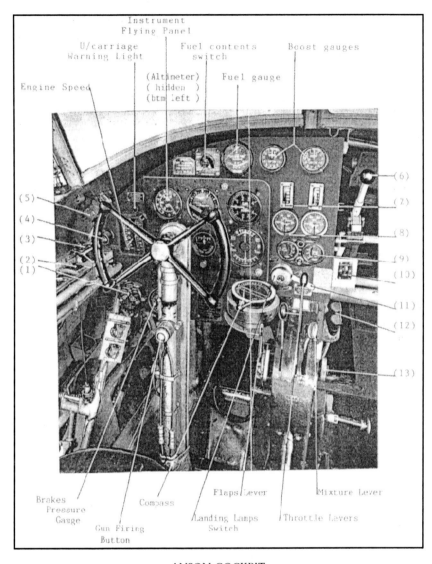

Instrument
Flying Panel

U/carriage
Warning Light

Fuel contents
switch

Boost gauges

Engine Speed

(Altimeter)
(hidden)
(btm left)

Fuel gauge

(5)
(4)
(3)
(2)
(1)

(6)
(7)
(8)
(9)
(10)
(11)
(12)
(13)

Brakes
Pressure
Gauge

Gun Firing
Button

Compass

Landing Lamps
Switch

Flaps Lever

Throttle Levers

Mixture Lever

ANSON COCKPIT

(1) Ident'n Lights Switch. (2) Pitot head heater switch. (3) I.F.F. Switch. (4) Bomb switch. (5) IFF Emergency. (6) Landing lamp dipper. (7) Oil Pressure Gauge. (8) Oil Temp Gauge. (9) Flap Indicator. (10) Recog'n Lights Switch. (11) Slow-running cut-out (12) Undercarriage Indicator (13) Throttle Friction Knob

"... and watch those instruments!"

Chief among these was the Cross-country Test, a triangular course of about 160 miles, with a south-westerly leg to a village north-west of Salisbury, then northerly across Salisbury Plain to the small airfield at Yatesbury where a landing and fuel check had to be made and documented, then a south-easterly return to Fair Oaks. I noticed that Wylie, the first turning point, was at a junction on the A 303, and if one passed about three miles south of Basingstoke this road would appear. It duly did, and though the route may not have been quite as direct as flying the appropriate compass heading, my logged time was within a minute of E.T.A. (estimated time of arrival). Salisbury Plain lay ahead.

The large open space indicated on the map was belied by the activity below. There were marked "Danger Areas" on each side of the track, and camouflaged vehicles, looking like toys on a parched back lawn, scurried, crawled, or tracked in haphazard array. Between these, teams of horses and the occasional tractor were cultivating land not yet requisitioned by the Army, turning pasture into ploughed furrow, furrow into seedbed, and already here and there, seedbed into close lines of green shoots, the harbinger of harvest.

Beyond the Vale of Pewsey and the Kennet and Avon Canal, two ancient white horses, cut into the chalk hillsides pointed the way forward. If on course, the one to starboard near Alton Priors, and the one further along the track to port, would both have their heads closer to the aircraft than their tails. If the reverse were true in either case, I would be on the far side of one of them and off course by twenty degrees or more. Fortunately it was heads, not tails, and so to Yatesbury on time, a good landing back at Fair Oaks within two minutes of E.T.A., and a growing interest in aerial navigation.

There remained the final Flying Test by Squadron Leader Arthur, the Chief Flying Instructor, and the written examinations. The need for proficiency in both was amply demonstrated by one colleague who, from early days, had been recognised as a natural with a Tiger Moth. We all envied his aerobatic artistry; we also knew that his navigation and airmanship were suspect, but we imagined his skill in the former would compensate for the lack of it in the latter. It was not so, and his name was absent from the list of forward postings. It was later rumoured that he had been attached to the incoming course for further training. We hoped the rumour became a fact.

CHAPTER 4

HIGH ON A COTSWOLD HILLTOP

At the end of the first week of April 1940, No.1 War Course at 18 EFTS was completed, and most of us were on our way to No.6 Service Flying Training School at RAF Little Rissington, Gloucestershire. The fact that the flying suits which winter and open cockpits had necessitated were returned to stores, naturally led to the supposition that we were to fly aircraft with enclosed cockpits. We would miss the direct contact with the elements, but how pleasant it would be to simply pick up a parachute, enter an aircraft and be ready for take-off without the need for pre-flight embellishment.

Although any onlooker would probably have described us as a cheerful group of young airmen in transit across London from Waterloo to Paddington, the casual and flippant attitudes which had been evident during previous mass-movements had almost gone, dampened by the news from Norway and Denmark, and the physical confirmation that London expected air bombardment. Every building of importance was protected by high banks of sandbags, and windows were latticed with adhesive tape. Cars were few, lorries many, several containing troops who swayed like bull-rushes in the breeze as the driver picked his way through traffic which was mainly concerned with the need to defend the capital against aerial, or even ground, attack.

The RAF Station at Little Rissington is situated 730 feet above sea level in the gently rolling Cotswolds, and there are few more attractive pastoral scenes than the flush of April green over such a pleasant countryside. We left the Paddington-Worcester train at Kingham, one of those isolated hamlets identified only by a railway station, and welcomed the bustle of the market-square at Stow-on-the-Wold as we passed through; we were to have remarkably little time to take part in it during our stay in the area.

Compared with the improvised nature of the facilities at Fair Oaks, Rissington was the epitome of pre-war expansion planning, much of it in Cotswold stone or harmonising brick: the Main Gate and Orderly Room, the large rectangular Administrative Block, the Officers' Mess with its facade of pseudo-Georgian windows and arched portico, and a Sergeants' Mess on the same lines, which we knew from past experience would now be too small for its purpose. As we lined up with kitbags waiting to move off to our quarters, we could only anticipate a distant billet, but where would this be in an open landscape two miles from the nearest hamlet? It proved to be just round the corner, for hidden by the side of the Mess were partitioned wooden huts, with ablution blocks adjoining. Gone were the marathon morning trails from billet to breakfast, but a look at the Routine Orders quickly dispelled any thoughts of prolonged slumber when we discovered that initial flying training would be at Kidlington airfield, north of Oxford; this meant taking breakfast at 6.30am.

A fine April morning, a comfortable 25-seater coach, and 30 miles of some of the pleasantest countryside in England, helped to mitigate the need to arrive at Kidlington by 8 a.m. The small grass airfield was already a hive of activity, operating as a satellite to Rissington, and taking those who were to train on the twin-engined Avro Ansons, whilst those likely to be posted to fighter squadrons flew American 'Harvard' trainers at the main base. They did not have it solely to themselves, however, as advanced training for both Anson and Harvard pilots of the preceding No 1 War Course continued there.

Training in the RAF to 'wings' standard on twin-engined aircraft was on either Ansons or Airspeed Oxfords and again we found the aircraft of our choice. Rumours about Oxfords from Brize Norton, a nearby SFTS, gave Oxfords a bad name on two main counts: poor single-engine flying in the not infrequent event of engine trouble, and a stall with an unpredictable outcome. The Anson, however, soon earned our approval of the sobriquet 'Anson is as Anson does', given to the aircraft in a corruption of the well-known phrase by pilots who had flown it on operations. As a training machine, it was spacious and comfortable, had no vices, and was robust enough to withstand ill-treatment. However, it had two disadvantages from the pupil's point of view: the substantial undercarriage – saviour of many a heavy landing – had to be cranked up manually, and this involved turning a handle 160 times. Although the undercarriage was left down for local flying and circuits and landings, on longer flights when it had to be raised one could only envy the Harvard lads who had merely to move a lever, whilst we had to turn this handle round and round until the blessed slip indicated that the last rotation had been made, and the wheels were locked up.

The second disadvantage was that each engine had to be cranked to start it. The engine nacelle protruded about three feet in front of the leading edge of the wing, and in the side of the nacelle was a hole into which the cranking handle fitted. On a signal from the pilot, the airman would turn the handle, and after about half-a-dozen cranks the engine would fire. The problems of running two airfields with a ground crew allocation more appropriate to one became apparent on the first morning at Kidlington, for our preliminary introduction to routine was a demonstration of how to crank an engine.

"Ah!" I thought, "sensible to give us an idea of what it's like to crank that handle – safety first to get out of the way once the propeller revolves."

"Now you, you, you and you!" – I was one on the roster – "will be cranking engines until you're due to fly. As we're desperately short of ground crew you'll just have to pitch in." So for two hours we cranked whilst others flew; then thankfully the positions were reversed.

Once in the air with Flying Officer Joy, my instructor, earthbound tasks were forgotten, for I immediately felt confident that under his tutelage I would enjoy flying this aircraft and I would fly it well. Such is the measure of rapport, and it intrigued me that with some colleagues in training, and later on operations, supreme confidence was there for the taking, whilst with others there were always doubts. My instructor at Fair Oaks had said "Call me Fred", but I had never felt that I had wanted to do so, even before he appeared in uniform, because he lacked effusive confidence. On this first flight in an Anson, respect was effortlessly established along with rapport, and even if invited to do so when on duty, I would never address this man by anything less than an acknowledgement of rank.

"There's a landmark for you, can't miss that from miles away!" he said, "When you're on local flying, keep it within sight, but don't make a practice of flying over it; too beautiful for that!" He was pointing to Blenheim Palace, a mere two miles to the west of the Kidlington circuit. With a wind from the west, on take-off one could hardly avoid flying over it. What a wonderful sight – still, at this stage of the war, in its peacetime splendour, with the formal gardens, elevations and columns of warm stone, open parkland and the lake beyond.

"Churchill was born there," – it had recently been announced that he was to be Chairman of the Defence Committee – "Look at that bridge across the middle of the lake, that's one of Vanbrugh's; the one at the south end was by Capability Brown. Can you beat that?" I certainly couldn't because as a lad of twenty, having seen little of real English heritage, I didn't then know the identity of either of the two gentlemen my instructor mentioned, but I found out that night and put another metaphorical feather in his cap.

The following day we remained at Little Rissington for a relaxed introduction to the lecture programme, which made the details of the concentrated timetable seem easier than they turned out to be: advanced map-reading, radio procedure, Anson systems, vectors, various types of bombs, and meteorology, in addition to the subjects introduced at Fair Oaks. During the lunch break several of the group went down to the hangars to watch the first American aircraft we had seen, the Harvards.

They didn't look particularly aerodynamic, with a blunt nose formed by the radial engine, and the long upright cockpit canopy already christened 'the greenhouse' which covered both instructor and pupil. Most aircraft can be identified, to the practised ear, by the sound of the engines, and the Harvard was unique in this respect. No one could mistake it! As it approached there came the usual drone, then as the decibels increased, an underlying throbbing counterpoint, coming to a shrieking or whistling crescendo as the aircraft came directly opposite the listener, subsiding in passing to a drone in the distance. Someone remarked that the noise from a squadron of them would be their most fearful weapon. We watched with envy as the wheels quickly disappeared after take-off, or were down within seconds at the appropriate point on the circuit when coming in to land.

"On a circuit like that we wouldn't have time to crank the Anson's wheels up, never mind get them down again before landing!" said Tom.

"If Ansons are still used on ops we ought to apply for another member of crew – undercarriage crank-handler!" replied another.

Day Three – Kidlington again, and more ground crew duties, this time removing the wheel chocks when aircraft were ready to move out for take-off, and helping refuel at the end of the day's flying. We began to appreciate the efforts of those who kept the aircraft fit to fly and then saw that they did so. In the first week or two we were quite exhausted by the time we returned to Rissington, but during the second week this fact appeared to be unnoticed by the driver of the coach taking us back.

He seemed to regard opening time for pubs as a personal invitation for him to win a race for the earliest pint, so that if he took his time on the journey we would be approaching, at the appointed hour, the last hostelry before reaching Chipping Norton. Some of the boys would be catching forty winks, and we who were awake had no reason to doubt that the driver's "I need a pee" was genuine. He stopped and disappeared into the pub. Five minutes seemed rather a long time for this activity, made the more obvious by growing pangs of hunger, particularly amongst those who had missed the afternoon cup of tea and a bun from the W.V.S. van.

He rejoined the coach, amid several expletives intermingled with a definitive use of English, but this made no apparent difference two days later.

Again he stopped, again remarked on the call of nature, and his retreat to the pub was joined by five of those who realised the true intent and couldn't wait until they reached the Mess for a reviving pint. Stoppage time on this occasion reached ten minutes and there was some concern amongst those of us in the coach that here was a growing habit which needed a corrective. It might well be fifteen minutes next time! Amid rumblings of rebellion and mumblings demanding a different driver, I decided there would certainly be one, at least for a short distance.

The road disappeared round a bend about a hundred yards ahead, so I got into the driver's seat, started the engine, and drove the Bedford 25-seater just round the bend so that it was out of sight, leaving the engine running and revving up occasionally so that sound, if not sight, would give the emerging loiterers a clue. After ten minutes, our spy peering round the bend reported the scene of consternation as they gathered in front of the pub. There was a great burst of laughter as he described the reaction of the driver, who first pointed and then moved towards the hill up which he had driven the coach, presumably thinking it had run back down it! With much gesticulation, his drinking companions persuaded him there was a likelier explanation.

The revving of the engine confirmed this to the malingerers, and by the time they staggered on to the coach the driver's seat was empty, and our faces patiently expressionless. The driver realised he was unlikely to be given the name of his substitute; and there were no more stops on subsequent journeys. He was replaced at the beginning of the following week – we supposed he had been called up or sent down – and the boys agreed that the beer in the Mess was just as good, and cheaper.

The second week of lectures at Rissington started with practice in the use of the main navigational aid of the time, the Course and Speed Calculator, by which the course to steer could be found by applying wind speed and the desired track to the machine. This was combined with instruction on the Link Trainer, as near as one could get to flying without leaving the ground, the current flight simulator. It was basically a box with controls and instruments inside which were similar to those found in a typical aircraft of the time. The pupil entered through a small door, sat at the controls, pulled down the hood, and carried out the instructions received through the headphones. By hydraulic linkage of the box to the base and electrical linkage of the instruments to the instructor's table, the simulated movement of the 'aircraft' in response to the use of the controls, and its movement through the 'air', was plotted on paper, chart, or map.

Aerobatic movements were not possible, but it was certainly the preferred way to practise spinning! Most flying in the basic stages had been a matter of positioning the aircraft in relation to the natural horizon. In the practice of flying by instruments alone upon which we were now embarked, the one which indicated the aircraft's attitude in flight – the artificial horizon - was one of the six in the Instrument

Flying Panel with which all Service aircraft were equipped. The other five instruments were the Air Speed Indicator, the Altimeter, Rate of Climb or Descent Indicator, Gyroscopic Compass, and the Turn and Bank Indicator. We quickly came to realise that the skilled Link Trainer Instructor was a very important person.

Much of the flying time at Kidlington was repetition of the sequence of instruction used during elementary training at Fair Oaks. There were two major, and several minor, differences. Although the Harvard pilots still enjoyed their aerobatics, such impositions on the dignity of an Anson would invoke, to put it kindly, structural objections. And for the twin-engine pilot, there was the introduction to single-engine flying, necessary if one engine should fail in flight. After a demonstration of the greatly increased drag which hindered an aircraft when the undercarriage was down, we fervently hoped that if, when flying solo, fate decreed an engine failure, please may it occur when the undercarriage was up! If it should happen to be down, the prospect of cranking 160 turns on the handle at the same time as going to rich mixture and increasing power on the good engine, trimming the controls, checking fuel supply and switches, oil pressure and temperature – it all seemed too long a list to accomplish successfully. Another significant difference was that, on both the Anson and Harvard, wing flaps had to be used during approach and landing. The inner half at the rear of each wing, (the 'trailing edge') had a six-inch section which was hinged to project downwards into the airflow, thus increasing the chord of the wing and enhancing the lift at the lower speeds used in landing. These aircraft also had brakes on the wheels, worked pneumatically from an air bottle!

The long hard days at Kidlington, interspersed with lectures and tests at Rissington, left us with little time and energy to do more than work, eat, and sleep. The whole tempo quickened as news over the radio and in the newspapers worsened. In the quiet moments of otherwise intense activity, like Servicemen everywhere, I came to value and look forward to letters from home, from relations and friends. In attempting to categorize them, they would be divided into three types: firstly, from mother, a neat letter in an almost copperplate hand. It would give little indication of her own privations or emotions, always ending with a metaphorical ray of hope and enclosing some woollen item or special delicacy. Secondly from Aunt Sarah, penned exactly as she spoke so that I could almost hear her cheery broad Lancashire accent, describing everyday incidents in a clutch of ill-assorted but amusing phrases. She wrote also on behalf of Aunt Alice whose material contribution was often more substantial – one of her delicious fruit cakes.

But the letters I enjoyed most were in the third category – those from a nineteen-year-old girl to a twenty-year-old boy, long imaginative discourses on any and every subject which in the end could be turned into a romantic reflection of times past or yet to come. The writer was an attractive auburn-haired friend of my cousin's I had known briefly before the war, with whom there had been a rather fiery relationship interrupted by my amourette with Brenda. As that faded, so this was rekindled, largely courtesy of the Royal Mail, so there was never any shortage of subject matter. I was looking forward to the long-weekend leave which was due at the end of initial training and the award of the flying brevet (the coveted 'wings'), when the rumour was put about that even this may be forfeit as a result of the recent debacles. It was the middle of May, Rotterdam had been heavily bombed, the Dutch Army had capitulated, the British and French forces which had advanced into Belgium a few days ago had begun to retreat, and the only news which seemed to offer the slightest hope was that Winston Churchill had become Prime Minister.

These events had little effect on the atmosphere in the Sergeants' Mess, where it was business as usual. Many of the old hands, having served in various parts of the Empire, gave the impression of 'this is what it's all about!' whilst the young blades merely wanted to join squadrons as quickly as possible. The need to pull together now becoming more obvious with each passing day, there was greater harmony between the ground crew senior N.C.O's and we 'jumped up' RAFVR Sergeants. Originally, relationships had been a little frayed, but as one no-nonsense lad remarked "A lot of them had only been LAC's or Corporals themselves before the expansion of a few months ago".

Following reports of the activities of neo-Nazis such as Quisling in Norway, fifth-column fever inflicted itself on some citizens, and particularly on minor officials. Towards the end of this disastrous month, four of us had the opportunity on a non-flying Saturday to visit Cheltenham. 'Dad' Owen, one of the older members of the course – he must have been twenty-three or four – had his Vauxhall saloon at the camp, and offered a scenic ride through the Cotswold countryside. We went by way of Stow-on-the-Wold, then stopped on the bridge which spans the River Dikker in Upper Swell, with a small lake on the upstream side of the bridge, where we watched the assorted ducks and moorhens disporting themselves. It was a hamlet of weathered golden-cream Cotswold stone, and every edge seemed to catch the midday sun in a glow, backed by the pale shadow of a niche behind it. On the Tewkesbury road beyond, we had just reached the entrance to quarries on the left at the top of a long upward sweep when we were suddenly confronted by a figure in dark blue uniform – a Special Constable. He held up his hand; we stopped.

The ensuing conversation concerned the fact that 'Dad' Owen's car had unmasked headlights, and during his night duties the constable had seen some flashing lights, particularly on the brow of the hill opposite.

"Now," he said, "flashing lights be well known as a signal to the enemy by these 'ere fifth-columnists, and what better than a car headlights, eh Sir? Now" he continued "you bein' RAF gents an' all, I don't say it's the sort o' thing you'd be up to, but...." he paused for effect, "suppose someone borrowed your car during the night an' you found it where you'd left it next morning. Would you be suspicious? Course not!"

Dad pointed out that we were from Little Rissington and it was a strict rule that all cars should be kept locked when not in use. We could see that the constable was putting his mind through the possibilities that someone had a duplicate key, or knew how to gain entry to a locked car, or found it unlocked, so Dad went round to the boot of the car to retrieve the headlamp masks he had taken off that morning.

"Look" he said, "I'm sorry, I cleaned the car this morning and forgot to put the masks back on. You can't clean the headlamp glass very well without taking them off. I'll put them on again in the car park in Cheltenham, and as for the flashing lights, have you considered that they could come from masked headlights on a car reaching the top of a hill slightly higher than you are? You may see them, but it doesn't mean they can be seen from above, and they disappear from your view as soon as the car is over the top."

Whilst the special constable was pondering this, Dad got in, and with a wave and a honk on the horn, we drove off. Looking through the rear window, I saw the country's guardian give us a smart salute. England would be saved!

Down we went into Temple Guiting, another village where the apparently undetermined grouping of mellow buildings created an attractive whole. The curve in the road through the village and the sharp bend round by the church suggested – not planned, but perfect. No lack of history here, for it had been the residence of the Knights Templars. So on past Sudeley Castle, burial place of Katherine Parr; Winchcombe, ancient walled city of Mercia, and into Cheltenham on the A 46 down Cleeve Hill, looking west across the panoramic sweep of the Severn valley.

If the broad Promenade in Cheltenham was any different to its peacetime self it was hardly discernible; gardeners were replacing the spent tulips and wallflowers with summer-flowering plants, and to the throngs on the pavement by the elegant Regency buildings the only direct evidence of perilous times was the billboard outside the newsagents: 'Belgian Army collapses – H.M.S. Curlew sunk'. But England still had its tea-shops, and , in this particular one just behind the Promenade, preference for Servicemen in the matter of cream with the scones. Then we enjoyed a relaxed saunter, went to the cinema, and returned to base – with the headlamp masks in place!

We were approaching the time of C.F.I. Tests, which, together with the written exam results, would determine the award of 'wings', so when sent off to fly solo, there was serious application to the task in hand. No more preference for sightseeing, enjoying the sweep of the wolds, or making imaginary attacks on an obelisk in the middle of some large wood. Now, one eye patrolled the local air space, whilst the other was on the instruments which would be keenly noted by the examiner. Watch that Bank Indicator, you're slipping in during that steep turn; the Rate of Climb Indicator - it's supposed to be 500 feet a minute; synchronise those engines; show you've trimmed the aircraft to fly hands off; your gyro compass is three degrees out compared with the magnetic compass; at least point to the oil pressure gauge to show you've seen that it's fluctuating slightly; must improve on that sequence of actions in the event of engine failure; watch the artificial horizon in that thirty degree bank right-hand turn, with a little more power to maintain height; most of all, I hope this is going to be a good approach – line up left a little – and landing, bump, bump, not bad!

Sufficient, in fact, to satisfy the Chief Flying Instructor when it came to the test, and, with reasonable success in the written papers, the 'wings' were mine, and so said all of us, as no one had failed at this stage.

For the long-weekend leave which celebrated this event, five of us hailing from the Manchester area hired a quite elegant Crossley saloon car which had a pre-selector gear change. There was a lever on the steering-wheel column which had to be placed against the appropriate numbered notch to pre-select the next gear likely to be needed, and when the clutch was depressed then raised, that gear would be the one in use. So, if in fourth gear, the lever would be placed in third gear position, and it therefore needed rapid thought if, say, it was being driven in third gear whilst pre-selected to fourth, when some unforeseen circumstance suddenly required second. After some engine-stalling in awkward places and gear-grinding in embarrassing ones, we became familiar with its idiosyncrasies without any apparent ill-effects to the engine, and it served us well.

Casting aside any cares we had about the French surrender to the Germans – "I shan't be off on a Dawn Patrol now!" – "Madamoiselle from Armentieres will miss me!" – "I'll bet she knew your father!" came a rejoinder – we traced a route along the Fosse Way through the lush Midland pastures, singing the songs of the moment, "Begin the Beguine" et al, accompanied by stirring sounds from the paper-and-comb specialists. As I had furthest to go, I took the car on to Rossendale, and started the return journey at six o'clock on the Sunday evening.

On the journey up in daylight, there had been no problems about the road to take, but as darkness fell on Sunday night and we passed into less familiar territory, navigational problems began. The threat of invasion, paratroopers, and fifth columnists, had necessitated the removal of all signposts on the roads and the obliteration of names wherever they may be in exposed places. There was no moon that night, and more by luck than by good navigation we took only one wrong turning, which we soon corrected courtesy of directions from an A.R.P. Warden. Until, that is, we approached a deserted crossroads 'somewhere in the Cotswolds', with twenty minutes left to midnight, the hour at which leave expired.

Which road to take? The beam from the masked headlights shone far enough to illuminate a telephone kiosk, and Phil was deputed to use it to maximum advantage. In the meantime, Tom was despatched to look for any signs of life. Phil returned first to tell us there was nothing useful in the kiosk, no Directory, no place-name, no exchange name and number in the dialling-plate, and no help from the operator. She explained, with some surprise at Phil's apparent ignorance, that it was perfectly correct of Post Office Telephones to strip the kiosk of everything apart from the actual instrument 'because you never knew who might be lurking about these days', but she agreed to put him through to 'a Police Station', where his call was regarded with the greatest suspicion.

"There's been an 'ay stack set alight last night, an' it might 'ave been a signal!" was the reason given for refusing information to anyone over the telephone.

Tom returned to say that there was a pub by the name of 'The King's Head' about a hundred yards away, but he couldn't make anyone hear. Phil thought that if he gave the name of the pub to the operator, she could be persuaded to say where it might be, but he found instead that she merely put him through to the police station again. Becoming desperate, he gave the constable the names of each of the five of us, (stressing the 'all Sergeant Pilots') and pointed out that we were all on operational flying first thing in the morning, pleading with him to ring the guardroom at Little Rissington to confirm our identity, and the fact that we were returning from leave. By this time, we were all crowded in and around the kiosk, and after a long three minutes we rang the police station again, and were treated to an apologetic explanation of how he was only doing his duty. At last, we had the directions we needed. We were at the crossroads of the A 44 and the A 424 south of Blockley.

Our opinion of the policeman changed whilst we were in the guardroom fifteen minutes after midnight: the duty corporal said he would not book us in as late, since the time of the constable's call showed that we would have been on time but for a slight error in navigation. "I hope you have more success with your navigation in the air!" was his parting shot.

COASTAL COMMAND PILOT

Navigation was indeed one of the more important aspects of the advanced course upon which we now embarked, flying from Rissington airfield over the higher, open reaches of the Cotswolds. Stow-on-the-Wold and Bourton-on-the-Water became the two chief landmarks, the former perched at 700 feet, its streets and honey- coloured buildings sloping gently away to the east from the long north-south line of the Fosse Way, with the steep fields on the west dipping down to the stream in the valley below. Bourton was easily identified by the several ponds on the east side, and the River Windrush flowing alongside the main street. Apart from the occasional dual check of application to a particular task, newly qualified pilots were paired together in roles which began to simulate the needs of operational squadrons. I was fortunate to have Tom Mycock as my co-pilot; he flew with precision, was as determined to do well as I was, he never panicked and he was always cheerful.

One of our first tasks was to carry out a detailed reconnaissance at 2,000 feet of the railway yards at Didcot Junction, where the Oxford and Birmingham line of the Great Western Railway leaves the one to Bristol. Our track took us close to Brize Norton, where we exchanged a wing-waggle with the pilot of an Oxford aircraft, then flew alongside him. He pointed to our Anson, gave us the thumbs up sign, and nodded his head; we nodded in agreement. Then he pointed downwards to his own 'kite', and, with a suitable grimace, gave it the thumbs down. Tom spread his arms in a sympathetic gesture, and we banked away gently, with that wonderful feeling of floating as the distance between the two aircraft lazily widened.

Our mentors had chosen a day when the marshalling yards at Didcot were full, and we were expected to record every detail. It was a sight for the sore eyes of any model railway enthusiast. There was a long train in the cream and chocolate G.W.R. livery standing at the station on the 'down' line, hauled by a dark green 'Castle' class engine – unmistakeable from the shape of its funnel and the polished brass steam dome.

"Let's go down and see which Castle it is!" Tom suggested. We saw the curved nameplate over the driving wheels – 'Truro Castle' – as we flashed by, then up again to start counting the wagons in the yard, and noting whether they were 'L.M.S', 'S.R', 'G.W.R', or carried the name of some industrial firm such as 'Dorman Long'. We tried to differentiate between those wagons which the little shunting engine was moving for unloading and those which were being prepared for onward movement. It was very pleasant floating around on a perfect day, adding the occasional observation to the prolific notes Tom was taking down.

"I suppose we'd be doing this rather differently if we were under fire!" I said, which, for the first time summarized a serious observation about what the future might hold. His reply was typical Tom: "We could probably do the job almost as well from 6,000 feet, above small arms fire, with a pair of binoculars, or better still, a camera!"

It was on our way back to Rissington that we encountered our first gremlin – that invisible agent of fate with the power to cause problems to aircraft which are attributable to no other source. The only embodiment of their form came from some pilot's imagination, a shape which had been accepted by this time throughout the RAF – peering over the edge of an aircraft wing, (as might be described in heraldic terms) the top half of an oval head with a single curly hair upstanding, embellished by the upper curve of two eyes, and on each side supporting, the ends of four fingers gripping the edge of the wing. This is not what we saw, but we knew one of them had visited the aircraft when, without any warning, there was a clanging sound down the port side and a sudden wobble on the elevators. With the oil temperature of the port engine dropping slightly, we discovered on returning to base that a small fairing on the port engine nacelle had come loose, but fortunately it had apparently caused no damage in the air or on the ground, as it dropped into a large area of woodland which we were over at the time. Tom was complimented on the detail of his report, and on his good fortune in being endowed with eyesight able to see the nameplate on an engine from 2,000 feet!

Whilst the Harvard pilots became familiar with the use of the gunsight in deflection shooting and simulated forward-firing machine guns, we twin-engined brethren practised the skill needed for a bomb to meet its target, by means of the camera obscura. This structure reminded anyone familiar with the farm buildings of Kent of an oast- roundel with a flattened top; there was simply a door within the circumference and an aperture in the middle of the roof. Inside was a raised section reminiscent of a draughtsman's table, upon which rested a chart and various instruments, and a means of opening and closing the aperture. With this open, and the building in total darkness, it was tantamount to the legendary mine-shaft up which one could look at the stars. If an aircraft flying over it emitted an intense light for a split second it would be seen on the table below and could be plotted.

Given the operational information we would have on approaching a target, such as the bomb's type, characteristics and falling pattern, also the height and speed at which to fly, together with the calculations which would have to be made in the air, when seeking to 'bomb' the camera obscura building we should be able to register a 'flash' on target. Easier said than done! In the strong thermal up-currents in that hot summer of 1940, the relatively low altitudes at which we flew precluded the likelihood of a stable platform from which to aim. Tom, lying prone in the nose of the Anson, watching the target move down the drift-wires on the bomb-sight, would press the bomb-release switch which activated the flashbulb, and some perverse air current would throw the aircraft a degree or two off course at the vital moment. Even when there was no apparent air disturbance, a look at the obscura plotting-table after landing reminded us we had a lot to learn. This simulated bombing was of two types: grouping the 'bombs' according to a predetermined pattern, or dropping a 'stick' in a single run over the target. I hoped that when the positions were reversed and I flew as bomb-aimer, I would have learnt something from Tom's commendable application.

The altitude test had to be flown solo. The aircraft was fully loaded to its maximum take-off weight and had to be taken up to 15,000 feet, as a test of the pilot's ability to remain compos mentis, able, without the use of oxygen, to react adequately to the effects of the rarified atmosphere. Given a fine day, and they were not in short supply that summer, it was a breathtaking experience in more ways than one, with the English landscape from the Severn estuary across to Oxford, and from Evesham down to Swindon, set out in rolling panorama.

It was becoming apparent throughout the Service that daylight bombing of enemy targets, with the aircraft then available, could not be sustained unless there was fighter cover, an element of surprise, or carried out as a short-range sortie. Accordingly, there was increased emphasis on night-flying training. At this time of year, and with the added 'daylight-saving hour', dusk could only be said to have fallen by eleven o'clock, and as the night-flying detail was sometimes at the end of a lecture sequence, we had now occasionally reached an eighteen hour day.

As at Kidlington during the basic night-flying, the flare-path consisted of up to ten goose-neck flares along the left-hand side of the landing strip, the orange-bright flames giving an eerie glow to the smoke billowing downwind, with a faint stench of burning paraffin wafting through the open side-window of the cockpit as the Anson drifted past on landing. Tales of enemy night-intruder activity before the fall of France led to some conjecture about the time it would take to extinguish all the flares in an emergency, and, more importantly to a pilot waiting to land, the time needed to light them again. In the event, when the threat became frequent reality, most aerodromes had concrete runways with landing-path lights embedded in them. Battery-operated Glim (Glowing Dim) lamps provided an immediate answer.

Towards the end of July, the news of persistent German air attacks on shipping in the Channel, with the implied threat of seeking air superiority before an invasion, increased the tempo of training still more, and, particularly amongst the trainee fighter pilots, the desire to get into action.

Following success in the written exams, we concentrated on the C.F.I. Test and the timed Cross-country exercises, firstly as pilot, and secondly as navigator, after which the Navigation Log would be strictly examined, particularly concerning estimated timings in relation to actual arrivals, and the documentation of landing at the distant airfield two-thirds of the way round the course. Tom was my co-pilot as usual; I navigated on the first test, and flew the Anson on the second. This gave me a wonderful, abiding memory of the Cotswolds.

It was an early morning take-off on a perfectly clear, still day, and the forecast was for yet more sunshine. As we lifted off from our perch on one of the highest parts of the Cotswolds, we could see the lower land enveloped in mist. The rounded hills, a patchwork of dark woods, faded green grass and the yellow of ripening corn, seemed like a quilt placed on a bed of silvery-white sheets. Valleys were lost in millions of shimmering droplets. The dappled cream buildings of Stow-on-the-Wold in streets sloping eastwards to the sun were silhouetted against the mist covering the Evenlode valley beyond. Bourton-on-the-Water snuggled somewhere under the blanket, but the nearby ponds were discernible as vague silvery patches blinking through the mist which covered the valley of the River Windrush down towards Burford. It was a different world of islands and mysterious depths, with here a church spire protruding, and there a strange column of smoke rising through the mist to spread out anvil-shaped upon reaching the warmer air above.

The sun had worked its own magic by the time we returned from our triangular course and the check landing detailed at Upper Heyford. The mist had gone, and with it the ten minutes of mysterious beauty which had been unique to Tom and to me.

The course ended with a brief statement of our postings: the Harvard pilots going mostly to Hurricane Conversion Units, with a few to Spitfires, and the Anson pilots to Bomber Operational Training Units, with two exceptions – Jack Hall (known as 'Henry' after the famous band-leader), and myself. We were posted to No 1 Operational Training Unit of Coastal Command at Silloth, to learn to fly Hudsons. To where, flying what? Two unknowns!

That was for later – now we were off on a week's leave, Henry, Tom, and I travelling up to London together. Henry's home was in Putney, and after a reminiscing trawl of Fleet Street pubs he went home. My only concern was to catch the last train home from Manchester, so Tom and I strolled through the streets to Euston.

The non-committal news was typical of a day in early August 1940: 'The enemy has attacked targets on the south coast and in the Channel, losing 31 aircraft. 20 of our fighters are missing.' No one was in any doubt that London would be bombed, and the walls of sandbags were still growing, thicker and higher, 'Air Raid Shelter' signs could be seen in every street, and nearly all transport was in Army khaki, A.R.P green, or London Transport red.

Manchester seemed a minor imitation of this as we walked from London Road station to Victoria in the evening twilight. Tom left the train at Prestwich, with something more than pangs of sadness within each of us; we had been together for a year, and had shared our flying with a zest which only comes from complete confidence each with the other. I never saw Tom again, but I was to read of the award of his Distinguished Flying Cross for a raid on Brest. It seemed appropriate that he was flying an Avro Manchester aircraft at the time.

Emerging after breakfast next morning, my first thoughts were of how little Rossendale had changed. There were a few sandbags piled in front of the village Police Station, and no more than half-a-dozen people in uniform although nearly all my friends had been called up, now presumably awaiting their first leaves. Otherwise the greatest impact of the war so far seemed to be in rationing. The timeless chemist's shop on the corner of the street leading to my Aunt's house retained its decaying Victorian aura, presided over still by an ageing one-suit- a-lifetime proprietor who never appeared without a trilby hat on his head. He had a kindly air but few customers to benefit from it. Whilst other chemists had been swept along by the 1930's tide of boxes, packets and tubes, he still dispensed by juggling the contents of brown bottles with large glass stoppers, which he took down from the rows of shelves behind the cluttered counter. The bottles had exquisite labels with gold borders describing their contents, which were imprinted on my memory as a boy: TICT LAVAND AQ, PULV TRAGAC CO, TINCT CAPSICI, DEC SCOPAR. Now, most of them seemed to be empty, and I wondered if they would ever be refilled with their substances.

On a visit to an aunt near Blackpool during my leave, I discovered that an Aircrew Holding Unit had been opened in the town, and again I thanked providence that I had been one of the early birds, for how could this place of past peacetime pleasures compare with Cambridge? Drilling on the Promenade instead of the Backs! But what of the Tower, the Winter Gardens, and Yates's Wine Lodge? Ah well, 'chacun a son gout'.

Flying Training at Little Rissington

Sergeants: North, Mycock, House, Rowlands, Hildyard, Page, Humphries, Palliser, Loveridge, Stone, Irving, Hine, Morrison, Jones,
Meeson, Watson, Holland, Hodgson, Owen, Marsden, Craddock, Rayner, Porter, Houghton, Hughes W.D., Buckley,
Peach, Brutey, Hayward, Hall, Hughes D.L., Read, Jarwood, Keighley, Roach, Massey, Syrett, Jessop

CHAPTER 5

SPILLS BY SOLWAY

So to the only part of the country with a State-owned brewery, apparently taken over during the First World War so that the strength of the beer drunk by local munitions workers could be controlled, to the eventual benefit of the troops at the front who were relying on their products. Taking the train from Carlisle to Silloth, the 'little jewel of the Solway Firth', marked a change from the part of the country which felt threatened to one which patently did not. The train to Carlisle had been filled almost to overflowing with rumbustious sailors and new-uniformed soldiers going on to Scottish bases. I then shared my compartment from Carlisle to Silloth with a local farmer who appeared to know little about the course of the war; he was concerned that the order to plough up as much pasture as possible to grow corn would affect a lucrative sideline – wasn't Silloth turf the best for golf-courses?

The town boasted a pleasant, though humble, promenade and a small dock and wharfage at the southern end. The RAF station lay behind with only a field separating the two, and most of the hangars on the side furthest from the town. Henry and I, together with a small group of Sergeant Wireless Operators/Air Gunners who were also new arrivals, were detained in the Orderly Room awaiting the Accommodation Officer's pleasure, when a sergeant pilot entered.

"What are you going to fly?" he asked, "Bothas, Battles, Ansons, Hudsons?"

"Hudsons" offered Henry.

"Ah!" he said, with a knowing grimace, "they swing a lot on take-off if you let 'em!" and he was gone, no doubt to bestow his encouragement elsewhere.

"Don't worry, he's only an Anson pilot stooging around with WOP/AG's," comforted the Orderly Corporal, but it was hardly the reception we expected.

The Orderly Officer handed us over to his corporal. "The Sergeants' Mess is full," he said, his sigh inferring it was all our fault. "You, like several others, have been honoured with a place at the town's favourite pre-war recuperative resort. Can't think why," he continued whimsically "so far no bod has emerged any the better! The Corporal will take you there."

We found this to be a reference to the Hydro Hotel, a smallish off-white building on the sea-front, with a pleasant outlook across the Solway Firth to the

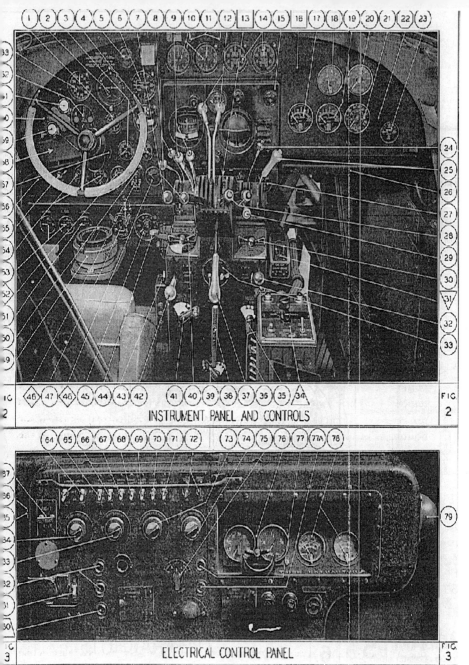

INSTRUMENT PANEL AND CONTROLS

FIG.
2

ELECTRICAL CONTROL PANEL

FIG.
3

◇MARKS I II III VI only ◇MARKS III V VI only △MARK I (series 3) only △MARKS III (series 1,3 4) V (series 2,3) only ▽ MARKS IV V VI only ○MARKS I II only

Hudson pilots, do you remember...? (see page 264)

higher ground of Dumfriesshire beyond. The exterior of the hotel, although far from sparkling, was better than the interior, which suggested a period of decline extending well before the outbreak of war. However, the sitting room – subject of an understandable special plea from the landlady – had sufficient hotch-potch chairs and was of a size to allow us to feel comfortable but not overcrowded, so we set about getting to know each other. It was the first time Henry and I had had the opportunity to discuss the outlook and techniques of aircrew other than pilots.

The sequence of conversion to Hudson aircraft followed the pattern of previous training: first, familiarisation. My instructor, known as Mac, was prosaic in his introduction:

" Have a good look at the outside, it's different; it's American. Twin rudders and fins; Fowler flaps, which don't just hinge, they also travel outwards to increase the width as well as the chord of the wing. A good reconnaissance machine – plenty of room for observing and taking photographs. Command seems to think it's all things to all men, but it's certainly the best kite in use in Coastal at the moment."

"What about the Blenheim?"

"What about it?" was the reply." If you'd rather meet Jerry on the other side of the North Sea in a Blenheim, good luck! They may be a bit faster and in some respects more manoeuvrable, but with a Hudson you've got a total of seven machine-guns covering all sides, even your belly if you winch down the flap in the bottom of the fuselage, and better single-engine flying, with feathering of the propeller on the failed engine on later models. The whole layout is so much better for longer flights."

It was indeed fortunate for the pilots who flew them that Hudsons were originally designed as civil airliners flying American routes, with instrumentation appropriate to the relatively advanced state of navigational aids in the United States at the time.

The cockpits of many British aircraft seemed to have been designed so that controls appeared where cables or pipes happened to intrude into the pilot's area. It wasn't until the Spring of 1942 that it was decreed that all Bomber Command aircraft should have an automatic pilot. One of the blessings of a Hudson was that it had such an aid – known affectionately as 'George', from the catch-phrase 'Let George do it'. It had been designed as a central feature of the instruments around the pilot. The control lever was one of several – throttles, variable pitch airscrew, mixture control, propeller-feathering button – centrally mounted on a dappled matt-black quadrant, below which protruded the hand-brake lever. The engine-rev counters and boost gauges were above the auto-pilot box, which had small bevelled knobs for setting 'George' in parallel with the aircraft's attitude, to allow a smooth transition from manual to automatic control.

There were, of course, limits to the manoeuvres which George could sustain, and there were few pilots who could resist the temptation to explore these knob-twirling limits in dive, climb, and turn. All lighting was rheostat-controlled, and the small spotlight in the centre of the canopy above, which could be subdued to a dim glow faintly illuminating the throttle quadrant, was a boon in the early stages of night-flying. The top of the canopy had a cover which could be pulled forward as a sunshade or blind – a blessing for those who were to fly these machines in hotter climates.

"Now you've seen it, let's fly it!" said Mac, and his hand flicked round the instruments in the lengthy check and setting sequence. I wasn't yet required to memorise the actions – I imagined a lonely vigil in a parked aircraft when I would be sitting in the cockpit alone with detailed check-notes – and it was the additions to commonplace checks which excited most interest:

"Tail wheel locked; auto-pilot off; auto-pilot vacuum selector valve, left; altimeter valve, static; carburettor heat controls, cold; airscrew pitch, coarse; fuel engine selector, both; manifold pressure valve, zero check."

There followed the use of the fuel hand pump to prime, master ignition switch on, then the starter and the booster were engaged simultaneously, round went the propeller as the engine fired, and the individual ignition switch was flicked on. As the engines roared during the pre-take-off checks, I was elated by the relative luxury of this latest aeronautical habitat, and spared a thought for the crank-handlers of the Ansons at Kidlington.

Performance in the air, as demonstrated by my instructor, was equal to the potential apparent on the ground, as we climbed, turned, dived, and seemingly floated over the silver-rippling waters of the Solway Firth, to become acquainted with the 1,868 feet high dome of Criffell mountain on the other side.

There were tales to tell in the Hydro Hotel that night as we recounted first experiences of the Hudson, but one fact was agreed: this aircraft certainly needed a pilot to land it, whereas the Anson almost landed itself. The next morning was unfit for flying, and as Henry and I returned to the hotel we were met by the landlady. She was a rather emotional woman intent on improving her features with the aid of auburn-tints, rouge, and bright lipstick. Sitting almost upon one of her high-heeled mauve shoes was a small white terrier-type dog of mixed ancestry. She gave it a concerned glance, then directed a much more generous gaze at Henry and at me.

"He does so miss his walkies if I'm otherwise engaged! I simply have to go out on an urgent errand, and none of the other boys are in – will you both be real darlings and exercise his little legs?" – and with that she had slipped the lead into Henry's hand and was gone. I tried to disappear through the open porch door, but Henry grabbed my arm with the reminder "One for Hall and Hall for one! Let's go!"

The little dog kept up well with the pace we set as we strode across the fields, his short legs moving rapidly as would an animated cartoon. Possibly he was also amused by the figure of fun Henry and I presented when walking together, Henry being about eight inches shorter than I but taking longer strides.

At the turning point we decided our docile charge had behaved well enough to be let off the lead, as we felt sure he would have a homing instinct. He certainly seemed to have a well-developed one, for the instant he was released he took off on the correct course to steer at a fair rate of knots. It wasn't until we reached the brow of a slight rise and could look down along his path that we discovered he had altered course by about twenty degrees, and his revised target was all too apparent – a swollen muddy stream and its equally muddy environs. In he went, he rolled, he sloshed, he even found time to bark his appreciation. By the time we reached the morass, he was being carried along by the current, crooning a tune which reminded one of a sea-shanty.

We set off to follow in a splashing extravaganza, cutting across a bend in the stream to arrive, fortuitously, at the spot where he decided to beach his body. It was obvious that he had long had his eye on that stream but had never before had the opportunity to sample its delights. He greeted us with a series of wet-hair-shaking vibrations which if measured on the Reichter scale would herald a minor earthquake, then he flopped on to his back, expecting to have his tummy tickled. Instead, he was rudely accosted by two aggrieved trainee dog-walkers who rubbed him and rubbed him again with bunches of the driest flora which came to hand. He seemed to enjoy it, except for the piece of thistle which pricked him in a tender spot.   We put him on the lead, and he became once more, in temperament, the docile pet the landlady adored; in appearance, however, there were signs that his docility had at some stage deserted him. By the time we reached the hotel, his matted hair had changed his colour from white to mottled brown, and his negative ambient odour had become very positive. The landlady had not returned, so we put him in the back yard, cleaned him up as best we could, and left for urgent duty (!) at the airfield. We stayed there later than usual that day, and forsook supper at the hotel in favour of a café meal which we were certain would be more peaceful. Retribution was delayed only until the following morning, when the lady's vocal output proved to be the equal of her pet's the previous day. Her concluding statement that she would never speak to either of us again was carried out to the letter, and when communication was necessary, one of the other lads had to act as interlocutor:

"Would you mind asking your friend the tall one why his room is so untidy?" or "Please tell your friend the short one that a parcel came for him today and I'll put it on the stairs."

Competence in take-off and landing was not difficult to achieve once we were familiar with techniques such as using variable-pitch propellers, mixture control, and selecting the correct amount of flap for the type of approach. Although still using a grass surface but with a heavier aircraft, after the hot dry summer the ground was as unforgiving to a bad landing as any concrete runway would have been. The need to pass aircrew through to squadrons as quickly as possible pre-empted operational training as such; it was still a matter of gaining experience by sending off two pilots as before – one to fly the aircraft, the other to act as navigator, and occasionally as bomb-aimer. There was no opportunity to operate with other aircrew as a team, and one might conclude we were being trained at a Conversion Unit rather than at an Operational Training Unit as such.

At the time, this mattered little, as we were as keen as anyone to get to squadrons, and the pressure on the staff meant that we were sent off for a couple of hours at a time to practise exercises such as splash firing the front guns at a target in the Solway Firth, or taking wind-drifts at different altitudes, simulating dive-bombing, or simply navigating from A to B. On occasions, however, Henry and I put pleasure before practice.

Jean, whose refreshing letters had been a lively link during my time at Little Rissington, was now working in Bootle, and on the last Sunday in August, 1940, having checked that I was on a two-hour detail with Henry, I telephoned her to suggest we could rendezvous at the end of Southport pier. I knew from peacetime visits that it was a long pier, so that whatever air manoeuvres we were able to perform would be far removed from any enquiring eyes in the town. To ease our consciences, we practised low-flying on the way down, skimming the dappled sunlit waters of the Firth, turning in a never-ending chase on to our shadow on the starboard bow, then as it disappeared coaxing the aircraft back on course for the distant Point of Ayre on the Isle of Man. Rising to 2,000 feet as it came in sight, with the wind-lanes on the open sea clearly visible to give a useful estimate of wind speed and direction, we set course for Southport pier.

As we approached at about 500 feet, I could see Jean waving some white object at the very end of the pier, so I turned away in a dive down to a height which in official terms might compromise safety, then round again to fly past at about the height of the pier. After repeating this manoeuvre, I became aware that not only had other onlookers joined in the vigorous waving, but, as we flashed by, the leader of the band playing in the Bandstand near the end of the pier seemed to be gesticulating in unison. I could imagine him conducting the musicians in some stirring tune in keeping with the lads who were even then battling in the air over southern Britain, and it was a time when people were cheered by the appearance of any RAF 'plane, so I gained a little height, then targeted the Bandstand.

Approaching in a dive with engines throttled back and windows open, we thought we could faintly hear the beat from down below; then as we passed over with throttles opening, we zoomed round in a steep left-hand turn. The band appeared to be still playing, but I couldn't see the conductor. We made one more pass and a wing-waggle, with a final wave to and from Jean, then flew across the vast expanse of sand towards the Ribble estuary. It was our first taste of public acclaim of the RAF in flight, and it was heady wine.

"What about Blackpool?" said Henry. The idea had already crossed my mind.

"Good idea," I replied, "there are three piers there!"

This was by far the best practice we had had in the tactics of low-level attack at sea, where the pilot is expected to 'skip' a bomb into the side of a ship, then pull up over it. We thought we would perfect it on the pier at St Annes-on-Sea before the triple jump at Blackpool. Again people waved, but I only had Henry's account of public reaction as we went over the South, Central and North piers at Blackpool, for in skipping them we had no sooner eased down after the first than I was concentrating on heaving up over the second, leaving us in no doubt that had the third been a ship, we would not have hit it with a bomb! Henry enjoyed this activity as much as I did, so he took over and managed to find a few more such targets along the coast on the way to St Bee's Head, whence a sense of decorum returned and we made our stately way back up the Solway Firth.

I telephoned Jean that evening; she had enjoyed it immensely, after recovering from the embarrassment of having the crowd realise that she was the main target, then having them join in the animation. I had, however, misread the gesticulations of the band leader, whom she thought was no less a personage than Joe Loss. They were meant to show his understandable annoyance while the band played on, and when I mentioned that he was no longer in view after we had targeted the bandstand, this was because he was striding down towards the end of the pier, presumably to get the aircraft number. His gesticulations were then of a different order, and he was entirely justified in his point of view!

The week ahead held the prospect of single-engine flying, then night-flying dual. Although Pilot's Notes for the Hudson could not be faulted in the statement that the aircraft flies well on one engine, it was the transition from two engines to one which caused a certain flow of adrenalin, particularly when flying with an instructor. Knowing the purpose of the exercise, and having reached a suitable height, there was usually something akin to a cat-and-mouse game going on in the cockpit after the instructor's demonstration. "I wonder when, and which engine?" you think.

You watch his every move out of the corner of your eye as he nonchalantly sits beside you in the right hand seat. Depending on his mood or personality, he might raise his hand to – scratch his brow, or suddenly lean forward to deal with a fly on the windscreen, or point to some other instrument close to the throttle levers – each movement seeming like the one which is going to close one throttle. But my instructor was more forthright; in the first demonstration we climbed to 4,000 feet, he went through the motions, then he told me he was closing the engine – "Now get on with it!" But I was a mouse to his cat in practise after that.

In late August, preliminary work began on the laying of concrete runways. We continued to take-off and land on the remaining grass areas, and dual instruction in night-flying began with sufficient space for the flare- path to be placed into wind. There was understandable urgency in building concrete runways now that ample evidence had shown that grass surfaces were unsuitable for faster and heavier aircraft. At Silloth, the contractors began to work at night under brilliant floodlights, presumably to beat the effects of the coming winter weather on a low-lying area, or perhaps at the behest of an optimistic Ministry planner. This first conversion course of Hudson pilots had to be hurried along to squadrons; whilst Fighter Command dealt with the threat in the air, Coastal Command had to be ready to join battle with any sea-borne invasion. Therefore, to complete the course as quickly as possible, solo night-flying was going ahead, but so was simultaneous construction of the runway, and the flare-path could not be placed directly into wind because of it. During the dual check-flight at dusk, there was little wind, but it backed and strengthened as the night wore on.

Two pilots were detailed together for night solo circuits and landings, flown first by one pilot, then the other. My co-pilot was Sgt Mitchell, and we agreed I should do two circuits and landings, then he would follow. As I carried out the final take-off check at right angles to the flare-path, I could see the smoke from the goose-neck spouts billowing out in the frequent gusts of wind, so I didn't expect a smooth trip. I'd had no instruction in any form of take-off and landing procedure other than directly into wind; apparently it hadn't been considered necessary, although it taxed the imagination to believe that all the instructors from the C.F.I. down had always flown from grass fields in that way. The very fact that runways were being made might have been food for thought; not that conjecture would help me now.

On take-off one subconsciously uses the rudder to keep straight, so in retrospect I was not really aware that I was having to deal with a tendency for the Hudson to drift across the flare-path line. Once into the take-off surge, with the control column eased forward to bring up the tail, the remaining line of flares became subliminal, with concentration on the flight instruments – air speed, rate of climb, altimeter, gyro compass, which I had set to zero degrees before take-off. Flying the downwind leg on 180 degrees, I noticed that we seemed to be getting slightly nearer to the line of flares down below when we should have been parallel to it, but then came the turn for the approach and landing – undercarriage down, airscrew pitch set, flaps down, retractable landing lights on, and easing back the throttles on the final approach.

The floodlights over the work on the new runway outshone the nearest landing-path flares, and those at the far end seemed to be moving slowly across the windscreen from right to left. To keep the aircraft aligned to the flare-path, I had been subconsciously moving the nose across, and on the approach path in the last fifty feet, I found it was pointing directly at the floodlit working area. I swung the nose of the aircraft parallel to the flare-path, and as we crossed the boundary I eased back the throttle and put her down. The actual touchdown seemed reasonable, but the Hudson immediately started 'crabbing', the undercarriage collapsed, and we slid along the ground amid the groans of metal fractures. My shin hit the edge of the compass base as I was thrown forward, I switched off the ignition and petrol, and hobbled down the cabin to follow Sgt Mitchell on to terra firma. I was left to wonder where on the circuit we had been joined by the gremlin responsible for this misfortune. I had come down to earth with a literal as well as a metaphorical bump, as this was the first time landing an aircraft had presented any problems.

British twin-engined aircraft such as the Anson and the Wellington had support on both sides of the landing wheels, which gave greater resistance against sideways stress. It was a weakness of the Hudson that only a single hydraulic leg on the inner side of the wheel took the strain. The fact that such weaknesses were not included in the familiarisation prior to solo flight now seemed to be an unfortunate oversight.

We were surprised to find the same flying detail listed for the following night, and without a dual check as a precursor. The only comment I heard was that it was well known that Hudson aircraft did not take kindly to stress on the undercarriage. I realised my emotions counted for little when compared with Sgt Mitchell's, for he was again detailed as my co-pilot, and the conclusion we reached was that as my faux pas had stopped the previous night's flying, the detail had merely been repeated en bloc. The landing area had been cleared, and during the day the wind again dropped, but as night fell conditions were much the same as before.

It was, indeed, a repeat performance. Sgt Mitchell must have regarded it as an uncontrollable nightmare after a frightening experience. There was one significant difference. In the final approach, when I pulled the nose of the aircraft away from alignment with the floodlit working party, as I had the previous night, I realised with a silent 'Eureka' that the flare-path (or, later runway) was the track I had to make along the ground, and the aircraft's heading was the course I had to steer to allow for the drift caused by the crosswind. Navigation training had taught me this when in normal flight in the air, but as it had always been possible to land into wind on grass airfields, the need to allow for drift in landing had evidently been of no consequence during instruction. Using the course/track technique, all that would be needed as the wheels were about to touch the runway would be to firmly swing the nose to point in the direction of the desired landing run.

However, a flash of inspiration which was to serve me well thenceforth so that I became something of a 'crosswind specialist' was of little use just above the ground on a wrongly committed approach, in an aircraft suffering a lack of what I now knew to be necessary correlation between the way the wheels were pointing and the way the aircraft was determined to go. Again, after the wheels collapsed and precautionary action had been taken, we scampered down the cabin and out through the door, to find our feet were only inches away from a growing pool of petrol. We were learning yet more about the Hudson – this time that the seams around the petrol tanks tended to rupture when the undercarriage collapsed in a certain way. This caused serious thoughts in both our minds, which my colleague felt needed immediate verbal expression – the last occasion on which I had any direct communication with him, although what he said sufficed for all time.

There was to be no further night-flying until at least the main runway was completed, and the C.O. felt obliged to record my guinea-pig experiences in my logbook as 'Damaged aircraft on two occasions when carrying out night solo; needs considerably more experience on type before undertaking further night flying'. I decided the time was inappropriate to mention the omission in the training programme which a flash of inspiration had now rectified, much less the blinkered view which prevented him from acknowledging the lack of it. It seemed likely that no thought would be given to the landing-drift problem until the runway was completed, but for my part I hoped I would soon have the chance to put the required technique into practice at an airfield already blessed with a runway. Within two months the exigencies of war were to come to my aid in this ambition. It was more than a year later that I saw Air Publication 1690E – Pilot's Notes for the Hudson, in which on page 17 it was noted that 'aileron control is sluggish at slow speeds, and rudder....may be the only efficient way of bringing up a wing which has dropped at low speeds.'

With much more interest now than had been apparent during the summer over the fall of France, we now listened avidly to the broadcasts relating the progress of the Battle of Britain. It was obvious from the repeated reports of RAF bombers attacking the French Channel ports, and the air battles over southern England, that invasion threatened. The contingency plan to avert this threat obviously included O.T.U's, for on the afternoon of 15th September, pupils and instructors were ordered to a briefing which allocated crews to all available aircraft, to be on immediate stand-by throughout the night.

I had realised that morning that it was one year to the day since I had received mobilisation papers, and whatever my thoughts then, the threat of invasion and spending the night under the wing of an aeroplane was not among them. This was not some Spartan response on the part of the C.O., but a necessity because our billets were too far from the airfield should immediate orders be issued. Each aircraft was to be crewed by an instructor and a pupil, and bombed up with 'secret' weapons. Fortunately, the night was balmy, but very long; the day's reports of Fighter Command's efforts lingered in our minds as we thought of 'single-engine' colleagues from Rissington who had by now been thrown into the fray. Not for the first, nor the last, time we were thankful for a plentiful supply of RAF cocoa during the night: unique in taste, but generous in warmth.

Evidence that no obstacle to the threat of invasion was forgotten came from a friend in the Army. He was responsible for making the best military use of the narrow-gauge Romney Hythe and Dymchurch Light Railway along its coastal line in Southeast Kent, which involved keeping steam up in the several locomotives throughout the emergency, ready to haul armed trucks to threatened points if needed!

"Panic over!" was our standing down signal at noon the next day, and training was resumed, but enthusiasm for it had been lost in euphoric thoughts of joining squadrons in action. Nor had we long to wait!

"Sergeant Pilots Hall and Rayner are posted to No 220 Squadron at RAF Thornaby after weekend leave. Get clearance and travel warrants." Henry and I hunted round amongst the instructors until we found a Wireless Operator who had served on the Squadron. He extolled its record, among which were:

The first successful U-boat attack of the war on 19th September 1939, by a South African pilot, P/O Selly, in an Anson aircraft;

The first operational use of a Sperry bombsight on 30th April 1940, when the ship 'Tyborin' was sunk from 8,000 feet;

The 'Thornaby Bag', developed for Air/Sea Rescue;

Other 'firsts' were the attack on 13th December 1939 by a 220 Hudson on two enemy destroyers in the North Sea, and on 27th December the shooting down of a Do18D seaplane;

Outstanding photographs on Dunkirk beach patrols;

The first sighting of the German prison ship 'Altmark', leading to HMS 'Cossack' entering Norwegian waters to release the Merchant Navy men captured by the 'Admiral Graf Spee'   Henry looked at me and raised his eyebrows in a grimace which meant 'We've got a lot to learn'. I agreed, and thought 'At last....'

We were to learn later of the Squadron's exploits during the Norwegian campaign, best recorded in the words of Mr William Berge, of Kristiansand, Norway:

"On that eventful day of Tuesday, April 9, 1940, when Germany invaded Norway, 220 Squadron of Coastal Command was the only known British squadron being part of the air battle over my hometown this day. The patrolling aircraft of 220 showed some low-flying which left memories to this day, and also gave the Norwegians a hope of help being on its way. The Squadron was flying the Lockheed Hudson Mark I on long-range reconnaissance missions in Skagerrak and along the southern Norway.

On April 9, 1940, three aircraft were sent out early in the morning to patrol Skagerrak, these being C, G & F/ 220. During the early part of the mission they received signals from Thornaby that neutral waters no longer existed around Norway, as we were now fighting German armed forces.

Aircraft G/220 came roaring in at low altitude over Kristiansand around 7.30 a.m. that morning, just as the attacking German ships were in the process of pulling further out to sea. It was fired upon by everyone on both German and Norwegian sides until the Norwegians spotted its roundels. The view of this single Hudson made the local Commander put a telegram through to Headquarters in Horten in order to know how to react to British/French aircraft, whereupon an answer was sent back informing that under no circumstances were Allied forces to be fired upon. When the German forces came sailing in from the west and in a new formation two hours later, the gunners on the fortress held their fire, in the belief/unsureness if they were the Allied assistance they were told not to fire upon. So the Germans were observed too late as such. The crew of this Hudson G/220 were: F/O Wright, P/O McNeill, AC Simpson, AC Turner.

Somewhat later two more Hudsons encountered German aircraft and ships, these being J & F/220, the crew of J consisting of Sgt Pilot Dacombe, Sgt Pilot Humphreys, AC Callaghan and LAC Mitchell.

And finally, in the later afternoon, two more Hudsons came in over our hometown, to be fired upon by the German pom-pom now being placed in the harbour. The machines were:

U/220 P/O Carey, Sgt Pilot Walsh, Cpl Hugill, L A C Dolson. F 'F/O Tullock, Sgt Pilot Knowles, AC Fawcett, AC Luckhurst.'

The Hudson

"Recuperating" outside the Hydro Hotel billet, Silloth, August 1940 From left: Tommy Edwards, Self, Andy White, 'Tich' Titchener, 'Henry' Hall

220 SQUADRON COASTAL COMMAND
Motto – "We Observe Unseen"

Below: How German Reconnaissance saw it in August 1940. Thornaby aerodrome

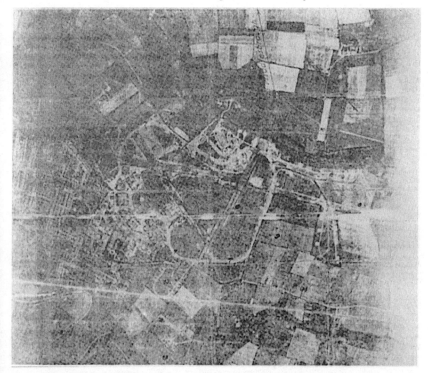

COASTAL COMMAND PILOT

CHAPTER 6

THE NORTH SEA AND BEYOND

oastal Command had been formed in 1936, and at the outbreak of war in 1939 its main function was to help the Royal Navy in the maintenance of our sea-borne communications, and the severance of the enemy's. In Area Combined Headquarters, Naval and Air Staff worked together. In September 1939 there was only one squadron equipped with Hudson aircraft, able to extend the foremost duty of the Command – reconnaissance over the North Sea against the greatest danger then perceived to our seaborne trade: the surface raider. Within a year, 'Security Area' flights across to the enemy-held coastline also included responsibility for first sighting of any invasion force.

The RAF Station at Thornaby-on-Tees owed its pre-war existence to the establishment of a squadron of the Auxiliary Air Force – No 608, equipped at the time of our arrival in September 1940 with Anson aircraft. No 220 Squadron, with its Hudsons, had several pilots who had seen action in Norwegian waters, along the Danish and Dutch coasts, and at Dunkirk. The Squadron Code – letters on the side of the aircraft denoting the squadron – were 'NR', which seemed most appropriate as it was based in the North Riding of Yorkshire!

The airfield was situated between, and almost bounded by, the towns of Middlesbrough to the east, and Stockton-on-Tees to the west, with the Racecourse and the River Tees on the far side. The day after I arrived I was given an air tour by P/O Sproston; it was the first time I had been in an aircraft which took off from a concrete runway.

"The balloons are up to welcome you! Don't make too wide a circuit. They're mostly over the I.C.I. Chemical plant at Billingham, and the docks – about ten to the square mile." From the ground before take-off they hadn't been especially noticeable because of the smog which was one of the pervading features of the area. Flying in the clearer air above the grey haze, the shining silvery balloons, each shaped like a fat sausage with four fins at the downwind end, and each pointing the same way as its companions as if held by some strange power, gave no indication of the lethal cables which tethered them to earth.

"If the wind is from the north or the east, there's likely to be pretty poor visibility, and even if it's from the west it's occasionally not so good," he continued "so you'll need to know the position of the Coronation pub – it's a good navigational aid, down there at the fork in the road." We were on a northeasterly course, and I could now see the coastline ahead, with the broad estuary of the Tees over to port. The familiarisation continued:

"When you come back from a North Sea sortie, and you see the barrage balloons shining above a sea of smog, it's a sign that visibility below a thousand feet will be pretty duff. So come in over Redcar pier," as indeed we were doing as I followed our route on the map – "and bear left on to the A 174, the road which runs west-south-west parallel to the line of the Cleveland Hills. Keep this road on your port side. Bear right after crossing the railway line" – we were now at a height of 700 feet – "and when you see the fork in the road at the Coronation, the airfield should be appearing on your left, and the racecourse on your right. Don't drift north past the racecourse, or you may have an argument with balloons, and unless your name is Weaver, it's likely to become Cropper, Ha! Ha! You'll need to do a split–A (tight) circuit to keep the runway in view, and down you go."

The demonstration ended with a perfect three-point landing; my confidence in the aircraft was flying high.

The Sergeants' Mess, although of wooden construction, was a cheerful, well-appointed place. The fact that it was on an operational station was apparent in a number of ways: there was a marked 'club' atmosphere, and ample evidence of accumulated and well-used Mess funds on the catering side – a late evening buffet table, usually of a joint of cold beef, cheeses, pickles, and good Vaux beer. For the first time in the Service, I had my own room in one of the long wooden huts adjoining the Mess. Also for the first time, the probability of a visit from enemy aircraft.

An occasional Luftwaffe 'plane would drone high across the area at night, or nip into the coastal area under low cloud during the day, sometimes preceded by an air raid warning. Little attention would be paid to the wailing sirens, and the Air Raid Shelters were seldom used. My first experience of hearing the local sirens occurred one evening when I was conveniently near a shelter, and having just read Station Orders which stated that personnel should take cover, I went in. I immediately realised that a better use had been found for the seclusion within. An officer with whom I had recently flown an air test was exchanging, perhaps maximising, emotions with a W.A.A.F officer. There was a very obvious reason why they had remained blissfully unaware of the air raid warning! Both were still wearing their tunics – was that sufficient, I wondered, to warrant a salute from a startled sergeant pilot? It was certainly a different view of him to the one I had in the aircraft! I withdrew quickly; I think he did the same.

October 1940 passed pleasantly and quickly. Firstly, local checks flights and training in crew duties with my co-pilot, P/O Ainsworth, and the Wireless Operator/Air Gunners (WOP/AG's) Sergeants Hamer and Lewis; then flying 'Security Area' patrols across the North Sea. Two pilots shared duties as pilot and navigator alternately and as my experience of navigating over the sea was minimal, and there was little time or opportunity for separate training, the system seemed reasonable.

The whole of the North Sea to the enemy-held coast was covered by aircraft flying parallel tracks about twenty miles apart in a direction and at staggered timings which would ensure that any enemy forces unseen by one aircraft would be picked up by another at a later stage of their voyage. The advantage to the Royal Navy was that this surveillance obviated the need for the Cruiser Squadron which patrolled the North Sea during World War One. Four other Hudson squadrons shared this duty, from Bircham Newton in Norfolk, North Coates in Lincolnshire, and Leuchars and Wick in Scotland.

Hudson aircraft had a rubber dinghy and the necessary equipment packed in the cabin door, which inflated from inside the door when immersed in water, remaining tethered to the door until manually released. New crews were given training in the use of this by simulating a forced landing on water (without aircraft!) in the Public Baths, diving in to board the dinghy, then to use the auxiliary hand-pump to top up the pressure, and paddle 'ashore'.

It was becoming obvious that the connotation 'Coastal' meant the enemy-held coasts as well as our own and several cryptic instructions were handed on from pilots whose experience was now more vital to newcomers than anything that had gone before.

"Remember 50-50" was the watchword, "When 50 miles from the enemy coast get down to 50 feet if you haven't already done so, to get under Jerry radar!" Exhilarating flying, apparently skipping over the waves at 150 knots, crossing the Dogger Bank when there appeared to be more sand than water, with small dappled waves idly lapping an aqua-tinted golden island.

When sheer bravado appeared to grip the Operations Room and a Battle Flight of three Hudsons in formation had to fly a triangular track to Lister Fiord in Norway, across the Skagerrak to northwest Denmark and back, even 50 feet seemed too high!

"If you're attacked by Me 109's get right down on the deck to protect your belly, but keep your wing-tips dry when taking evasive action!" There were times when the reference was pertinent not only to the aircraft; the human belly also suffered the occasional reaction!

"You're in a reconnaissance squadron, so when you see something really interesting don't break radio silence, unless of course you are about to be shot down – in which case send your message in plain language and end with a prayer; otherwise come back and tell us."

During the dismal days of late 1940 and early days of 1941 when the fortunes of the RAF, like the rest of the country, seemed at their lowest ebb, the 'Hornli' daylight sorties of three aircraft were a rather cheeky way of letting the enemy know that the offensive spirit remained with us. Had we been attacked by an equal force of German fighters, it would have been very unlikely that all three aircraft would have returned. Fortunately, in my experience this did not happen; on a few occasions others were not so lucky, although there seemed to be no attacks of more than two fighters, and we began to wonder about the effectiveness of co-ordination between the German command in Norway and that in Denmark. As our approach to the coast of southern Norway was observed by the occupying forces and the necessary action taken, did our consequent turn on to a southerly course, away from the area threatened, lead to disinterest by the Germans there?

"Over to you, Wehrmacht Denmark!" could have been the sentiment, but without the corresponding message relayed across the Skagerrak to the forces in northern Denmark. Perhaps the German war machine was not infallible after all! Realism, however, intruded by suggesting that the invading armies and anti-aircraft defences had only been there a few months, and conditions were likely to improve for them, and deteriorate for us. So it proved, very soon.

"Offensive patrol – Lister Light Norway – Skagerrak – Horns Reef. 24/10/ 40. 3 aircraft formation" noted the Intelligence Officer at the Operations Room de-briefing of the sortie in which my aircraft was No 2 (on the right of the V formation).

Airborne 0810 hrs. Landed 1340.

Weather poor to 3 degrees east. Landfall 1038 Lister Light. 1112 N. Denmark.

Photo reconnaissance Agger to Blaavands Lighthouse. North of Horns Reef about 100 fishing smacks.

Wake of submerged submarine – N.E. to S.W.

1145 – 2 Flak (anti-aircraft) ships 6 miles south.

No cloud cover. Patrol not extended over land."

A little more had been added to our slowly increasing knowledge of enemy dispositions.

On 7th November I for one came back wondering what had happened to the Luftwaffe. The leader of our offensive patrol of three aircraft buzzed around the entrance to the Skagerrak between Norway and Denmark long enough, it seemed to me, to invite certain retribution. It came not, although visibility was virtually unlimited, so I chose to think it was a demonstration of getting under enemy radar defences. Certainly, from the height we were flying, the heavy Skagerrak swell seemed to be reaching for the wing-tips.

On returning from one sortie when the Billingham smog was thicker than usual and had been lavish in its spread, we were diverted to Acklington airfield near Amble on the Northumberland coast. There was a Blenheim with a collapsed undercarriage on the runway, so we had to stooge around until it had been removed. The bare countryside had the bleakness of late autumn about it on this dull, cloud-hanging day, and I realised how lucky we were at Thornaby to have a wide choice of social activity – inside the camp a very good Mess which could have sufficed alone, but outside the camp within a five-mile radius there was entertainment catering for a population approaching 200,000 citizens. As a result of accepting the pleasures that Teesside offered, I was becoming impatient at the delay in clearing the runway down below, for that evening I had arranged to meet Dorrie, a most attractive fair-haired girl and I needed to telephone her in abject apology before she was due to leave for our date.

I had met her in the Corporation Hotel Ballroom in Middlesbrough. I was there with some of the boys from 608 Squadron, and we were enjoying a breather from the dancing and a pint of Vaux's Best Bitter at a table next to a group of stevedores from the docks, whilst eyeing some charming girls seated at a table next to the dance-floor. A pretty fair-haired lass caught my eye, and I thought a smile might help to establish contact.

Lefty, the prankster, had other methods, and being behind the rest of the group but able to attract the attention of the girl opposite, he held up a pint of beer in one hand, and in the other a bottle of Worcester Sauce, brought with someone's tomato juice. With much gesticulation he enthralled the girl with his obvious intention, nodding his head with eyebrows raised in a "Shall I?" query. The girl, perhaps of a more cautious nature, put her hand to her mouth to smother a faint giggle, had a precautionary look around, then nodded her head in encouragement. At this, Lefty vigorously shook Worcester Sauce into the beer, looked at Andy, his intended victim, then across at the girl, and with a smirk and turn of his head towards the backs of his colleagues, showed what a great joke this was going to be. The girl looked away, but when she turned back towards Lefty with another smothered giggle his enthusiasm knew no bounds. At last, beginning to shake with subdued mirth and fearful of spilling his heady brew, he put the glass back on the table, pointing surreptitiously to the colleague he expected to sample the concoction.

A large hand appeared, picked up the glass, and with a distorted, muffled croak, Lefty became very aware of the awesome demeanour of the stevedore holding the doctored beverage. He smiled, and Lefty half-rose from his chair and with hand outstretched began a stuttered warning with "Er..er" but froze as he watched the stevedore look across to the girl now submerged in a paroxysm of mirth. He turned back to Lefty with a mystified grimace and a shrug of the shoulders, then again became one of the heavies. His back was now towards Lefty, who remained statuesque with hand outstretched, able to see only the thick upper arm and elbow of the hand holding the glass.

We became aware of these activities when the girls could contain their mirth no longer, Lefty began a low gurgling, and we all watched spellbound as the glass met the lips. The man was evidently a proper drinker, and the entire contents had disappeared before he stopped, held the glass quizzically before him, then took a sniff. What followed was quite unexpected and was quickly recognized as Lefty's lifeline. With a "This beer's off!" the drinker plundered his way to the bar, whilst his pals alternately eyed him and their own glasses of beer with equal disbelief. Grabbing Lefty, still posing as hesitation personified, we fled, and re-grouped in the next street. Acting as look-out and peering round the corner, I saw the girls emerge, still shaking with laughter, and beckoned them to join us. Later, towards midnight, as I walked the two miles back to the camp after seeing Dorrie home, I mused that a kindly fate had ordained that Lefty's exuberant misfortune should lead later to an evening well spent.

The first threat to this pleasant fly-by-day, eat, drink, and dance-by-night existence came with an order that there would be five hours' night-flying training for each pilot lacking operational night-flying experience. The second threat, in mid-November, was more drastic, although paradoxically it removed the need for night- flying dual as far as I was concerned. We had been ordered to St. Eval airfield in Cornwall as one of three crews on detachment, and we had a rather unfortunate act to follow. Of the four aircraft sent on previous detachment on 6th November, weather and navigational problems caused one crew to make a forced-landing on a beach, a second crew had to bale out with one member sustaining a broken leg, and a third experienced difficulties when eventually landing.

We flew down in open formation, across the York plain, over the pinnacles and gorges of the Peak District, then the Welsh valleys looking remarkably parallel and similar, and the wooded coastal fringe of North Devon and Exmoor. Compared with the largely undamaged, almost urban, appearance of Thornaby airfield from the air, St Eval had little to commend it. The runways seemed to be intact, or had been well patched, but German bombers had apparently been determined to ruin repair and domestic facilities. We sergeants found it was back to sleeping on the floor on palliasses, four to a room in one of the few married quarters which had been built. The only furniture was the floor.

The Sergeants' Mess lacked the 'lived-in' feeling of the one at Thornaby – St Eval had been more 'bombed-in' than 'lived-in' – and as an airfield recently opened for operations, it lacked the important attribute we had come to regard as essential on the well-established RAF Station – a Mess which over the years had been endowed with funds, and a Mess Committee of experienced senior N.C.O's who had set out to make a home of it. We knew our sojourn was depriving us of the last pre-rationing weeks of Thornaby buffets! We also realised the rapid change in the need for suitable airfield locations – the takeover of French ports by the Germans had not been foreseen in re-armament planning.

In this and other ways we could see the problems facing those whose efforts were bringing military expansion to fruition. Buildings do not a Station make, nor aeroplanes a Squadron; St Eval at the time was very much a place of detachments, pitifully so for twenty of our ground crew shortly after our stay, all of whom were killed by a direct hit from a German bomber on an Air Raid Shelter.

Our first breakfast in the spartan Mess was not what we might have expected. There was a sudden drone and the unmistakeable beat of German aircraft engines, followed immediately by a hurried exit by several diners – through a window by one fellow who surely couldn't hope to reach a shelter in time – then machine gun crackling, a powerful 'whoo-oosh', and more crackling as the German rear-gunner left his own visiting card. Within two minutes the bacon, fried bread and beans were again being demolished, and the whole place settled down in the knowledge that further visits were unlikely that day.

This move to St Eval in November 1940 was part of a response to the expected German use of the Brittany port of Brest as a base for their warships. Intelligence reports suggested that the 'Admiral Hipper' was the first to do so, so surveillance of that part of Brittany and the coastal fringe was begun, which was the start of the massive RAF effort against the port which became the most heavily-defended area in Europe.

Our first sortie – my turn to fly, my co-pilot's to navigate – was a midnight rendezvous with the guns outside the port, with the Wireless Operator glued to the A.S.V. (Air to Surface Vessel radar) to monitor any ships down below. Once the course of the patrol had been established, our ambitious navigator decided to

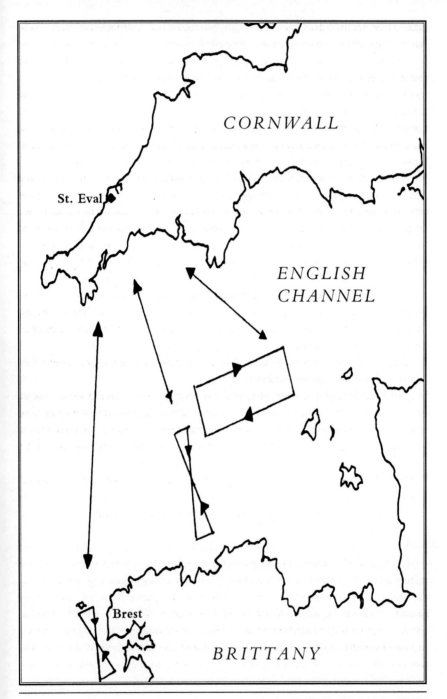

St. Eval

CORNWALL

ENGLISH
CHANNEL

Brest

BRITTANY

make a first practical attempt at astro-navigation, but his 'shooting the stars' led to calculations that we were over Switzerland.

"Perhaps that's Lake Geneva" he mused, as we looked down on the southwestern approaches of the English Channel, now overlain with a soft moonglow. No lake could have bettered the sight before us at the end of the sortie as we approached the south Cornish coast at about 3,000 feet with the full moon now behind us. With a high tide and an on-shore wind, the whole coastline from Land's End to St Austell Bay was etched in a flickering white line of surf, as prominent headlands stood like beacons with darkened coves behind.

But the beacon we expected to be homing on by this time – the one at the airfield – was unlit. By now down to 2,000 feet, it became obvious that St Eval was suffering an enemy intruder hoping to get a landing aircraft in his sights, so we would have to hang around and hope we could get down before fuel problems led to a diversion. Now it was 'Qui vive!' – one eye on the airfield, one helping us avoid the intruder, and one on the rolling low clouds which had appeared on the southern horizon!

Suddenly, the rear gunner called that he had seen the flash of the red beacon light which stood near the intersection of the runways. As we turned it disappeared, but we took it to be a welcome greeting and went into the circuit with the runway now dimly visible beneath us.

"They'll put the runway lights on for a few minutes when we're on the final approach," I suggested hopefully.

They didn't, but the single beacon light came on again, giving some help in estimating direction and distance to the pale outline of the runway we were now approaching at one hundred feet, and with retractable wing lights on we managed a respectable landing, thankful that the intruder evidently didn't see us. Before we finished taxying, the beacon light went out.

"Don't tell them about that at Thornaby," joked Chris "or they'll be saving electricity too!"

"Who cares?" I replied, "I've done my five hours night-flying!"

Basic though our accommodation was in the intended married quarters, we were glad to get away from the Mess from time to time when off-duty, and, in hindsight, the lack of outside distractions gave us greater cohesion as a crew. Palliasses made acceptable card-tables whilst lounging on the floor around them, and the therapeutic relaxation they offered was quite different from being obliged to sleep on them. In one of the facile discussions which helped while away the waiting hours, Chris suggested it would be more sensible if the wireless operator acted as Captain of operational aircraft. After all, he reckoned, once in the air, he was the link with higher command, he would be the one to receive instructions and pass them to the pilot or navigator, who would merely carry them out. The rear gunner, who was also qualified as a wireless operator, agreed. My co-pilot was in the Officers' Mess, so I was in danger of being 'outgunned'. I sought to shoot first and perhaps defend my corner by introducing a little levity.

Hudson aircraft, considering the opposition at that stage of the war, were well-armed, but with the anomaly that there were more gun positions than crew members. Two fixed Browning machine-guns fired forward and had to be aimed by the pilot in the way of a fighter aircraft, and there were two Brownings in the power-operated turret at the rear. There was one Lewis gun on each side of the cabin mounted so that it gave a wide field of fire through an open window aft of the wing; also one Lewis gun to protect the underside which, when in use, was positioned on a hinged flap which had to be wound down so that the gun may be fired through the opening. Five crew members were needed to be fully effective when attacked, but we only had four. The co-pilot (navigator) would man one of the side guns, the rear gunner the turret, and surely – I said – Chris wouldn't suggest that the pilot should leave 'George', the auto-pilot, to fly the aircraft whilst he manned the other side gun! In any case, the pilot had to 'aim the aircraft' at the target when firing the front guns. If the W/Op were captain and considered his first duty to be communication, would manning his set be more important than helping avoid disaster by manning the side gun? He might well need to leap from a side gun to the belly-gun, in order to deal with the enemy aircraft he had just managed to miss shooting down!

Whilst the two wireless operators were considering this spiel of semi-nonsense, which was nevertheless making them think a little more about operational responsibilities, I continued quickly with the 'coup d'etat' – experience had shown that whether the co-pilot or any crew member was commissioned or of a higher rank than the first pilot, who would in many cases be a sergeant, the latter, the one actually in charge of and flying the machine, would be the one having to take decisions affecting the safety of the aircraft. It led to some strange situations, as when a Wing Commander flew in a sergeant's aircraft, but it worked; to query it among relatively novice volunteer aircrew surely indicated a sense of responsibility and pride in their own tasks.

Life on the ground in the late autumn gloom offered little excitement, occasionally enlivened by a fleeting visit from an inquisitive German aircraft. The subdued delights of Newquay were available to the few more permanent residents with a car. It was hardly more exciting in the air, with more night patrols in the Channel and off Brest watching the flak-fireworks and occasionally playing cloud hide-and-seek with an enemy fighter. There was a daylight escort to a damaged tanker into Milford Haven, slowly wallowing its way to safety, and necessary as a result of U-boat activity and aircraft attacks in the southwest approaches; then a sudden call for a night cross-over search off the French coast for 'enemy forces' as the Ops Room vaguely put it.

In this type of search the anticipated position of the target became the joint apex of two opposing triangles, so that the aircraft crossed diagonally from the side of one triangle to the other, then turned across the base of the triangle for a distance equal to the maximum effective radar 'visibility', then returned along the other diagonal, again crossing the expected position. On this occasion, the screen remained blank. Was it just a supposed sighting of enemy forces, we wondered, by some agent on the French shore; was it, indeed, an early indication of the limitations of 'Mark One' radar surveillance?

We were glad to return to Thornaby in good time for Christmas, and I quickly sought verification of the fact that I had done my quota of night-flying, to the envy of those who had not completed theirs. I subdued the inclination to take my log-book back to the Silloth C.O. for an amendment to the comments with which he had obliged me to leave his training unit.

Christmas in the Sergeants' Mess in 1940 became the one best remembered throughout the war. The Mess was handsomely decorated, the Yuletide fare appetising and plentiful, the nose was pleasantly assailed by a Drambuie-based bouquet, and bonhomie flourished in every corner. Andy and the friends now with 608 Squadron whom Henry and I had first met at Silloth, were on stand-by duty and confined to camp, so after the midday Christmas dinner, Andy suggested we should bear his festive good wishes to his aunt and uncle who lived four miles away in Norton-on-Tees. He need not have troubled to encourage us to undertake this task, by regaling us with an account of their wide interests in supplying Teesside with the staff of life and associated confections. We were already satiated. However, being warmly received, we discovered our capacity for Christmas cake and claret hardly diminished. Henry and I felt it quite unnecessary to touch the sandwiches we took with us on our flights the next day!

The last patrol of 1940 suggested a festive lull had overtaken North Sea proceedings. There were no ships to be seen, not even the Danish fishing boats which usually appeared at some stage of the flight. Harold, the rear gunner, spotted a Me 110 twin-engined German fighter as we turned for home, but either he didn't see us brushing the low cloud, or the Christmas spirit had prevailed. Seagulls were dipping low over the Dogger Bank, no doubt picking fry from the silvery shoals in the shallow water. Harold – Aitch – reckoned dogfish must have given their name to the Bank, but as a result of some previous private research I was able to put him right.

"A Dogger was a two-masted bluff-bowed Dutch fishing boat!"

"Coo! Fancy that!" was his scurrilous reply.

"Brains will out!" and "Yes teacher!" added the others.

On 27th December we learned that the weather and enemy intruders were still causing trouble at St Eval. One of our aircraft on detachment ran out of fuel as a result of being unable to land, the crew had to bale out, and the Wireless Operator and Rear Gunner were drowned. The aircraft crashed to the east of Trevose Head.

New Year's Eve brought a more optimistic report across the Atlantic. A Hudson for the RAF, given number T 9465 and named 'Spirit of Lockheed Vega employees' was presented to the people of Great Britain by the employees of Lockheed Aircraft Corporation and Vega Airplane Company, on 22nd December 1940:

'The gift of this airplane was made possible by the spontaneous and voluntary donation of two hours or more time on the part of each of some 18,000 Lockheed and Vega employees.'

Many Hudsons were now in RAF service, but the Atlantic was still a formidable barrier to speedy delivery, and there had been times during the year when operational losses exceeded replacements. It was heartening news, therefore, to learn that on 10th November, 7 Hudsons led by Capt D.C.T.Bennett – later to become better known as the Air Vice Marshal commanding Bomber Command's Pathfinder Force – had taken off from the large new airfield of Gander in Newfoundland. Ten and a half hours later and 2,100 miles to the east, they all landed safely in Northern Ireland. There had then been three more flights in formation by the end of 1940; arrangements were then made for the aircraft to be flown from Burbank, California, to Montreal by U.S.A.A.F. pilots, and from there by RAF Ferry Command. Prior to these efforts – made possible by the installation of extra fuel tanks – it had taken up to three months for each Hudson to reach England from California; and they took up shipping space which was desperately needed for other purposes. During the coming year one of the pilots taking part in the ferrying was to become a colleague of mine, and he regaled us with stories of the lavish welcome the ferry boys received in Hollywood, dining and dancing with Rita Hayworth and other gorgeous film-stars of the era. By 1944, a total of 41 squadrons had been equipped with Hudsons.

On New Year's Eve, following the last uneventful patrol of 1940, I counted my lucky stars and found they were numerous. I had lived, for wartime, in comparative luxury interspersed with a growing acceptance of a straw palliasse as a somnambulant friend. I had been a welcome visitor to several rural communities and the best of University cities, and flown over much of beautiful England at a height which enhances an eye for detail – the Hog's Back , Windsor Great Park and Virginia Water, the Cotswolds, Oxford, Blenheim Palace, Solway Firth, the Lake District, Lancashire and Cumbrian coasts, Flamborough Head, the Yorkshire coast around Whitby, Cornwall – and parts of Norway and Denmark. And so far as I was then aware, none of the colleagues I trained with had 'bought it'. It was to be my 'Annus mirabilis'.

There was a small private-car petrol coupon allowance for aircrew when on operations, and part of an old Bellman-type hangar at Thornaby was used as a garage by the fortunate few. Early in January 1941 snow fell heavily and the thick layer and ice which collected on the hangar roof proved too much for it to bear, and part of it collapsed on the cars beneath. Fortunately my Morris 8 was tucked in a corner and escaped the debris; doubly so, as leave was imminent.

A few days later, with Aitch, my rear gunner who came from Bolton, we set out to cross the Pennines. The roads were passable until we reached the approach to Blubberhouses Moor leading to Skipton, and after much wheel slippage we were stuck at the bottom of a sharp incline. The engine was steaming from the frustrated efforts we had made to try to keep moving, so 'H' went to a snow-encrusted cottage nearby to ask for water. Before he could knock the door was opened, and he disappeared into the cheery glow within.

"They say leave it till morning; we're invited to stay the night!" he shouted a few seconds later. I needed no further bidding – I slammed the bonnet-lid closed, grabbed our bags, and joined him. Our kind hosts were a middle-aged couple who obviously cared a great deal about their home, and even more about the freedom to live their lives as they wished.

"He fought in the last one," the lady confided, "and we never thought there'd be another so soon after. We're right behind you lads – let's put a real stop to it this time!"

After a wonderful meal, a sound sleep, and bacon and egg for breakfast, we were on our way the next morning. Difficulties literally melted away. In one of our rare serious moments, I asked 'H' if such warm-hearted support had any effect, or was he just in it for kicks?

"I may have volunteered without really knowing what I was doing," he replied, "but I do know now."

"Me too," I agreed, and we were silent for much of the journey as we drove through the snow-tipped grandeur of the Pennines.

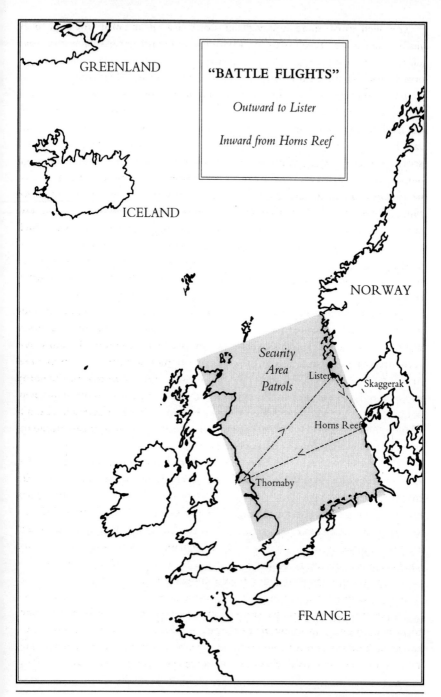

GREENLAND

"BATTLE FLIGHTS"

Outward to Lister

Inward from Horns Reef

ICELAND

NORWAY

Security Area Patrols

Lister

Skaggerak

Horns Reef

Thornaby

FRANCE

The need to continue to cover the North Sea led to some forays in dicey weather, but if the Meteorological people promised a cloud base no lower than 800 feet, we coped, although the Coronation pub and the A 174 experienced some very low-flying Hudsons from time to time Along the enemy-held coastline and up to 50 miles from it there appeared suspicious-looking large fishing-boats, and it was soon established that they were packed with virtually everything but fish, from radio and jamming equipment to machine-guns and mines. Along the Danish and Norwegian coasts there were also increasing numbers of heavily-escorted ships carrying Swedish iron-ore plying back and forth. One of the reasons for the Norwegian campaign in April 1940 had been to attempt an interruption to the vital supply of this ore to Germany. In the early months of the war, iron-ore from Sweden and Norway accounted for two-thirds of Germany's needs. The mines in the north of Sweden produced large amounts of high-grade ore, which went by rail to Lulea on the Gulf of Bothnia. When this port was ice-bound in winter, it was sent to Narvik on the west coast of Norway, and from there by sea to Germany. As the demand for iron-ore increased, the ore-carriers were escorted by 'flak-ships' equipped with every type of defence against air strikes.

During a sortie in February 1941 we found what we presumed to be an iron-ore convoy off the Danish coast, 20 miles west of Ringkobing. Cloud base was at about a thousand feet, and I was flying at 50 feet when we sighted the ships. We were armed with two 250 lb anti- submarine bombs, and two 250 lb General Purpose bombs, so I decided we would use one of the A/S bombs first, then drop the G/P bombs in a second run. If the A/S bomb struck the ship or was reasonably close, it would cause sufficient distraction to make the second run easier, and if it fell in the water too far away to cause any damage, it would still cause turbulence sufficient to adversely affect the defensive gunfire.

As we came within range of the convoy's guns I took the Hudson up into cloud and circled about 180 degrees, so that when we emerged we approached the ships from the opposite direction from where they had last seen us, gaining those vital few seconds of indecision and adjustment among the gun crews. We dived low as I pushed the airscrew pitch controls into high revs, gave the engines full boost, and selected as the target the largest ship of about 7,000 tons in the middle of the convoy. The bomb fuses had been set at an eleven-second delay so that we would be clear from a low-level attack by the time the bombs exploded.

In the co-ordinated action which had become second nature, I pressed the Browning gun firing button to let off a few rounds – 'just' as has been said more than once 'to let them know we're serious' – then pressed the bomb release. I hauled back on the control column to lift the aircraft over the ship. The rear gun clattered its message for a few seconds, then we came round again on an east-to-west heading as quickly as possible for a second attack. We dropped the two G/P's – on target according to the rear gunner – and we were away, up into cloud again, on course for home.

As on other occasions, a lone action meant no confirmation of a damage claim unless there was an opportunity to take photographs, which was difficult in low-level action with the clumsy cameras we had at this time, without the risk of enemy fighters appearing during the manoeuvring for camera angle. The risk entailed in doing that was in any case contrary to the dictum 'reconnaissance requires a return journey', and we could rest assured that the discovery of the convoy would lead to further attacks on it. There was some justification in claiming this a 'probable' as another aircraft on a sortie the next day reported a similar convoy with one ship fewer, but an attack was prevented by enemy fighters. These, together with enhanced anti-aircraft gunfire, were increasingly evident in support of iron-ore shipping as its importance to Germany became vital. As the historian Denis Richards noted "as a healthy occupation for aircrew in 1941, bombing German ships by day had much less to commend it than bombing German towns by night," although this was soon to change as the need to defend 'the Fatherland' increased along with Bomber Command's great effort.

Among the gifts celebrating my 21st birthday in February was a copy from my mother of "The Complete Air Navigator" by the same Capt D.C.T.Bennett who had led the first flight of Hudsons across the Atlantic. I read later in his book "Pathfinder" that on his honeymoon in 1935 whilst on the S.S. 'Hobson's Bay' from Southampton to Brisbane to allow his wife "to be inspected thoroughly.... by his relatives in Australia" he "managed to write one whole chapter of this book, but even that was a struggle with a ship full of passengers violently and aggressively engaged in the waste of time." I proceeded to learn more from his book than my training and experiences had so far been able to accomplish.

Crossing the North Sea to drop a bomb, fire a gun, or report and/or photograph enemy movement, was an accepted, often eagerly undertaken, task. To do it to scatter thousands of leaflets (code name 'nickels') over German- held territory in daylight was regarded by many as akin to delivering a supply of toilet paper. Bomber Command pilots had been doing it at night, intermittently, since the outbreak of war, as part of their familiarisation and reconnaissance. Our task on the 1st March 1941 was to spread the leaflets from 37 bundles of nickels over the province of Ringkobing, to the north of Esbjerg in Denmark. The message, so far as we could tell, was an exhortation to the Danes to keep smiling, chin up, the Americans were beginning to help us, so it wouldn't take long for this dreadful business to be resolved. I hoped that the Danish people would find some humour in the situation, rather than irony, for here we were papering them with platitudes a mere eight months after fleeing the Continent! The sortie was also to be a reconnaissance flight, for there was a belief that we were becoming strong enough to be more aggressive over coastal Europe – a theory that was to be frustrated by the approaching crisis in the war against U-boats, and the consequent need to divert effort to counter-measures in the Atlantic.

Approaching the Danish coast as low as possible, I took the Hudson at mid-cruising speed through the gap into Ringkobing Fjord, then climbed up to within easy reach of the cloud-base at about 1,800 feet, ready to be swallowed up by it should fighter 'planes appear. A hasty return to the deck would have been necessary if the area had anti-aircraft defences, but we had been assured at the briefing that this was unlikely. The water in the fjord had the shimmering appearance of being almost ice, indeed there were one or two patches round the edges which merged with the pristine white of the flat, snow-covered landscape.

The area appeared to be sparsely populated – a few small villages and isolated farmhouses, and we reckoned there must be about a thousand leaflets for each inhabitant. Opinions within the aircraft regarding the real purpose of the mission varied as the nickels fluttered down. The rear gunner reckoned the Danes were short of litter for their pig-sties; the W/Op suggested it was meant to encourage the males to row to England to avoid being made by the Germans to pick up all the leaflets; my co-pilot, a little more seriously, said he understood how the locals would feel about waiting for American help; whilst my thoughts continued along the 'bottom' line.

A German soldier enlivened the whole proceedings. He was the only moving object we had seen, so he attracted various forms of attention. I took the Hudson down to 300 feet and we were circling round when there was a shout from Chris who had been casting the pearls:

"The Command motto is 'We search and strike' – hold her steady and I'll let him have an unopened bundle!" he yelled.

I did so, but his aim did not warrant promotion to Bomb Aimer! However, there was no denying that the soldier was moved by this attention. He dismounted from his bicycle, took the rifle from off his back, assumed the classic kneeling posture, and took aim at us in the best Wehrmacht manner, slowly turning as we circled round him. In our separate and highly-individual ways we were very amused and reacted accordingly, but when we landed we discovered that there was a bullet-hole in the tail of the aircraft. His aim had been better than ours!

On the 8th March we had news of the first casualties from amongst those with whom the bond of comradeship had become strong. The previous day, an Anson

---

of 608 Squadron took off from Wick at 0750 hours bound for Dyce and Thornaby, but had to force-land in the sea at 0840. Three of the crew were lost, including Tommy Edwards and Andy White, whom Henry and I had first met at Silloth. Andy was the Scotsman who had sent us as Christmas Day messengers to his relatives in Norton. It was a grievous loss caused by one of those accidents inseparable from defying gravity as aviators.

On the 12th March, Henry, Harry and I took two Hudsons up to Wick in northern Scotland on another detachment. 269 Squadron was being redeployed to Iceland to help alleviate the desperate situation in the North Atlantic by flying anti-U-boat patrols from there, and we were to replace them at Wick. Although at that stage of the war Coastal Command had expanded more rapidly than Bomber Command, the unexpected German occupation of the whole of Western Europe demanded more response than the Command was effectively able to provide.

Five D.F.M's and eight D.F.C's were awarded to Thornaby-based aircrew during 1939 to 1941.

Thornaby Christmas 1940 Menu

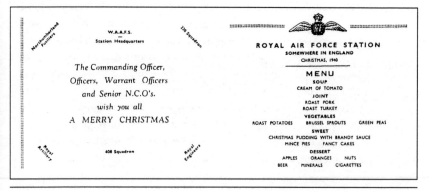

COASTAL COMMAND PILOT

Making the smog. The River Tees and the I.C.I. factories

Parachute Exits and Emergency Equipment

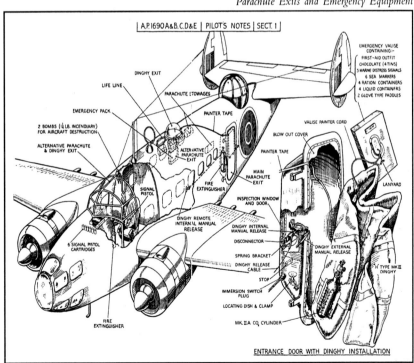

Dinghy training – Ainsworth, Rayner, Lewis, Hamer

Typical 220 Squadron Photo Rec'ce. Sylt, N.W. Germany

En route to Wick 12.3.41

CHAPTER 7

OCEAN SWELL

The Operations Room at Wick told a different story to the one at Thornaby. Instead of the tracks of the now redundant anti-invasion patrols across the North Sea, or the position of an east-coast convoy needing air cover, or a symbol representing an enemy convoy hugging the Danish or southern Norwegian coasts, Wick showed Atlantic convoys with the last-known position of some of the gathering U-boats, and perhaps enemy activity north of Stavanger in Norway. 1941 had opened with weather which was equally bad for U-boats and for aircraft, but the increasing number of new, longer-range U-boats, and reinforcements of the Luftwaffe's four-engined FW 200 Condor aircraft had prompted Hitler to boast on the 24th February that the blockading forces of the German Navy and Luftwaffe would be successful within sixty days.

Churchill's Battle of the Atlantic Directive had been issued on 6th March 1941, in order to give priority to the war against U-boats, surface-raiders, and long-range enemy aircraft. In March, more than 500,000 tons of Allied shipping was sunk, in April it was to be 644,000 tons, of which almost 300,000 tons was by aircraft alone. They were carrying out their damaging attacks by flying from enemy bases taken over in northwest France and southern Norway. Blenheims from Bomber Command took over some of the Hudson North Sea duties, so that Coastal Squadrons could be moved north and west. Thus, for me, Wick.

In flying a mission to the east from Wick, the main problem, as from Thornaby, was German fighters, flak-ships, and shore-based guns. To the west, it was the terrain, the weather, and the occasional clash with a U-boat or long-range Condor. Whereas flying from Thornaby we sought to avoid confrontation other than with the chosen target, flying from Wick on anti-U-boat patrol we quickly realised that enemy opposition of any kind would help relieve the monotony. Unfortunately, U-boats were a mere speck in the ocean, and with the paucity of search equipment at the time, seldom seen.

Thornaby to Wick was even more of a contrast than Thornaby to St Eval! The magnificent wilderness of northeast Scotland, the mountain peaks to the west across the forbidding expanse of heather, pond, and bog! It soon became apparent that the great advantage to squadron life and morale in being based on an isolated station was the greater cohesion between all personnel. We relaxed in various forms of amusement which were rarely seen, much less heard, outside a Service Mess. Henry, Harry and I were fortunate enough to meet Robbie, a fisherman, during one of our strolls around the harbour; he and his wife invited us into their cottage, one of a trim, stone-built line along the broad-flagged quay, and they gave us a meal of the most delicious fish, caught that morning. The taste of it lingers, never bettered, but equalled when their wonderful hospitality extended to further visits.

Mountains and atmospheric conditions frequently interfered with transmission and reception of the coded Morse messages handled by the W/Op, and we had no Radio/telephonic communication. Even on the ground, we were still in the era of the green flashing Aldis lamp for take-off "Go!" To a pilot used to flying low, the mountains of Scotland got a great deal of respect. Bad weather and night-flying needed a positive, prepared response in the absence of any external navigational aid other than radio-direction-finding from a known radio station ('QDM' in the RAF Morse Code). Wick got me into the habit of always plotting on to my local map, safe bearings for take-off and landing approach, which were to save my aircraft and crew almost two years later.

It could be said that it saved us on the 19th March 1941. We were detailed in aircraft 'K' for a dawn anti-U-boat patrol, which meant taking off in darkness with a Met report of visibility 'moderate to poor; large amount of low cloud; frequent showers; wind fresh westerly'. Taking off into wind was therefore to the west with mountains up to 3,500 feet ahead. I reckoned it was better to reach the height needed well away from them, and my prepared track allowed for this by crossing to the Pentland Firth over the low land between Wick and Thurso, then taking up the required westerly course over the waters off the north coast.

When we took off at 0610 hours, we had barely reached 500 feet before we entered cloud, so I continued a climbing turn to port until we were on track for the Thurso turning point, thence westerly up to 4,000 feet. We descended later to 1,000 feet about 20 miles beyond Cape Wrath and found conditions much improved, but with the sleeting rain of heavy showers mingling with clear patches as far as the eye could see – good U-boat hunting weather, so please let there be one skulking around!

After four hours of fruitless scanning by four pairs of eyes over hefty broken-topped waves, we discovered on the return journey that there had been a gremlin abroad. Chris drew my attention to W/T traffic from which he concluded that Hudson 'L', which had been airborne 15 minutes before ourselves, was not answering the call from base. The pilot's task had been similar to our own, and he should have been approaching base as we were, but we had neither seen the aircraft nor heard anything from it. In the Operations Room after landing at 1253 hours, we were grieved to learn that the captain of 'L' had evidently been trying to keep under the cloud base, and had crashed into the Old Man of Hoy, the great stack of rock which stands sentinel to the Orkney island. All the crew had been killed.

A brisk walk beyond the airfield to allow the wind on some headland to act as balm after the sadness of such misfortune was not unusual, so the two 'H's' and I set out for the cliffs at Noss Head to the north of the aerodrome. From the edge of the towering cliff we looked across the magnificent sweep of Sinclair's Bay. This was seagull country with a vengeance – we scrambled along the barely accessible ledges to collect a few eggs whilst the birds demonstrated dive-bombing techniques of a high order, screaming down to hover and squawk above the rapacious thieves carrying off their unborn offspring. These eggs had a tangy taste, perhaps too strong for a more civilised palate, but, we thought, undoubtedly a food of last resort should the enemy blockade succeed! Certainly more acceptable than the dried, powdered 'eggs' which wartime recipes were deemed to require.

The local railway line provided an interesting day out. Helmsdale was about 40 miles to the south by the scenic coast road, but about twice that distance by rail, owing to the loop which took the line towards the gaunt mountains of the west before joining the river valley southeastwards to the coast. The well-worn but comfortable carriages were hauled by a locomotive which was as much like the Rev. Awdry's Thomas the Tank Engine as one could wish to see. With suitable restrained toots on the whistle it announced its impending arrival at a length of platform and perhaps a small wooden shelter, which might go by the name of Georgemas Junction, or Scotscalder, or Altnabreac, or Hotel Forsinard. South from the last-named, it squeezed its way between the shoulders of imposing heights until, accompanied by the road and river twixt two-thousand-foot mountains on either side, the small but significant station at Helmsdale crept slowly into view, its importance recognized as a mandatory stop rather than a 'halt-if- needed'. That was 75 miles in four hours from Wick, but time well spent by anyone appreciating the grandeur of mountain, loch, stream and valley which only the Highlands offer.

For those travelling further south, yet another loop took the line from the coast above Dornoch Firth inland to Lairg, at the southern end of Loch Shin, then along the southern shores of the Firth to Tain, another 37 miles. Travelling time from London to Wick was 24 hours; from Manchester 20. When returning from leave a few weeks later, I determined to travel overnight to Perth, so that, in the flush of

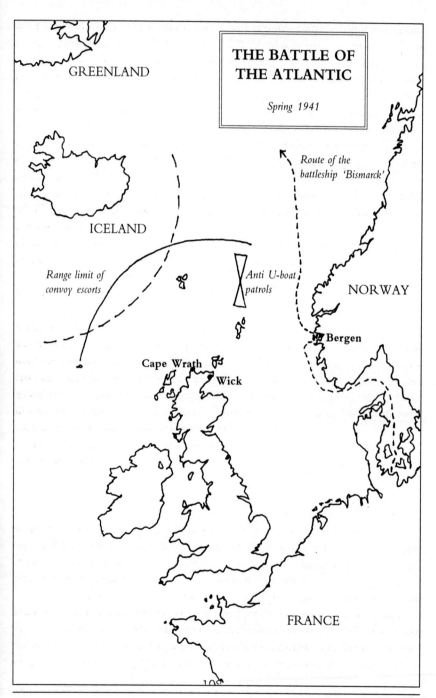

GREENLAND

THE BATTLE OF
THE ATLANTIC

Spring 1941

*Route of the
battleship 'Bismarck'*

ICELAND

*Range limit of
convoy escorts*

*Anti U-boat
patrols*

NORWAY

Bergen

Cape Wrath

Wick

FRANCE

COASTAL COMMAND PILOT

Spring, my journey through the austere beauty of the Grampians would have the benefit of sparkling daylight.

A sortie on what seemed the blackest night in March led to a sighting which was fixed in my mind for several days. We were airborne at 0300 hours as part of a search for a scattered convoy, and had reached a point 100 miles out over the Atlantic in the kind of darkness which seems to be painted on the outside of windows, when the Wireless Operator reported a blip on the A.S.V. receiver which suggested an object about ten miles ahead. As he guided me towards it, I became aware of a flashing orange spot slightly to starboard and, turning towards it just as Chris called "Ten degrees starboard", the flickering became so haphazard that I assumed it must be something burning. We approached at 500 feet and soon found that the flames seemed to be leaping at us, spreading fingers of fire which gave the glow of Hades to the underside of the billowing columns of smoke. I took the Hudson round full circle, and in the blazing cauldron around it we could see the slanting outline of a stricken tanker – stern aloft, bows in the water – licked by the flames and the encircling froth of the sea which would surely claim it soon.

As we flew round a second time, flame belched forth from several parts of the hull and steam erupted as if some sea-dragon were defending her prey. On the fringe of the inferno I could see a darker outline and, steering towards it, we yelled as if one voice "It's a boat!" I went in as close as I dared, but it appeared to be empty, rocking erratically as the rings of flaming water spread outwards with each shuddering dip of the dying ship. A lifeboat without any hope of saving life, the torpedoed remains of an explosion which in a few seconds must have turned a ship into a crematorium. There was something compelling about the raging mass of flame, smoke and seething water, but we had to move on; and when, in a final look back, it disappeared from view, silence was broken only by the drone of the engines as we continued a fruitless search, and we thought of those who would never be found.

Having joined the RAF to fly, there was nothing more frustrating to aircrew than very bad weather which prevented it. A case of 'Even the birds are walking' led to a sojourn in the Mess, cards, shove ha'penny, table tennis, or even a spate of letter-writing. Occasionally, by the end of such a day, these activities would pall, and an 'incident' would be the excuse for a bout of internal 'hostilities'.

Mike, one of the more eccentric and successful pilots, had a session in mind when he collected a double whisky from the bar and took a soda syphon to the table; in this way, the whiskies which could be expected to accumulate as a result of successful wager, poker, or as a last resort, payment, could be personally diluted to the level he preferred. He was joined at the table by his co-pilot, who stretched his long legs on the inside of the table leg, so that when he arose to go for the next round of drinks, the table began to move with him. The soda syphon, perilously near the edge, fell into Mike's lap in a way which depressed the handle, and a short squirt of the contents covered his trousers around the top of his left leg. Thus amused, his assailant chuckled "Have you wet your trousers Mike? Now we know which side you dress!"

Having considerable experience in leading offensive action – and in handling soda syphons – Mike promptly hosed him down, then, realising there were interested onlookers around him and generous to a fault in this respect, he jumped on the table and in the accepted overgrown-schoolboy fashion, sprayed haphazardly around the room, to the accompaniment of "Shoot 'im down!", "Get 'im!" and "Bomb 'im with a meat pie!"

Happy bedlam ensued, until the Orderly Sergeant and the Orderly Officer entered. A pause! The Orderly Sergeant grimaced and looked very orderly, the Orderly Officer smiled. Although of the ground staff, he was at heart 90 per cent aircrew, the minus 10 per cent which had clipped his wings being poor eyesight. He crossed to the table, took the syphon from Mike, told him to dismount, and with the syphon at the ready and war-cry proclaimed, he manoeuvred Mike so that his back was to the door. At the moment it opened and his target was flung aside, the Orderly Officer delivered a jet of soda water, but the figure at which it was aimed had been replaced in the open doorway. The sleeve which rose to wipe away the deluge carried the broad blue and black ribbon of an Air Commodore. An expectant silence descended.

"So you got here ahead of me; got caught by the C.O's good lady!" he said to the Orderly Officer. "Just having a look around," to the stunned incumbents. "Could do with a quick snifter!"

The Orderly Officer, with considerable aplomb and an unusually rapid response, asked if he might get a double Scotch for the Air Commodore.

"Proceed to the bar and make it a treble!" came the reply, which offered secret hope of an armistice to the O.O. The whisky was duly served.

"And soda!" commanded the recipient.

The barman wrinkled his nose, shook his head, and was about to confess that no soda syphon remained in the bar, when five of them quickly appeared on the bar top from various parts of the Mess. The O.O. was reaching for the nearest one when the Air Commodore moved his outstretched arm aside. Then, appraising the syphon containing the most soda water by deliberately putting his hand to the level in each, he placed the chosen syphon by his glass and gave it the briefest dash. He turned to the O.O.

COASTAL COMMAND PILOT

"Your tunic is wet, old man – better take it off!"

There was a grimace of satisfaction on the O.O's face as he did so, as this unexpected concern on the part of an officer of Air Rank appeared to reinforce the belief that his misdemeanour had been forgiven. As he turned back from placing his tunic over a chair, the Air Commodore, now alarmingly armed with the soda syphon, pulled the top of the Orderly Officer's trousers out, pushed the nozzle of the syphon into the gap, and pressed the trigger. The Mess erupted, and the Air Commodore was left in no doubt that members would consider it an honour if he would accept their hospitality as often as possible.

When flying east for low-level approach along enemy coasts to see, search, or strike, the four- or five-hour flights would be in daylight. Occasionally, such a sortie might require a take-off in darkness, but such action as there might be against a ship with a backdrop of mountain or fjord had to take place, in early 1941, in daylight or brightest moonlight. Flying to the west from Wick on patrol or convoy-escort duty was meant to provide anti-U-boat cover throughout daylight hours, and was soon to extend to the full twenty-four hours. There were times when the armourers might well have known the type of operation planned before the aircrew at their briefing. At Thornaby, a Hudson in a state of readiness would invariably have been bombed up with 250 lb General Purpose bombs. The same could be said of pre-flight preparations at Wick at the time of our first operations from there, but the emphasis quickly changed to priority against U-boats during the Spring 1941 crisis. The armourers were fitting 250 lb anti-submarine (A.S) bombs as standard, with an occasional need for G.P. or armour- piercing. It was about this time that airborne 250 lb depth-charges (D.C's) became available, and they were much more effective against U-boats than the bombs had been.

An escort sortie was very much a solo operation; we were in a Command which usually operated, at this time, on the basis of co-ordination of single aircraft with other mobile forces – convoys, ships, relieving aircraft, and the sea-borne enemy. If you preferred to be aloft as one of a flock, you had been hatched in the wrong nest. If you preferred to drop your bombs as ordered and then hare for home, or fire your guns and do a victory roll, there were better opportunities. Our Ops Room briefing would indeed be brief – take-off time, last known position, course and speed of the convoy or ship, an estimated rendezvous time, a parting time (i.e. relief aircraft arrival time) and any information about a possible quarry. The rest was up to the crew: courses to steer, best height to fly, method of search if not met spot-on, which was much needed if detailed to escort an independently-routed liner which might be zig-zagging and varying speed. Decisions!

On 31st March we were airborne at 0530 on an Atlantic escort task, and about an hour out from Cape Wrath, that majestic northwesterly outpost of the Highlands, I handed over to Terry, a newcomer to the squadron, who continued the patrol at 1,000 feet whilst I stood look-out in the astrodome halfway down the cabin. The smooth tone of the engines seemed to falter, and looking forward I could see the nose of the Hudson dip a little, and by the time I reached the cockpit the propellers were merely idling their way around. One of Neptune's gremlins was beckoning! With a distraught look at me and the W/Op, who had left his seat in alarm and was standing behind me, Terry pushed the throttles forward and back two or three times to emphasize the lack of power. He jabbed a finger at the fuel contents gauge to show that the tank which it indicated, and which was the one he believed he was using, was three-quarters full, whilst I pumped the handle of the auxiliary fuel pump, but to no effect.

Turning to the W/Op I yelled, "Broadcast an SOS in plain language, get a fix (position) and then add it to a repeat as soon as possible!" In turning back to the front I noticed the Fuel Tank Selector quadrant on the console to the right of the throttle levers. The Hudson had four fuel tanks, two in each wing, which were selected as needed and in a prescribed order, by turning the lever on the quadrant. A glance at the fuel contents gauge showed that it was indicating the amount of fuel in a different tank to the one selected on the quadrant. I assumed that when Terry last checked the fuel amounts, he left the indicator showing the fuel in a tank other than the one actually in use. A quick turn of the selector to another tank, a few rapid primes on the auxiliary hand-pump, and the engines roared back to life. We were now less than 200 feet above the waves, and they loomed alarmingly as we gathered speed and climbed away. Aitch, the W/Op, tapped me on the shoulder.

"I haven't got an acknowledgement to the SOS," he said.

"Well," I replied. "We can only assume that it has been received somewhere, so you'd better send a message cancelling it – and in plain language so they know the panic is over, and we don't need assistance. Tell them we're continuing the patrol."

I went back to the tail gunner to explain what had happened, only to find he had remained blissfully unaware of the incident and the W/Op beckoned me as I returned. He greeted me with a grimace which suggested righteous dissatisfaction with the state of wireless technology, cocking a thumb over his shoulder as he said:

"Ground station's reply was 'What SOS?' They didn't bloody receive it! If I'd wanted to be drowned, I'd 'ave joined the ruddy Merchant Navy!"

Looking down on the convoy later as we circled protectively around it, on a rare day of blue sky and sun-tinted sea, with the ships moving sedately forward and the occasional flurry from a shepherding corvette churning a white zig-zag on the water, Aitch might have thought it wasn't a bad job on such a day. But we knew that out of every one hundred days, ninety-nine would be worse, many much worse, for the lads down below. After an uneventful four hours during which the convoy, typically, moved about twenty miles and we covered more than five hundred, we flashed our parting message by Aldis lamp to the Senior Naval Officer's ship: "Going home. Good luck!" Came the usual reply: "Good hunting! Thanks!"

We landed at 1230, and in the de-briefing Aitch was asked by the Signals Officer to explain the mysteries of a signal which no one had received. He replied that, being airborne, he had no means of knowing whether the ground operator was asleep or not! Rational thinking was more in evidence when we explained the circumstances leading to the transmission, and our position and height – probably below 400 feet at the time. The cancelling message, on the other hand, had been transmitted when we were above 1,000 feet. A glance at the map showed that a line between our position and the ground station passed over the mountains, and the amicable conclusion, therefore, was the panacea which covered most such ills – ground interference. As Terry so rightly put it, the mountains were big enough to take the blame!

By the late Spring of 1941, the pattern of German air attacks was one of single or small-scale nuisance flights against coastal areas by day, and large-scale bombing of urban areas by night. Occasional marauding aircraft would approach the coast near Wick or the Naval base at Scapa Flow, overfly the airfield to keep a tally of our operational facilities, then dart away. Some of these interlopers considered it necessary to leave a 'message' – at times this was very inconsiderate! Three of us had invested in bicycles as a readily available means of local transport, which, with others, from time to time led to rodeo-like activity on the open spaces between the huts. At each end of these tracts of grass were concrete paths leading to the end doors of the huts, standing about three inches above the grass, obstacles which the cycles had to be persuaded to jump when crossed at full speed.

The chase was on towards the path nearest the Mess when a machine gun burst spread a line of flashes and ricochets along it. The leading cyclist applied his brakes hard, then skidded into the sharp edge of the path, whereupon two of those following immediately behind crashed into him. A Junkers 88 flashed by as the pilot opened up the engines to clear the airfield, leaving a tangle of cycles and cyclists in a mangled heap on the ground. The opportunity to 'pay our respects' was not long delayed! Reconnaissance had shown that Norway was snowed in, which made it unlikely that fighters would be airborne, at least not until the runways were cleared, so that if we were lucky enough to have an aircraft ordered off on some North Sea task within a short time of this uninvited intrusion, the crew would be briefed by the aggrieved cyclists as well as by the Operations

Room. A quick visit to Stavanger airfield in southern Norway was agreed; the 'courtesy call' was returned in full.

At the end of April 1941 the rest of the Squadron joined our detachment at Wick, and we began to receive more Mark III Hudsons, which many pilots believed to be the best of the six Marks made. Returning from leave, I was ordered to collect, with Jock, a W/Op who lived locally, a new Mark III from Prestwick, one of the reception airfields for machines from U.S.A. Taking off for Wick in the late afternoon of a clear Spring day, we flew along Kilbrannan Sound. To starboard lay the shadowy undulations of the Isle of Arran, with minor cascades of sparkling water plunging to the sea, whilst to port stretched the long finger of Kintyre, which we crossed near the hamlet of Clachan. Traversing the clear blue fingers of Lochs Tarbert, Caolisport, and Sween as the sun sank low behind the islands of Islay and Jura to port, we flew along the Firth of Lorn, then low along the quayside at Oban. There was some activity among the boats and a few people were walking along the promenade; we were surprised to get a cheery wave, and assumed it was a reflection of good relations with our larger brethren of Coastal Command, the Sunderland flying boats which were based there.

As we flew along Loch Linnhe towards Fort William, with the sun behind us now touching the horizon, Ben Nevis appeared in a huge russet glow. We passed over the series of locks at the entrance to the Caledonian Canal as the mountain walls began to close in on both sides, whilst the trees on the slopes shimmered pink, each apparently with fairy-lights twinkling in the uppermost branches. The gently rippling water kaleidoscoped through shades of blue to pale orange, then the whole picture became slowly darker and more intense as we approached the end of the loch, and Inverness. By the time we passed into the Moray Firth it was quite dark out in the North Sea, but as I circled for one more look, a faint glow beyond the dark outline of the mountains was all that remained of a light which had enhanced the natural beauty of one of the most attractive areas of Britain.

Within a few days, on the 4th May, in a rapid change of weather which is never unexpected in northern maritime latitudes, we flew through hanging leaden skies and sheets of rain to escort a large convoy suffering the attentions of U-boats. About half-way to the rendezvous, flying at 1,300 feet just below the cloud base, we sighted a lumpen shape lying fore-and-aft to us so that it lacked the conformation of a distinct conning-tower, in poor visibility three or four miles ahead. It was about to disappear beneath the waves as I opened up the engines and started a shallow dive.

We knew that by the time we were in a position to attack, our quarry could be anywhere within that half-mile square of sheltering water and going deeper. We were carrying four 250 lb depth charges, and my eyes were still fixed on the spot as my hands went through the drill – into the shallow dive, more revs still, bomb doors open, bomb-button from 'safe' to 'fire', select – ah! how many depth charges should we drop? All of them, with little hope of a 'kill' or real damage at this time interval, though we might give the U-boat a good shaking? But the convoy we were detailed to escort was expecting something more than an aircraft minus depth charges to help bring relief from attack, something able to deal a lethal blow at any marauder, rather than an escort able only to machine-gun an attacker if we should be so lucky as to find one on the surface.

Select two! – there they go; a warning to the U-boat commander that we know he's there, and shortly so will the Royal Navy. We had two depth charges left, hoping to use them to better purpose, but, as luck would have it, no further targets for them that day. However, we were able to spread the warning without breaking radio silence, by Aldis lamp messages not only to the Naval escort, but to a flying-boat which was returning to base. He would pass the message on to his relieving colleague, and to his Operations Room.

By the end of the month, the immediate crisis had been alleviated by the air escorts and sweeps which stretched 500 miles out into the Atlantic. In actions by destroyers and corvettes, the Royal Navy had sunk U-boats commanded by the German aces Prien, Schepke, and Kretschmer which greatly affected the course of the battle. It was Prien who on 14th October 1939, had taken U47 into the Royal Navy base at Scapa Flow and torpedoed the battleship 'Royal Oak'; the Navy had replied in kind.

The main U-boat hunting-grounds now moved further west, and to the relatively unprotected areas such as West Africa. The central Atlantic was beyond the range of the Coastal Command aircraft then available, apart from the Sunderland flying boats, but it was also out of reach of the German FW 200 four-engined Condor aircraft, and without their reconnaissance, their co-operation with the U-boats, and their attacks on shipping, the threat was easier to contain.

During a sweep on the 6th May, we met one of these predatory eagles. On many of their flights between Brest in France and Stavanger in Norway the large Condors went undetected and undeterred. They reported on Allied convoys and bombed shipping as the occasion allowed. With a top speed of 230 knots, a bomb load of 3,600 lbs, and armed with three 13 mm and three 20 mm cannon, they were a menace.

About 100 miles northwest of Cape Wrath, in only fair visibility with cloud base 2,000 feet, a convoy which, unusually, had not been mentioned in briefing loomed ahead. Suddenly, as if rising from the waves, a large aircraft flew on an easterly course across the beam of the convoy, followed by great plumes of water thrown up between the ships. It was obviously an unsuccessful bombing-run. With a "Better not give him a second chance!" we gave chase, with full revs and throttles wide open as we strove to make the best use of our slight advantage in height. There was little difference in top speed between the two aircraft, but the shallow descent towards our quarry helped to narrow the distance between us, whilst from behind me came the cries of the chase:

"Giddiup! Giddiup! Come on, let 'im 'ave it!" and "You can do better than this!"

In combat, particularly in a defensive action, one had to decide whether to jettison the bomb-load on the altar of a little extra speed and manoeuvrability. Here, the immediate need was to drive off the marauder, but the abiding reason for the sortie was the protection of shipping against U-boats, so the depth-charges remained on board. The two front guns in Hudson aircraft were fixed, one on each side of the bulbous nose, fired from the button on the pilot's control column. When, after what seemed an age of urging, we were within extreme range, my itching finger pressed it, and the tracer bullets from the front guns seemed to be lost in the flaring reply from the Condor's rear gunner. We had closed a little more before the second burst, when the tracer appeared to be reaching the enemy's rear turret, and there was no immediate response. Taking the pragmatic view that the gunner might well have been changing the magazine on his gun, particularly if he had also been firing at the convoy, we moved slightly to port for the possibility of a rear quarter approach which allowed the anxious-not-to-miss-a-part-of-it rear gunner to continue the attack.

The turret at the back of Hudson aircraft protruded above the fuselage more than most, and this allowed a field of fire of almost a full circle, apart from the automatic cut-out as the guns swept past the twin rudders. The tracers from the rear guns were flashing by in a low arc – "he's firing from the hip!" yelled the W/Op from the side-gun position – when the Condor's rear gun sent tracers dipping at us slightly to starboard. It was now obvious that the German pilot was climbing slowly towards the cloud base, so, to curses at losing the opportunity, I slipped back behind the target and opened up again with the front guns. After a few seconds the return fire stopped, and black smoke began to trail behind the Condor, but just as we could sense a celebration, our quarry was stolen from us by the clouds; at first a wisp or two floating down the long fuselage, then billowing grey-white plumes enveloping the whole until it was gone.

After the excitement of the chase, a few silent grimaces expressed our disappointment, and we made our way back to the convoy. At least we had persuaded the crew of the Condor that they ought to make for their Norwegian base as quickly as possible, and whilst in the cloud they were not to know whether or not we were directly escorting the convoy they had attacked. We had hardly returned to its position before the Senior Naval Officer's Aldis was flashing, in typical Naval parlance.

"*Did you do him dirty?*"

Chris flashed back our reply: "*Apologies! Regret he got away into cloud, with tail between legs. Are you well?*"

Answer: "*Fine! And thanks!*"

Reply: "*Our pleasure!*"

Checking the convoy whilst circling, we counted one merchant ship apparently surrounded by four small escorts, which seemed rather extravagant, and prompted the question – what could the precious cargo be?

"Maybe it's a load of bombs and depth charges going to Iceland," said Terry.

"Better still, a month's beer supply!" replied Chris.

"More likely a week's!" came from the rear turret.

After an uneventful patrol which seemed very dull as a sequel to its exciting opening, we discovered during de-briefing back at base that it was a small flotilla relieving an Iceland base. Terry was right when he said there would have been many disappointed UK- bound sailors in Iceland, as well as on the ships, if the bombs had found their targets.

One of the advantages of flying at various times of the day or night was that when off-duty a visit to the Sergeants' Mess during mid-afternoon would find it much more sparsely populated than at other times, and it was at Wick that I first experienced the delights of Sgts Mess 'afternoon tea'. The rationing suffered by civilians also afflicted the Services, although there was every reason to believe there must have been extra rations of carrots, reputedly to enhance night vision, and of bread and cheese to provide sandwich sustenance during a sortie. There was no set meal between midday and supper, but bread, margarine, and jam were put out 'on the side' during the afternoon. The one item needed to turn this plain fare into a satisfactory snack was not available, unfortunately, during the summer months. For this essential item was the humble, round-bodied, Nissen-hut type, coke-burning stove. What a delight for a group of off-duty airmen, on a dismal wintry day, to meet in the Mess at the approved peacetime hour for afternoon tea, stoke up the stove to a cheerful glow, open the bottom flap, and fill the room with the appetising smell of toast made to perfection as only glowing red embers can. A hurried spread of margarine and turnip-embodied but still fruity jam, and the wait till supper was very pleasantly bearable. The practice became just a pleasant memory at a later date, when, upon being commissioned, I discovered it was not *de rigeur* in the Officers' Mess, perhaps because there was no suitable stove available.

On the 21st May 1941, my crew and I returned at 0922 after a night and dawn Atlantic sweep, followed by the routine of Operations Room de-briefing, Dining Room, and bed, to be awakened in the late afternoon by much hustle and bustle. At 1330 that day, a Photographic Reconnaissance Unit (P.R.U) Spitfire had photographed German warships near Bergen in southern Norway; it was known that the enemy had envisaged a link-up between forces from Norway and the Scharnhorst and Gneisenau from Brest, but the latter had been severely damaged in the torpedo attack for which Flying Officer Kenneth Campbell was awarded a posthumous V.C. But the northern enemy forces were now on their way into the Atlantic in an attempt to improve on the 115,622 tons of shipping which the Scharnhorst and Gneisenau had destroyed during their raiding before arrival in Brest. There had been reports on the 20th, through diplomatic channels from Sweden, of the passage of warships down the Kattegat, and first assumptions were that the largest unit was the heavy cruiser 'Hipper'.

It was no surprise, therefore, to enter the Ops Room and see "STRIKE HIPPER" heading the aircraft and crew list; equally no real surprise to note the frustrating omission of my aircraft and crew, as we were not 'on readiness', having completed a sortie a few hours before. However, the anticipation was contagious, for it was an unusual Squadron event, at that time, for ten of our aircraft to be directed at the same target at the same time. It was the first time I had seen this happen during my service with the Squadron, and its effect was heightened by the fact that the aircraft were to be bombed up with armour-piercing bombs. There was no doubting the importance of the target, which was later confirmed as the 'Bismarck', the most powerful battleship afloat.

It seemed as if that 24 hours encapsulated the way Coastal Command was stretched to the limit during mid-1941: dawn would see aircraft searching for U-boats and FW 200's at maximum range westward over the Atlantic; dusk would find a strike force preparing to attack targets off the Norwegian coast.

Not for the first time, nor for the last, the promise of the hunt was to be negated by what one historian, on this occasion, reported as 'bad weather hampering air action'. The ten Hudsons departed at 2300 hours, but covered most of the journey in cloud, and proof of reaching the enemy coast, but not the target, could be read in reports of the attempt:

Aircraft G: Heavy and light flak, and searchlights through gap in cloud. Saw docks at Bergen, dropped 4 – 250S.A.P. bombs. Heavy concentrated anti-aircraft fire.

Aircraft U: Dropped flares. 2 bursts of flak, 2 searchlights. No bombs dropped because of cloud.

Aircraft A: Heavy anti-aircraft fire. Dropped 4 250S.A.P. bombs on 2 ships.

Aircraft F: Dropped flares. Heavy anti-aircraft fire, Searchlights through cloud.

The ten aircraft returned in the early morning, with disappointed crews and minus a few bombs, prevented by a layer of cloud from gaining recognition as the first wave of aircraft to strike in the saga of 'The sinking of the Bismarck'. Well, not quite! The Bismarck had sailed from Bergen at 2200 hours on the 21st May, an hour before the first Hudson left Wick. In his book "Pursuit", Ludovic Kennedy notes that as the enemy forces were heading north, "Look-outs reported, far away to the south, enemy aircraft dropping flares and bombs over Korsfjord", (the entrance- fjord to Bergen). Operations in a Hudson squadron were often frustrating, but sometimes very interesting! On this occasion, the Bismarck was sunk six days later, to the honour of the many air and naval units which took part. 220 Squadron's contribution and the magnificent effort of the ground crews at short notice, was hidden in the words 'bad weather'.

Clouds often interfered with intention, but occasionally offered salvation. The last eastward sortie I was to fly before posting was typical of both situations. After setting course of 050 degrees from Duncansby Head, north of Wick, with wind speed and direction checked from the sea-lanes down below – the lines of the swell or breakers – and with guns tested, on such a trip we would often rely on the sensitive fingers of the Wireless Operator to find a radio station broadcasting music. Some 'twiddlers' were apparently gifted in this ability, whilst others seemed to lack the important attribute, and as a breed they were judged accordingly, always assuming they were equally good on the key. Was this wartime, up in the blue alone, a silvery expanse of sea below, the strains of "Who's taking you home tonight?" or "Little White Lies" played by Geraldo and his Orchestra, and accompanied by a raucous quartet in the aircraft? Frequently, the enemy or the elements, or some combination of both, left us in no doubt before the end of the flight.

The first contact to disturb the festival atmosphere was a large trawler of the kind the Germans now liked to pack with radio and guns, but on close inspection the sight of fishing nets, Norwegian registration, and a cheery wave and grin from a bearded Nordic face, established its identity sufficiently to avoid molestation. At this time of year there was a fair chance of covering cloud appearing before making landfall, and as usual we were not displeased to see it as we approached the enemy-held coast. Nor were we displeased to see a Dornier flying boat of the type Henry had shot down recently. Here was our chance, we thought, to even the score, but the Dornier crew had evidently seen us, managing to escape into cloud before we could do more than exchange a few rounds. However, our clouded curses quickly changed to appreciative accolades when the rear gunner spotted a couple of Me 110 twin-engined fighters skimming the sea towards us, and as we were just below the cloud into which we had chased the Dornier, they saw no more of us than we had of it. Fair exchange!

Towards the end of June 1941 Johnnie Lane and I were called to the Adjutant's office. Johnnie had joined the Squadron just before I had, a pre-war 'weekend flyer' as I could just claim to be, and although not one of my closest friends at that time, we had much in common, and fate had decreed that we would spend the rest of his Air Force days together.

"Rayner and Lane, you go on embarkation leave in a couple of days. You are posted as instructors to a Hudson Operational and Ferrying Unit which is due to open shortly in Canada. Documents and sailing instructions will follow shortly to your leave addresses." So to my last Westward sortie from Wick with the old crew I would be sorry to leave – Collins, Lewis, Hamer. A last chance on this tour to derive maximum pleasure from dropping *all* our depth charges with malice aforethought.

Setting course northwest from Cape Wrath, even the best 'twiddlers' among the Wireless Operators would find it difficult to provide background music. At the heights we flew the mountains screened out the radio waves, although occasionally some freak reception hundreds of miles out would superimpose a snatch of music on normal reception, known to the initiated as 'bouncing'.

Arriving at the spot in the ocean to which our calculations had brought us in the hope that here we would rendezvous with the large convoy and half-a-dozen escorts we were due to meet, there was nothing to be seen but angry water. Had we miscalculated, perhaps because of the changeable weather, or was it the convoy, delayed by an attack or ahead of time for some tactical reason? The former possibility was always the more likely, so we decided on a square search based on ten-mile legs with the first leg along the convoy course as briefed, followed by a 'creeping line ahead'. After half-an-hour into the square search, we found the convoy some distance to our starboard. On reporting to the S.N.O. the Aldis lamp on his destroyer flashed in reply:

"Kindly help escort vessels inspect area 5 miles starboard. Possible dirty deeds afoot."

We saw the corvettes busily scurrying to and fro, at times seeming to disappear under battering waves, whilst we commenced a wide sweep beyond them. If the activity was meant to make attendant U-boats lose contact with the convoy, it apparently succeeded. Until nightfall, that is, for as we eventually turned for home with the usual "Goodbye and thanks!" from the S.N.O., we knew that at this stage of the Battle of the Atlantic, Coastal Command had few facilities specifically designed to help protect shipping against U-boats at night. The Leigh Light which would later provide airborne illumination of U-boats at night was not yet in operational use; nor were the advanced radar sets which would be developed from Bomber Command's H2S type. So, down below, they were virtually on their own now!

As he watched the convoy disappear whilst darkness fell, the rear gunner echoed the thoughts of many such partings:

"Come what may, I'd rather be in my little turret up here than anywhere down there!"

I was about to add a comment, when I realised that very shortly I too could expect to be in a ship crossing the Atlantic!

As Johnnie and I left the Squadron for embarkation leave, the latest news was of the rapid advance of the German armies on the Eastern Front, following their invasion of USSR, which had commenced on 22nd June. There was considerable speculation about future operations against the likely German supply routes to their forces advancing towards Arctic Russia, and the need for air escort to any Allied convoys supplying the Russians through Murmansk. These additional opportunities for offensive action by the Squadron added to our regrets about leaving.

220 Squadron at Wick – April 1941

Back Row: Sgts Davison, Moss, Hamer, Cooke, Cullen, Money, McLaren, Milton, Mills, Jackson, Faucett, Drew, Diplock, McHugh, Lloyd-Jones, Boardman, Walshe, Walker, Greenock

Middle: Sgt Taylor, F/Sgt England, Sgts Cornish, Jackson, Sgt ?, Shane, Nobel, Travell, Ramsey, Heppell, Hall, Rayner, Viner, Ashworth, Ramsden, Laverack, Dunn, House, Lange

Front: P/Os Clench, Tate, F/Os Jackson, Negus, Halstead, F/Lt Simpson, S/Ldr Gilbert, W/Cdr Carr, F/Lt Raw, F/Os Mallinson, Wood, P/Os Ainsworth, P/Os Nair, Birchall, Cansdale, Jackson

CHAPTER 8

NOT CANADA!

"Canada! That's a long way to have to send parcels to you! I wonder if you'll ever get them in the wide open spaces, particularly in winter?" mused Aunt Sarah, as I explained recent events to her.

"Even if you do," added Aunt Alice "my cakes would be stale!"

I told them how much I had enjoyed the cakes and woollen 'comforts' they had sent, but I understood food was not rationed to the same extent over there. From the other side I might even be able to return their favours.

"Many of your friends have gone overseas," Aunt Alice continued. "We want to feel we're doing something useful. What part of Canada are you going to?"

I wasn't able to answer; there had been no further instructions, and as word had got around in the village I would have welcomed the opportunity to be more specific, to be able to vary my answers to the inevitable questions.

The opportunity came very shortly:

"Previous instructions cancelled. Report RAF Silloth forthwith. Adj. Wick".

Thus reduced from an intrepid voyager, to a Cumbrian prodigal's return, I filled the remainder of the day with revisionary farewells, left my mother to explain to others that on my next leave I would be unlikely to have a Canadian accent, and caught the afternoon train next day.

Changing to the main line to the north at Preston, I arrived at Carlisle to find the last train to Silloth had left some time before. I asked a porter the time of the first train next morning. We were standing on the exposed part of the platform, and he pointed to four carriages in a siding nearby.

"D'you see yon carriages?" he said, "they'll be the 6 a.m. out to Silloth. They'll not be locked. Why don' ee go across there, an' kip down in one?"

I left him in no doubt of my gratitude for this accommodating information, and managed a fitful five hours sleep from the six hours of snug occupation. I became a regular midnight caller when returning from leave whilst stationed at Silloth.

The airfield had changed a great deal from the embryo of ten months before. There were three splendid runways with built-in night-landing lights, and a much larger concrete handling area, with extended maintenance facilities. Whereas its main purpose in 1940, given the urgency of the time, was merely to convert pilots to Hudson aircraft, it was now organised in two sections – one for conversion, and a complementary one for operational training, where newly-qualified navigators, wireless operators and air gunners would join pilots to make combat crews, later posted as such to squadrons. The Air Staff had directed that in Coastal, as in Bomber Command, the days of two-pilot crews were over, except on very-long-range flights.

Johnnie Lane arrived the next day. We discovered that the training unit in Canada to which we had originally been posted was not yet ready; in the event, it was ultimately used for other purposes, and the increased demand for Hudson crews to man the expansion of squadrons was met by establishing No 6 O.T.U. at Thornaby by the end of the year. Johnnie and I were allotted an aircraft with dual controls – the right hand control column and rudder pedals were fitted across the entry down into the navigator's den – and we were then sent off to practise right-hand seat flying and instructor's patter.

After giving a few familiarisation flights to pilots from the new intake, neither Johnnie nor I felt able to enthuse about our new role. To have to leave the squadron for the adventure of helping develop a new unit in Canada was just acceptable – it had a certain cachet – but we agreed we would have objected if a crystal ball had been on the table alongside the posting order in the Squadron Adjutant's office that day! Most of the staff at Silloth had changed, and I was denied the pleasure of showing my night-flying total to the officer whose ill-considered note had spoilt my stay as a pupil. However, Johnnie and I were happy to find that the Conversion Flight was now commanded by Squadron Leader Hodgkinson (later Air Chief Marshal Sir Derek), who had been one of our outstanding Flight Commanders on 220 Squadron.

Hardly had the right-hand seat warmed to my incumbency than I was detached to No 1 Beam Approach School at RAF Watchfield near Swindon. As one of the many radio and radar aids which the boffins were developing for operational use, the Lorenz system was deemed to be most suitable, at the time, to assist an instrument approach in bad weather down to 100 feet, so that the pilot could then land visually.

A continuous radio note was directed down the runway from the far end, and this beam became Morse 'dots' on one side of the runway and 'dashes' on the other. The two together produced the continuous note. The volume of the dots and dashes faded with distance from the central line, so that on picking up the signals, the pilot knew which direction to take, and, moving along the line of continuous note, he then became aware of distances from the runway by the superimposed shrill marker beacons along his path. It was a technique practised in the Link Trainer during earlier training, but without the opportunity to use it in the air. The aim now was to qualify as an instructor in the technique.

I was happy to find that the aircraft in use were trusty old Ansons, and that on such a concentrated course of instrument flying there was no need to wind up the undercarriage! After dual instruction, we learner- pilots flew in pairs – one acting as look-out to the other, who would be concentrating on instruments and the beam sounds under the hood. It was a relatively small grass airfield, and if given the go-ahead for an actual landing by the co-pilot, one had to whip back the hood smartly upon hearing the 100-foot marker, and quickly adjust to the external situation in order to skim the boundary and put the Anson down without the need for harsh braking.

My co-pilot was Bruce, a philosophy student before volunteering for aircrew. He was a night-fighter pilot whose squadron was converting from Blenheims to American Douglas 'Havocs', counterpart to the 'Boston' light bombers. Knowing that, when he returned to his unit, he would be flying aircraft with a tricycle undercarriage – with a nose-wheel instead of a tail-wheel, which required a slightly different aircraft attitude in landing – he regarded his time at Watchfield as an opportunity to practise the different technique. It soon became apparent to both of us that after touching down we approached the far boundary of the airfield much too quickly after one of his 'two-point' landings compared with the usual 'three-point', or 'tail-wheel-down' landings, and although his efforts improved with practise, we seldom finished the landing run more than a stone's throw from the boundary hedge. On one occasion, he seemed mesmerised by the changed alignment, whilst to me the nose seemed to be dipping and I had to yell "Get the tail down and brake!"

We were fortunate that July was at its brilliant best during the ten days at Watchfield, since it enabled us to complete the course quickly, but also because what the station lacked in Mess life, and what the area lacked in entertainment, it made amends for in providing a couple of rustic pubs with beer much superior to that provided by the State around Silloth. Bruce and I were surprised, but not ungrateful, to find that the airfield 'died' on the Saturday afternoon, and we strolled along lanes amidst ripening corn and meadows patched with pockets of buttercups and daisies. We were in no doubt that it was the hottest day of the year, so we spread ourselves on the ground amongst them in the shade of a hedgerow oak. The sound of grasshoppers came as a chorus from all parts of the field, whilst several cattle lay under great oaks lazily chewing cud. Bruce searched in vain for one of the insects.

"Those grasshoppers like you to know they're about! Out of sight, but we certainly know they're around, whilst the cows...."

"Bullocks," I corrected, "they're not female! They're males which have suffered the indignity of being of no further interest to cows!"

"Ah, yes," he replied, with the slightest grimace of annoyance at the interruption to a line of thought which was more serious than I anticipated.

"Grass hoppers and cattle under English oaks...." he went on, "Have you read Edmund Burke, the piece from his 'Reflections on the French Revolution'? I think he was suggesting that once the cattle stir themselves, it's likely that the noisily chirping grass hoppers caught under their mighty hooves will be silenced. And who's done more hopping in great jumps after much squawking than the Nazis, and who's been chewing the cud for long enough? Get it?"

"I've got a glimmer," I felt obliged to admit; and I resolved to look up the quotation as soon as possible. When I did so, I realised that Bruce was yet another remarkable person to add to those I had met since joining the RAF:

"Because half-a-dozen grasshoppers under a fern make the field ring with their importunate chink, whilst thousands of great cattle, reposed beneath the shadow of the British Oak, chew the cud and are silent, pray do not imagine that those who make the noise are the only inhabitants of the field; that, of course, they are many in number; or that, after all, they are other than the little, shrivelled, meagre, hopping, though loud and troublesome insects of the hour."

Mindful of the adage 'Still waters run deep', I was conscious of the fact that in my case they were as yet quite shallow.

By the time I returned to Silloth, Johnnie was already putting his pupils through the sequences of the conversion schedule, and I was soon doing the same with those allocated to me. Overall, they were a mixed bunch – one or two from squadrons needing just the conversion part of the course, a few Czechs and Poles, and the remainder, including Canadians, Australians, and South Africans – the first great surge of volunteers from the Commonwealth – straight from the Flying Training Schools set up under the Empire Air Training Plan. It was interesting work, and involved a camaraderie quite different to that on the squadron: an ability to inspire confidence, and establish immediate rapport. However, we missed the thrills and variety of operations, and shamefully admitted that the only excitement seemed to come when gremlins were abroad among the pupil pilots. One began to understand why, from time to time, orders from higher authority stressed the fact that non-operational losses in aircraft and crews were much too high. Occasionally a solo landing attempt would come to grief because the pilot came in too fast, bounced, closed the throttles in panic, then flopped one wing low on to the runway and spun off like a top; another might forget the limit set on the safe use of flap being unable to control the ensuing over-steep approach, occasionally resulting in a splintering fireball on the runway which claimed its dreadful toll before the fire-crew could reach it.

The operational section, where crews were brought together as a unit, had their difficulties with night exercises, as navigation over the British seaboard was so different to night-flying over the flat lands of many of the training areas abroad, where there wasn't even a blackout. We suggested that some of the problems arose because of the lengthy interruption to flying which the fledgling pilots suffered during their return voyages from overseas training; it was obvious that nothing could be done to mitigate the effect at the time, owing to logistic pressures, but in due course Advanced Flying Units were established in U.K. where the returning pilots would have refresher courses before going on to Operational Training Units.

On our first Saturday off-duty together, Johnnie and I took the train to Carlisle, admired the Castle and Lowther Street, noted that Constance Cummings was shortly to appear at the theatre, avoided the pubs which dispensed the State brew, and returned with the small items of personal shopping which would last for a week or two. However, when the Hair Tonic and shaving cream needed replacing, I decided to shop locally, and explored whilst Johnnie was still on duty, finding a smart chemist's shop on a corner near the station. It was obviously a place deserving of regular custom, for the charming assistant who greeted me with an encouraging smile was a lovely dark-haired girl whose picture might well have replaced Jane Russell's on the cover of 'Picturegoer'. I decided I would purchase one item now; the second could wait for another visit. When I told Johnnie, he received my description with mild reserve and considering himself, with some justification, a lady's man, decided that his toothpaste needed replenishing as soon as possible.

On the Tuesday, low cloud brought flying to a halt by mid-afternoon, and an eager stroll took us along to the chemist's shop. It was half-day closing. Enthusiasm diminished, Johnnie began to doubt that a girl as attractive as I had described would be found in such a place. Nevertheless, he decided to accompany me the following day, when a preliminary observation through the shop window brought forth a complimentary "Gosh! Why didn't somebody tell me?"

There was no time to point out that I had done exactly that, before he entered the shop and joined the queue waiting to be served. Whereas those in front of him remained almost static, J's head followed the girl's every movement. On one occasion, she had to pass between us to retrieve some item, and 'J' turned through a half- circle as his gaze followed, and then slowly turned back again. I merely wished she would trip on something so that I could display my chivalrous side. On the only occasion I had ever seen 'J' unnerved, when she turned to serve him he meekly asked for a packet of razor blades, which was the nearest item to him, then, embarrassed by his apparent fixation after receiving his purchase, I guided him out of the shop.

"What about the toothpaste?" I asked.

For a moment he looked blank, then

"Tomorrow!" he said with a wink.

Our appearance the next day caused some agitated observation by the proprietor, who obviously considered he had a protective role to play. He hovered. The shop was well-patronised, and our original tactical plan of casual, then meaningful, conversation with the raven- haired goddess obviously needed amendment. After a whispered revision, 'J' asked for toothpaste, I objected in favour of a different brand as she was reaching for it, she again obliged, this time with a faint smile as she began to realise the true purpose of our mission; 'J' reverted to the original choice and we went into a triangular huddle to discuss the relative merits. The proprietor hovered, with intent. We decided a tactical retreat was sensible, and emerged with two tubes of toothpaste.

It was late on Saturday afternoon before we could put plan number three into operation. We remembered it was commonplace for customers to approach chemists' counters holding slips of paper – prescriptions perhaps, or even requests for certain items which might cause embarrassment to the purchaser if spoken aloud. 'J' and I each proffered our slips of paper, and our dark lady of the chemist's took them in a way which suggested it was by no means the first time that airmen had sought to make a purchase in that way. My note was succinct – 'May I meet you this evening?'- 'J's was competitive – 'Better still, meet me instead!'

The protective hoverer was approaching when the telephone rang and he disappeared. The last customer left the shop as she read the notes and smiled, then leant across most invitingly and whispered

"You're both very sweet" – we glanced at each other sheepishly – "but I'm engaged to a Navigator due home from an overseas posting. He didn't have time to give me an engagement ring; we're being married during his leave. And anyway, I live in Carlisle, I'm only here for this week, I'm really based at our Carlisle shop".

All we could do was wish her a sincere 'Good luck!' and back slowly towards the door as the manager – obviously demoted from proprietor now we knew the circumstances – reappeared ready to pounce. His protective instinct could now return to a watching brief.

"Pity her fiance's a navigator and not a pilot!" said Johnnie, as if his romantic proclivity was evident throughout the breed.

The routine of dual-instruction from the right-hand seat continued into the declining autumn days, and when putting a pupil through the rigours of stalling the aircraft, or carrying out single-engine flying, we were expected to wait for a cloud-base of 5,000 feet, or at least gaps up to that altitude. The Lake District offered a selection of distinctive landmarks over which to carry out these procedures, and on this October day, with a pupil whose handling on the circuit had been exemplary, we climbed over Aspatria towards Bassenthwaite Lake, leisurely practising precise climbing turns to give a rotating panorama of the fairyland below, with its bowed bridges over twinkling streams and walls of rounded boulders. We could see occasional huge piles of them where they had been left after clearance of the land for pasture many years ago.

The gremlin must have been on the pilot's shoulder by the time we levelled out over Derwentwater. I demonstrated the closing of one engine, the action to stop the incipient swing, the increase of power required from the good engine, the need to trim, the diagnosis of the engine-trouble, and the 'feathering' of the propeller on the failed engine to stop it idly rotating and increasing the drag. I re-started the failed engine, and handed over to him, and after a few minutes of comfortable flying to allow him to get the sequence sorted out in his mind, he saw my hand close the throttle on my side. His corrective reaction was perfect, and I complimented him on it; opening up the engine which had been 'feathered' was equally good, and once more we floated leisurely in an orbit around the gossamer lake below.

There was a broad-brush pattern of russet and gold edging the blue-grey waters, and on the lower slopes were the regimented lines of conifer green. I was mentioning the difference between these and the pale yellow of deciduous larches, the pilot nodding his understanding as he gazed below, when the engine I had been closing in demonstration suddenly backfired and lost power.

Knowing that we had plenty of height, there was no great emergency, but he acted with alacrity, closed both throttles and promptly pressed the feathering button of the wrong engine, leaving the aircraft without power. The one which had been losing revs began running rough as if it wanted to break free, the oil temperature rose rapidly, so I suggested he should switch it off and feather it. He looked at me in amazement, so I reminded him that we had plenty of height for our return to the airfield. Nose down to maintain minimum flying speed, for a few seconds there was the sensation of being in a glider, with a faint eerie whistling of the wind replacing the engine noise.

"Now for some real single-engine flying!" I suggested. "Trim for 110 knots, start up the good engine, re-trim against it, see what boost and revs you need to give us a rate of descent of 200 feet a minute, and we should be approaching the circuit at Silloth at about 2,000 feet in 15 minutes."

As we approached the airfield, I saw no point in making a single-engine landing if two could be used, the oil temperature was almost back to normal, so I cautiously carried out the re-starting drill on the troublesome engine, and, after an uncertain squeaky rumble or two, it started. The approach to the runway was straight-forward and the engine was equal to the diminishing demands asked of it, until we were taxying to the hangar, when it started popping with the revs fluctuating again. The fitter later reported that there had been a shortage of oil to the engine owing to a slight leak, and to have run it any more than we did would have caused serious damage.

Not only had the station's flying facilities improved over the past year, but support services also, and we were now encouraged to take 15-minute sojourns under an ultraviolet lamp, briefly clad and wearing dark goggles, on the officially-sponsored assurance that it would help to keep us healthy, increase the vitamin C in our bodies, and generally be a substitute for daylight during spells of night-flying. Of greater importance to the converted, however, it came to be seen as very pleasant relaxation!

Occasionally there would be visits to the airfield by groups of Air Training Corps cadets, and one of these included the son of the friends to whom we had been introduced whilst at Thornaby. The Air Cadet section of his school's O.T.C. were camped by the eastern shores of Lake Windermere near Bowness, and if, by any chance, 'I happened to have an aircraft in that area the next day, they would be very pleased to see me'. I was detailed for an hour's familiarisation with a new intake pilot, so I gave him some straight-and-level, climbing, descending et al, which, surprise, surprise, took us to the middle of Windermere, where I took over 'to demonstrate low-flying'. At about 50 feet we flashed by the pier at the Grand Hotel, then lower still towards the ferry which crosses from The Nab to Ferry House.

At this height, and without a map, the waters of the lake apparently disappear beyond Cockshot Point, as the long straight edge of Belle Isle appears to merge with it, and my passenger's face showed his concern that we weren't going to clear it. However, his expression turned to one of relief as we rounded the point and swept in a right-hand turn towards the village of Bowness, with its cluster of pleasant boarding-houses and cottages dominated by the square bulk of a large hotel a quarter mile from the shore.

We could now see the tents of the cadets' camp between the road north to Windermere and the shore, and boys in Air Force blue seeking the vantage point of the rising ground behind. We turned away to port, sweeping past the narrow northern edge of Belle Isle to allow a low fly-past over the camp, then, with a wing-waggle we were gone, up the lake and away, before any complaints could materialise about disturbing the peace of this tranquil haven from the clamour of war. Gently climbing at cruising speed to give my Canadian passenger an ever-widening view of the beauty of this unique area, we were high enough as Ambleside passed across the starboard quarter to see the autumn-tinted bracken of the slopes soften into a flecked red-and-gold patchwork of wood and pasture surrounding the fell-shouldered valley through Rydal Water and Grasmere.

Leaving the lake northwards at a steady 2,000 feet, the road along the rising valley floor came up towards us between the heights on each side before we descended again to skim the waters of the ever-deserted Thirlmere, forlorn in its utilitarian role of supplying most of Manchester's water. Pointing to Skiddaw, now visible to the northwest, I suggested we should fly towards it at a height just sufficient to miss its 3,054 feet summit, thence alter course to Silloth for a dual approach and landing.

Interesting interludes such as this occasionally relieved the routine of helping fledgling pilots develop the skills which might assist survival, but Johnnie and I still had no doubts about where we would rather be. Confirmation of what we were missing came in news from 220 Squadron shortly after the 29th October 1941.

On that date, nine Hudsons from the Squadron took off from Wick at 1600 hours and landed at 2200 after completing what was acknowledged as 'the most brilliant shipping attack of the war by a single squadron' at that time: the 'Alesund Strike'. At the entrance to Storfjord in Norway, Alesund was sheltered by a number of small islands, and, backed by mountains, offered enemy shipping a relatively secure anchorage. Not that night. 7 ships were sunk!

A moonlight strike at optimum strength such as this depended for success on a number of factors: a full, or almost-full moon at the right time of night and of month, shining from an appropriate place in the sky; precise and speedy information of the disposition of the enemy convoy sneaking along the Norwegian coast and fjords, provided by agents and their equally brave radio operators, or by photo-reconnaissance aircraft, or indeed by a previous Squadron patrol; a lull in other operations for a few preceding days to allow maximum strength to be deployed in the strike, and a careful plan of attack to create maximum impact in minimum time to avoid confusion in the air, but to create it among the ships.

There was a sequel to the Alesund strike. *The Times* of 17th October 1990 carried an Obituary of Leif Larsen, DSO, DSC, CGM, DSM & Bar.... "a Norwegian fisherman who became his country's best known resistance figure, smuggling Allied agents, arms and supplies into occupied Norway during the war.... No one, British or foreign, ever received quite the range of British military decorations Leif Larsen did."

Several of his adventures are told in *The Shetland Bus*, written by Lt/Cdr David Howarth RNVR (Thos Nelson & Sons), which was the name given to the constant sailing of small boats between the Shetland Islands and Norway, taking equipment and returning with agents, refugees etc.

One epic account tells the story of the "Nordsjorn", a fishing-boat, which left Shetland on 19th October 1941. Twenty four hours later it made landfall on the Norwegian coast at Stadtland and sailed towards Kristiansund on a mine-laying mission. On the 21st, following severe storms it began to break up and was beached near Gripholen. The crew of seven, headed by Captain Larsen, decided to head for Alesund, some 70 miles to the south, the home of one of the crew, to obtain a boat to return to UK.

After six days of dangerous movement evading the Germans, tramping through forests, climbing the peaks, and crossing fiords by whatever means were available, they arrived at the house of a neighbour of the Björnöy family, whose son was a crew member. They stayed for two days; then Björnöy's father told them of a boat named the "Arthur". They decided to take her that night.

"But early that evening" Lt Cdr Howarth explains, "Frau Björnöy ran in, alarmed. They must hurry! The Gestapo were here! They had been asking the children if they had seen five men in oilskins and seaboots. Just now they were searching a house down the road. It was a matter of minutes.

At that moment the air raid warnings sounded. Immediately after came the crash of RAF bombs from the harbour, and the German defences went into action. The five men picked up their clothes and ran for a rowing boat which they had seen on the beach. They took it and hid with it in the lee of the land till they were sure there was no one on board the 'Arthur'. Then they rowed quietly out and climbed aboard.

The 'Arthur' was lying close inshore, so they crawled about the deck on all-fours to inspect her. Björnöy looked over the engine, Larsen searched for charts, and the others measured the oil in the tanks and found food and bedclothes. She was completely equipped for the journey. There was even a new suit of sails in the cabin! Björnöy's father came out to them with more food and charts and a log, and told them where a barrel of oil was cached.

Under cover of the noise of the air raid they started the engine and slipped quietly out into the darkness. They stopped to pick up the barrel, then headed for the Sound which led to the open sea. The Sound had a seaplane base on one side and a German watch-post on the other; but the RAF were keeping the Germans busy, and safely through the Sound the 'Arthur' set course for Shetland." Their safe return for future clandestine activities was probably more important than the effects of the raid itself.

That results such as those from the Alesund strike were achieved without loss was, in large part, a tribute to the experience and training of the crews, most of whom had been trained on the Squadron as Johnnie and I had been, before the advent of integrated training at OTUs. In our current daily routine of attempting to guide successors, 'J' and I found some slight reward in the knowledge that crews were well prepared for the various roles expected of them in General Reconnaissance Squadrons. A deflating substitute for the real thing; even so, not without some danger. The narrowing headwaters of the Solway Firth, and the large sandbanks such as Blackshaw Bank on the Dumfries side, and between the estuaries of the Esk and Eden rivers, provided ample space for practising the twists and turns of evasive low-flying. On a calm, damp day, the water would sometimes be glassy, which made height in a steep turn difficult to judge. It was on such a day that one of the instructors dipped a wing in the water, and in an instant the Hudson was on its back, the two occupants lost in a foaming mix of sand and water.

On 11th December 1941 Germany and Italy declared war on the USA. The American Congress declared war in return and provided for American forces to be despatched to any part of the world. These events followed the Japanese bombing of Pearl Harbour on the 7th December, and the declaration of war on Japan by the USA and Britain on 8th December. The intervening three days between these declarations and that of the Germans on the 11th were fraught with suspense, as we were led to wonder if the Americans would use all resources to fight Japan, and avoid waging war also on Germany, leaving us woefully short of American aircraft, particularly in Coastal Command, where three-quarters of our equipment came from the States. However, the declarations of the 11th brought the second year of war to a more optimistic conclusion.

When we returned from Christmas leave, bad weather interfered with the flying programme, and we had the day off on New Year's Eve. Johnnie and I felt we needed exercise as an antidote to the effects of seasonal fare, so we decided to climb Skiddaw, all 3,054 feet of it. It was not the best of days, but the fact that the top was covered in cloud led to the decision that we would simply go as far as conditions allowed. We left the main road by Spoony Green Lane, skirted the wood lying under Latrigg Hill, then joined the pony track by the side of White Beck and the unremitting steadily-ascending path lay mistily ahead. Not the most welcome sight on a raw day when stamina had been threatened by festive indulgence – a track with some interesting minor diversions would have served better. Reaching the shrouded heights, we decided to carry on so long as we could see the path in front of us. It was with some surprise that we suddenly found ourselves beside a cairn of large stones on level ground sprinkled with snow, and a brief reconnaissance showed that the surrounding land tended to fall rather than rise. We could claim to have reached the top, and took a photograph to prove it. All that it revealed when developed was the outline of a hardly-recognisable figure on a whitish foreground against a grey backdrop.

We arrived back at the airfield in time for a late supper, and during the meal a steward came across to say there was a telephone call for me. Harry was ringing from the Squadron at Wick. Henry had not returned from an offensive patrol near Bergen in southern Norway on 23rd December, and there had been no further news. It was a cruel way to end 1941, and neither Johnnie nor I could face the developing festivities which would see in the New Year.

We retired to our rooms; I found it difficult to make a fair summary of good events and bad during the second full year at war. There had been strong rumours, and occasional published confirmation, of losses among colleagues from Training days, but Henry was the first great friend to go. A strange belief developed that one's close colleagues would be no more likely to suffer the ultimate misfortune than would oneself. Perhaps 1941 was best described with tongue in cheek as a year of ups and downs. With an hour to go to midnight, I took out my pen-and-ink drawing of a Hudson, and busied myself with that.

During those seven days between Henry's non-return and our notification of it, he had been taken half-way across occupied Europe. He recalls the experience in these words:

"It happened on 23rd December 1941 at approximately 1420 hours. We had completed an uneventful reconnaissance – landfall Stavanger then up the coast to Bergen, when the Fates took a hand. Weather was lousy – sleet, snow, mist, with a few brief patches of clear, just enough to keep us on track along the coast and a couple of hundred feet above the water. Two of us – Harold Hamer and I – were fresh from leave and relishing the excitement of ops once again. Harold had been my regular W/Op for some months now. Stan, the rear gunner, was on his second or third flight; Henderson, my second-pilot was new to the Squadron – we had met him in ops that morning.

As we prepared to set course for home he had a look of "Is this all?" on his face – and so the seed was sown: not directly back, but along the way we had come, Bergen-Stavanger then Wick. So we flew south.

We had just reached our turn-off for Wick, when the curtain of mist was drawn aside and we were in the clear – three hundred yards to port, the coast. A mile to starboard, steaming north, a large convoy headed by a naval escort! Little time to identify; my reaching forward for the bomb-door lever coincided with a sharp explosion in the cockpit. I was flung forward on to the control column and the instrument panel.

My next recollection was of awakening in a smoke-filled cabin, with the 'plane's nose in the water, bubbling in from the front. Of Henderson and Harold no sign. I slid back my cockpit window and must have clambered through the 24 by 18-inch opening, then found myself on the wing. I snatched off my helmet – still attached to the 'plane by the intercom plug. The Hudson was sitting on the water, nose well down. The rear door was open, with Stan peering down at the water some ten feet below him. The 'plane lurched ominously – I shouted "Jump, she's going!" and found myself in the water as the tail reared up above me. I frantically kicked away and watched, fascinated, as it rose to its high point, hesitated, and then slid silently into the depths.

It was time to take stock – the Mae West was inflated, no problem there. A rise on the crest of a wave gave a brief glimpse of the dinghy already some hundred feet away and drifting fast. Down into a trough and up again, this time to seek the coastline, perhaps a couple of hundred yards away – but in the high and cold seas running it might as well have been a couple of hundred miles. Down again, and up again, this time to see a rowing-boat pulling out from the shore. "Thank God!" I shouted to Stan, and we concentrated our efforts on shortening the distance. Then we were heaved into a twenty-foot boat, manned by Sven Hellisto and his son (I met them again five years later in 1946). They took the oars to return – I made signs to them that there were two more. We scanned the seas and spotted first Harold, then Henderson, both apparently lifeless, borne by their inflated life-jackets. We heaved them aboard, and our saviours pulled for the shore.

Was there a chance to lie low somewhere? A look ahead quickly put paid to any such idea: a sizeable group of green-uniformed soldiers stood awaiting our arrival. We touched shore on a shelved area among the rocks, and the soldiers stepped forward, two by two, for me and Stan. Hustled into a waiting car, I glanced back to see Harold and Henderson being carried from the boat, and our two fishermen being walked up through the rocks to a wooden house.

In a few minutes we reached a small military medical centre, where we were stripped of our sodden clothes and stood naked, shivering uncontrollably. I realised for the first time how cold I felt – the outside temperature was well below zero – then we were dried, wrapped in hot blankets, and put to bed in separate rooms. There remains only a pattern of confused memories: a visit from an officer who spoke excellent English, which he explained was due to a recent spell as a schoolmaster in Holloway, London. His interest was specific – what had we been doing, in what 'plane, from where? My reply of name, next-of-kin, address and service number did not deter him. He returned several times till nightfall.

The door of my small room was left open, and in the lighted room outside the heavy incessant pacing of a guard was accentuated by his shadow moving up and down the open door. It was becoming unbearably hot under the heavy blankets – probably very necessary to sweat out the effects of my immersion, but uncomfortable. I wanted to sleep. Then came a visit from another officer, who introduced himself as being in charge of the 25mm gun battery that had brought us down. Apparently his first victim! He was more solicitous; I suggested moving the radiator away and closing the door. He agreed, and left, wishing me a good night. I slept until morning.

An orderly brought my clothes, dried and wearable, but minus pipe, tobacco pouch, and a counterfeit shilling I had always carried in the fond belief that bad money always turns up! Breakfast was coffee and bread sparsely buttered, and jam. The orderly gave me a piece of paper and asked for my address in England – seemingly his first victim too, and souvenirs were required!

With an escort of three soldiers we were taken by car through a white landscape, and then through town streets brightly lit for Christmas Eve, past a railway station, up a hill to a door let into a high wall. The town gaol of Stavanger! Into separate cells, a bed of boards, a combined stool and table not unlike a school desk, a heavy door with iron bolts and grating, a cold stone floor.

On Christmas morning came an early awakening with bread and coffee to precede our departure, this time on foot down the hill to the railway station. The guards, again three, had little to say amongst themselves, appeared to speak no English, and soon made it very evident that they wished to hear none. It was thus a very uneasy party which boarded a train and steamed off into Christmas Day – to us, destination unknown. The occasional glimpse of the sea as we emerged from the frequent tunnels through the mountains told us we were heading south. After two or three hours we left the train and boarded a waiting single-decker 'bus, already filled with a mix of uniformed passengers. The bench at the rear was empty, apparently awaiting our arrival, for as soon as we were seated the 'bus set off. I sat in the corner near an emergency door, then a guard next, then Stan, and the other two. We lurched round a corner and all four swayed against me. I leant heavily on the door, and with an audible 'click' it became partly disengaged from its latch. My immediate thought of a dramatic escape was dispelled by a glance outside. We were driving through a mountain pass, I was on the valley side and below, dropping sheer from the road, was a two hundred foot ravine! But would my escape be forced upon me as my companions lurched against me at the next sharp turn? I reached for the door to close it – and stopped. How would that be interpreted by the guard? I turned to him, opened my mouth, and was told, quite clearly, no talking! There followed many heart-stopping miles until we reached our next destination, to continue once again by train to Oslo. There, a police van took us to a modern office block.

Stan and I were put into a large sparsely-furnished room, with a small peep-hole in the door winking its warning that even now we were not alone. Our two days there ended with the appearance of two guards, who took us by car out of Oslo to Gardemoen airport. Inside the terminal building we were handed over to a Luftwaffe officer, whose English was adequate enough to tell us that we were bound for Berlin, which was quite a surprise after being given no information at all. He later explained that he also had been shot down near Sola – by German batteries! – and was now grounded for health reasons.

Time came to depart: there were two Ju52's on the apron. Our fellow-passengers were all military, mostly officers. Our escort told us he was going on leave, so we were an additional and probably not very welcome chore. As we boarded I noticed that the other aircraft was receiving a special party in dark uniforms, in the centre of which was a large imposing figure, wearing an impressive cloak with heavy silver chain.

Inside the aircraft, there were two continuous benches down each side, backs to the fuselage, facing inwards. Two RAF airmen occasioned the curious glance, but no more; we were evidently not the first! We took off and flew low over the water towards Denmark, landing at Alborg for refuelling. We waited in a small terminal building, where we learned, before embarking again, that the other aircraft was overdue. Retribution?

On to Copenhagen where we landed at lunchtime. Our escort explained funds were limited and we sat in a canteen with a glass of milk and a bun each. An airman from the Ju 52 approached, and spoke to our escort in German. We were invited to join the crew for lunch, but our escort remained seated – the invitation did not include him. In the large kitchen, where the crew members were enjoying their meal, we joined them for goose, vegetables, and an ample supply of lager beer. What an unexpected opportunity! There was a young Dane in attendance and as we left he offered his hand, saying "Good luck!". I thanked him, took his hand, and felt in my palm a folded piece of paper. On rejoining our escort I asked for the toilet where I hastily inspected the paper – it was a 5-Mark note!

Soon we were airborne – destination Berlin. The cabin-heating was very poor; the cold and the plentiful lager had its inevitable effect and I asked where the loo was. Alas there wasn't one! The next hour was a fidget of crossed legs and crossed fingers, mostly legs! An officer sitting opposite grinned, and reaching under his seat made a gesture of offering me his hat. He nearly lost it! At long last we landed, and quickly I stood beneath the fuselage and answered the call. I can truthfully say that the first thing I did on arriving in Berlin was to piss on it!

On the way through the city in a coach we encountered a diversion to avoid a closed street down which I saw damaged buildings and debris. The officer seated in front of me – the one who had offered his hat – turned and smiled. "And no damage was done!" he said with a wry smile. We left the coach at a railway station, busy with trains and teeming with people, the majority in uniform. In a large cloakroom we had a good wash – and saw ourselves for the first time since being shot down. I had a shock – the mirror showed that my left eye was black, blue and shiney – a relic of the crash! A stubble of beard did not improve matters!

Our escort took us to a large canteen, crowded with troops. He found an empty corner table, told us to sit, and left to fetch some soup. We were attracting a fair amount of attention – no doubt the RAF blue did not help. By the time he had returned we sensed an air of hostility, and before we had finished the soup the escort was approached by someone in authority. He turned to us and explained we could not remain in the room – "the table is needed". So we left, but with a problem for the escort – where to put us? Solution – a left-luggage room, where we lay down on the racks among the kit-bags! I was on the upper shelf, with Stan below. As troops entered, to leave their luggage or claim it, the procedure was the same: "Heil Hitler!" as they entered, then "Heil Hitler!" replied the check-in clerk seated at a table. I could hear Stan's sotto voce comment below me! So we passed the time until the return of our escort.

We hurried for our train, and went to the end compartment of the last carriage. It was occupied by two soldiers, feet up on the seats. There was an angry exchange with our escort, and they left, none too graciously, as the compartment was reserved for us; the thought of having priority over the German Army was gratifying, but not for long! We were in confiscated French rolling-stock, and the heating-system was incompatible with the adjoining German carriage, so we froze! All praise to the escort, who lent me a spare woollen sweater he carried in his baggage. We cat-napped through the night, finally arriving at Oberausel near Frankfurt in the middle of the following morning.

The final lap of our extraordinary journey halfway across Europe was by normal public transport. On a single-decker tram we clattered, strap-hanging, through the streets of Oberausel together with folk going about their daily business. The tram stopped, we alighted, and walked the last few yards to our 'home' for the next few weeks: the Luftwaffe Prisoner Transit and Interrogation Centre, Dulag Luft. It was our first view of a prisoner-of-war camp: the double barbed-wire fence enclosing the single-storey barracks, the high forbidding watch towers at each corner – the prisoners already inside looking curiously at the new arrivals. We did not enter the camp, but were guided to a large brick building standing outside.

Within seconds, Stan and I were separated, and I was put in a bare cell-like room furnished with bed, table, and chair, and the door closed behind me. A minute later a guard appeared to ask for the return of the borrowed pullover – I had completely forgotten it, and had no further opportunity to thank our escort for the loan. Then came an order – the days of requests were over! – to completely change into khaki (apparently French) kit. My RAF uniform was then removed and I was left alone with my thoughts."

So began three-and-a-half years' sojourn as a 'guest' of the Third Reich.

Early in 1942, 220 Squadron was withdrawn from operational duties to convert to Boeing 'Flying Fortress' aircraft and the link with the old days was severed, not least because such aircraft were to be used by Coastal Command only in the war against U-boats. 'J' and I were rather disappointed to think that none of the pilots we had trained would now be going to 220. Harry, the Squadron's 'champion ship-buster' had been posted as an instructor back to Thornaby, which had become No.6 OTU, to assist in supplying crews to Hudson squadrons in the Mediterranean, the Middle East, and Africa.

Up to that point, none of the NCO pilots of our vintage had applied for commissions, largely because of what one might call egalitarian camaraderie. Now the time to do so seemed appropriate. Two items of good news lightened the heavy winter days, during which more time seemed to be spent in brushing the low clouds in weather tests than in instructional progress. The first item was that Henry had not 'bought it' but was a prisoner of war in Stalag Luft III, where his promotion to Warrant Officer would eventually reach him.

The second was that I was called for interview by the Commissioning Board at Blackpool on the 18th March. A Hudson awaiting an Air Test was put at my disposal, and I flew into Squires Gate aerodrome at Blackpool, then joined a small mixed group of aircrew and ground crew personnel awaiting the call to the presence. Being successful, I felt this was an occasion to celebrate, but I had to return with the aircraft for night-flying, so, as it was only fifteen minutes flying time to my family home in Rossendale, I would celebrate in the air over those quiet hills.

Few people have the opportunity to fly in salute over their alma mater, to celebrate an important event in the life of a past-pupil, as I was now set to do. The valleys of the imperfectly named 'Forest' of Rossendale resembled a capital letter 'E', with the vertical stroke running east-west, and the other three north-south; moorland rising to over 1,000 feet intervened and surrounded the whole. The base of the 'E' and the vertical line was the valley of the River Irwell, on its way to Manchester and the Mersey, and through the other valleys ran the tributaries which had been as essential to local prosperity as the tall mill chimneys which stood sentinel over the lower reaches. Although no stranger to the moors, the middle valley had encompassed my birth, my home, my schooling, and social deliverance – and mad dashes down the hill to the station to catch the 7.45 to work.

From the air, there was so much more moorland than valley! Knowing the extent of the moors, it ought not to have been a surprise, but it certainly was. At least, I knew that the surrounding hills were about similar heights, and I decided to approach from the west about fifty feet above the highest of them.

The first run was across the three valleys, parallel to the longest one, then a sweep to the left to position the aircraft for a shallow dive into the middle valley from south to north. It needed a tighter turn than I had expected at the head of the valley, over the high moor where a decoy airfield had been built, whence to the north I could see the sprawl of Burnley at the bottom of the hill beyond. I was now in position to go down the valley in a roaring shallow dive which kept the Hudson parallel to the gradient of about 400 feet loss of height in four miles.

The Grammar School I had attended stood at the top of a rising road to the left of my track, with a fine facade facing down the hill, and as I flashed by almost as low as the upstairs windows, I supposed that the 'exhibition' would be more readily accepted by pupil faces at the windows than by teachers whose lessons had been temporarily interrupted. As the school swept by, I was almost immediately at the T-junction of tributary and Irwell, when I had to heave the Hudson up in a steep climb to clear the gap 1,000 feet up on the path to a spring in the hillside known as Waugh's Well, which I had trodden many times. Then away north west to Silloth and the relative calm of night-flying.

A report of the visit followed by letter, and reactions appeared to be varied but generous, one going so far as to say it was the best way to advertise an approaching "Wings for Victory Week" (lucky timing!), another that you couldn't beat a British aeroplane! Many onlookers guessed who the pilot might be, but among those who didn't were the person who sounded the Air Raid Warning siren, the Police Sergeant who emerged from the small local Station blowing his whistle, and the concerned ladies who waved a large white sheet 'to show where the football field was' in case the pilot needed to make an emergency landing! My Aunt Lorna suggested that her daughter should "go out on to the lawn with the table cloth and wave it, so that if it's your cousin up there, he'll know we've seen him and then perhaps he'll go away!"

"As I flashed by almost as low as the upstairs windows..."

Johnnie Lane

Harry Ramsey at Hudson controls en route to Wick 12.3.41

As soon as I got Henry's POW camp address I decided, rather fatuously, that I would attempt to establish a code between us which would allow him to send the sort of message which he might prefer to keep from the eyes of German censors. The idea was that he and I would compose our letters so that the first and last letters of each line of writing would make up the secret words, but of course the problem was that I had to explain this to him in confidence. The opening sentence – 'Hope this reaches you (in thought) as it leaves me' was, I optimistically hoped, a coded message in itself, and I decided to use his preference for 'Gold Block' tobacco as the centre piece of this exercise in double entendre. Thoughtlessly ignoring the lack of it in his straitened circumstances, I asked him to imagine rows of 'Gold Block' tins on his tobacconist's shelves, and in serving his customers, the tobacconist took one tin from the end of the left, then the end of the right, top shelf; similarly on the next lower shelf, and so on, until the 'bottom line', below which could be seen his name. Needless to say, Henry was completely baffled by this, but his reply indicated that my letter had helped him while away several weary hours.

Being now a Pilot Officer, once more I encountered the problem of accommodation such as in the first year of the war. There were insufficient sleeping-quarters in the Officers' Mess. Paradoxically, the Sergeants' Mess at Silloth had been extended to take the increased numbers of sergeant aircrew, although staff and pupils were still partially segregated: the staff members had their own section of the Mess, and single rooms, the trainee sergeants had barrack rooms. Various views were expressed about this arrangement, but to me it seemed to have the advantage of enabling teacher and taught to relax free of the need to be anything other than realistic in relationships. If one took the trouble to make them, there were plenty of opportunities for pleasant social contact.

Easter 1942 became one such occasion. Sergeant Ken Hanson was an Australian pilot who had just finished his conversion course with me, and had started crew training with two compatriots and a Canadian when he discovered that Pete Castell, another instructor, and I were going to Keswick and Derwentwater on our next day off. As none of the four had been able to visit the Lakes but were very keen to do so, we arranged to take them with us. Ken had been enthusiastic about the beauty of the setting when we had flown over Bassenthwaite and Derwentwater during stalling and single-engined flying exercises, and his appreciation of this piece of 'olde England' flowed freely as we strolled down the main street in Keswick towards the Moot-Hall. About fifty yards from it, on the right-hand side of the street was a small garage with a sign above the doorway advertising "SIX SEALED BRANDS". On each side of the arch stood a petrol pump with a handle which had

COASTAL COMMAND PILOT

to be rocked from side to side for the delivery of petrol, and standing by the first one as if to consolidate the notion that this was an old-established business, stood the tallest and oldest 'penny-farthing' bicycle imaginable.

Hanson was on it in an instant, propping himself up with a foot on the huge stone slab on which the pump rested, his service cap across his head instead of fore-and-aft, right hand tucked into his tunic, his features bearing a passable resemblance to a mobile Napoleon. We had a camera, and each in turn posed on the 52-spoked steed with no objection from what appeared to be a deserted workshop. The owner was certainly justified in supposing that no-one was likely to ride it away.

Sustained by a lunch arranged around one of those delicious, fat Cumberland sausages, we hired two rowing-boats to venture out on to Derwentwater. Hanson's Canadian navigator, Smithy, suggested a race to St. Herbert's Island, about half-way down the lake, – the three pilots in one boat, the three aircrew in the other. There were two pairs of oars to each boat, and a helmsman. Approaching the island we pilots were just in the lead, but the opposition was closing fast, and when within arm's reach, the Canadian leant across and grabbed the side of our boat. As we pulled harder on the oars, he lost his grip and water again separated their prow from our stern.

Dissatisfied with this failure to grapple successfully, Bluey, the other pursuing oarsman, stood up, indicated his longer reach, and moved towards the front of the boat. Unfortunately, Smithy, moving towards the vacated seat at the rowlocks, chose to move down the same side of the boat, which started to dip menacingly down to the water. They grabbed each other, and like a pair of ballroom dancers, shuffled across the boat to try to right it. But too far, and water lapped in before they could chase back again! The oarsman lost the oar he was using as a boat-hook, and with it one which had been loose in the rowlocks. By now, the side was well under water, and in trying to stop the other oar from floating away, they leant too far and the paired sailors, statuesque on the brink for a second, then swaying as if in muscular spasm but unable to avoid the inevitable, slid into the water.

We were still about thirty yards from the island, which suggested a depth of water at least sufficient to require the trio to display their swimming talents, whilst Pete, at the helm, turned our boat to the floundering crew. Struggling to recover from the undignified positions in which they had been cast into the water, and amidst a plethora of curses and a flurry of foam, the three heads, shoulders and torsoes slowly emerged like dripping sons of Neptune, embarrassed by overdoing the heroics when the water was only four feet deep! After a brief interlude of hilarity, we successfully retrieved the floating items whilst they turned the waterlogged boat aright, then dragged it to the shore of the island, where we beached both boats and reviewed the situation.

The island, and indeed the lake, was deserted, and in the undergrowth among the trees there were dry twigs which could be used as kindling, so we decided to light a fire to dry the three sets of wet clothes. Pete and I were despatched to the mainland for food, and on our return we could see the smoke rising through the trees. As we approached the island it became obvious that the 'colonials' were making the most of the situation: one, we thought the Canadian, seemed to be attempting to send a smoke signal, which we managed to read as far as four short puffs equals 'H' and three long puffs 'O', but the rest was lost; a second body was standing naked, just visible by the fire between the trees, sending unintelligible semaphore; and the third was catching the sun on a mirror, flashing the morse, as far as we could tell, for 'Good show!' They would certainly not have been stranded on a desert island for long!

"The third letter was 'W'," explained the Canadian, "isn't 'HOW' reckoned by you Brits to be the customary Red Indian greeting?"

By the time we had eaten lunch the thinner garments were dry, so vests were donned, followed by much cavorting to keep semi-naked bodies warm whilst the thicker uniforms dried, then trousers, and scavenging for more dry tinder, and finally dry tunics to complete the rehabilitation of the shipwrecked sailors. There were reasons for a disinclination to race back to the landing- stage in Keswick; meanwhile, the late afternoon sun dipped behind the island which for four hours had been the nudist colony of the Lakes. We did not even have to pay extra for the extended adventure, as the boatman had told us that he would be obliged if we would simply tie up the boats when we returned, as we had been the day's only customers.

We were too late for supper when we arrived back at the camp, but fish and chips and a lengthy drink provided many an opportunity for jovial use of the words 'wet' and 'dry'!

I was to learn much later with great regret that Ken Hanson and his crew were reported missing in action from a sortie in a Hudson near Celebes, Indonesia, in July 1945, a month before Japan's surrender.

Kent Hanson (3rd left) and crew

Ken Hanson in Keswick Easter 1942

Derwentwater "S.O.S."

*Water-nymphs drying out. St Herbert's
Island, Derwentwater*

*Back to normal. Ken, Self,
Pete, Smithy, Bluey, Dave*

CHAPTER 9

FILMING FICTION
AND FACING FACT

The year so far had kindly provided monthly interludes in the humdrum routine of flight instruction, and these incidents seemed set to continue. In April the Crown Film Unit arrived.

The film 'Target for Tonight', about a Wellington of Bomber Command, had been well received at cinemas throughout the country, and 'Coastal Command' was next on the list for publicity. Squadron Leader Hodgkinson detailed Johnnie Lane and me to join him in a meeting with the location director, to be briefed on the schedule of filming. The story line was to follow a lengthy patrol by a Sunderland flying-boat (the star of the film); a brush with long-range enemy fighters, and the appearance of a pocket battleship intent on raiding Allied convoys. Hudson aircraft were to attack the battleship, followed by Beaufort torpedo-bombers. A screen portrayal of "We search and strike!"

The Crown Film Unit had to move around stations as appropriate resources became available, and this was intended to be the first of two visits to Silloth – on this the first occasion to film various aspects of the flying techniques involved, then at a later date, the attack on the 'enemy warship.'

The first 'take' was meant to provide a link with a scene already in the 'can', of nine Hudsons in a formation of three 'Vic's', taken against a background of the grim Icelandic coastline. In the film, this was the base from which the Hudsons were to set forth, and our first task at Silloth was to provide aircraft in the same formation for continuity.

The people in the town were to witness the unusual sight of nine Hudsons manoeuvring into squadron formation in the skies above, and until we had a chance to explain the reason for the flying display, local opinion had it that 'something big had come up'. It was also quite an occasion for several of the pilots who had little experience of formation flying, but after half-an-hour's practice the nine aircraft wheeled about the sky with some precision, and the cameraman decided to shoot. He had his camera mounted on a Heath-Robinsonish tripod in the doorway of a tenth Hudson, the door having been removed, and the aircraft flew across the line of the formation so that he could get an approach shot, then turning down the line for a 'passing shot', and, having sped round behind, 'takes' from the rear quarter and front quarter alongside. The onlookers must have been equally impressed by the way the formation went into line astern to fly round the circuit before landing, and at that point the knowledgeable viewers would realise that it could hardly have been something big as we had only been out of sight over the Solway Firth for about an hour.

Pete and I were the subjects of minor inquisitions by our landladies when we returned to our billets that evening. As a result of the lack of accommodation on camp, we had each been given a room in adjoining houses by two very kind families. They were neat terraced houses in the middle of a row at the end of the road which led down to the airfield. Hospitality extended to wonderful late breakfasts after night flying – bacon, eggs, tomatoes, fried bread – always served with a smile and an approving nod at our hearty response to the meals put before us. Mrs Todd's house was a second home to Pete and to me.

The Crown Film Unit seemed well pleased with first results, so 'J' and I were detailed to provide the next phase of their filming schedule. They wanted shots of a Hudson in a diving attack, then of a 'stricken' aircraft trailing smoke, and of the underside of another as the bomb-doors opened for the release of the bombs. For the first, I had the cameraman with his tripod in the doorway of my machine, whilst 'J' provided the dives from varying heights and different angles of attack. Rehearsals exposed problems to be solved. The camera's traverse angle was limited, firstly because the Hudson was a twin-ruddered aircraft, and the fin on the same side as the camera allowed less than a 45 deg sweep to port, and secondly because the need for stability of the tripod meant that the camera could not be fixed so that it extended beyond the line of the fuselage.

We decided that our camera aircraft would have to be positioned to allow the filming to start as the attacking aircraft was above and beyond the tail-fin, with the camera following its dive towards our front, and as it reached our height we would go down with it, turning inwards so that as 'J' levelled out fifty feet above the sea, we passed over with a final shot of his aircraft skimming the water. This worked well and the next day the positions were reversed for the shots of the 'stricken' aircraft – 'J' flew the camera Hudson and I made the 'flaming' dive. The arrangement was that the camera aircraft would signal when ready in position, and as I started the dive, the airman armourer who was shut away in the fuselage of my machine would detonate a smoke canister, leaving the red plumes of smoke to trail out through the open windows in the cabin. We had immediate confirmation that it had been very effective, for as we finished and crossed the seafront on our approach to the airfield with the red smoke still billowing forth, many anxious faces were turned up towards us, and the doors of the town's Fire Station were being opened, presumably in case this stricken aeroplane crashed on the town! The airman opened the cabin door and called "Was that O.K.?" I turned as I gave him a thumbs-up signal, then couldn't restrain a howl of laughter. His face was the colour of a Red Indian, and his shock of hair, brown when we took off, was an even brighter red! He was known as Rufus for several days.

The idea of opening the bomb doors for filming from below needed more thought, and we eventually decided that it would be better for the camera aircraft to fly straight and level, leaving the other Hudson to manoeuvre in close-up to get the desired shot. The mounting on the tripod allowed good elevation, but to fly alongside and slightly above the camera would not achieve the desired result, as the bomb-doors when open would block the sight-line into the bomb-bay. We decided that I should approach from the port beam in a shallow dive, with the bomb-doors starting to open as my aircraft passed over the other. Then from behind, I would turn and fly as close as possible above 'J's' aircraft, almost on the same course but drifting slowly to port so that my machine would gradually come into range of the camera below. Then I would open the bomb-doors and drop the mock-up bomb. The problem here was that, flying from the normal – left-hand – seat, I would not be able to see the Hudson below once I had crossed to its port side, still flying as close as possible. In the event, as I drifted across the aircraft below, and being in a dual-control machine as used for instructing, I moved very tentatively from the left-hand seat to the right-hand, arms outstretched with one hand on each control column, so that, on my right I could now see the cameraman below. I was then in a position to receive his signal for the appropriate moment to press the bomb-release button. Fortunately, the C.F.U. chaps were satisfied with the first attempt, for they had to leave the following day to continue filming with the Sunderland flying-boat crew.

"You're not going to try that manoeuvre with a Sunderland?" I joked as they left. I had to admit I wasn't particularly keen to repeat it myself, as during the few seconds when only feet separated the two aircraft and I was unsighted, I half-expected to hear a jarring sound which would indicate unpleasant, perhaps calamitous, contact.

Within a few days of their departure, I was subjected to a painful interruption to my flying duties – my Wisdom Teeth decided on a rapid appearance. The patter between instructor and pupil was beyond me, so I sought a meeting with the

Dental Officer. His Appointment Book left few gaps unfilled, and a theory was put about that the local State beer rotted the teeth. I could only assume a contra theory, as my Wisdom Teeth were emerging in pristine condition, one on each side of my lower jaw. My first attempt at getting an appointment was regarded by the assistant as jumping the queue, so I retired to the Mess to await the sympathy of the bar steward. Spying a dictionary among the volumes on a corner shelf, I decided to define more closely this painful affliction:

"WISDOM TOOTH – Molar usually cut after twenty years of age (cut one's wisdom teeth – to gain discretion)". The definition was entirely specific – I was now 22 years of age; the saw which followed, suggesting that I had now reached the age of discretion had yet to be proved. Certainly valour was in the ascendant the next day when the pain drove me back to the dentist with the cry "Get the damn things out; I don't mind if your lancing would qualify you for the Lancers, but do something quickly!" He did! With my mouth locked open he said:

"I think we can manage this without full anaesthetic, don't you?"

I gave him an answer after he had performed his torture, but it was then of no consequence; at least I spat into his bowl with some vehemence. My misery was ameliorated by visits to the Sick Quarters, not simply to cosset myself in dental resuscitation but to bask under the ultraviolet lamp in the 'sunshine room'. It was presided over by an attractive member of the W.A.A.F.

The not unwelcome interruptions to the instructing regime in the month of May 1942 were not yet complete. On the 25th the whole RAF Station was agog at the receipt of a signal ordering the preparation and arming of as many Hudsons as possible, with stand-by crews made up of instructors and pupils as necessary. Given the preponderance of pilot instructors, all crews would have an experienced pilot, but most of the navigators, W/Ops, and Air Gunners would be in various stages of training.

The operational requirements completed, we were ordered to fly across to Thornaby airfield. There we were told we were to be part of a 1,000 bomber attack on an enemy target still to be decided. Similar arrangements had been made among the staff and pupils based at Thornaby O.T.U., and it was expected we would be able to contribute about two-dozen Hudsons to this raid. It was a pleasant return to the scene of past activities – a grand reunion whatever the outcome.

On the 28th there was a flurry of activity – air testing, practise firing, instrument checking, even some compass swinging, and a book was opened on the most likely target. One of the aims in sending a much greater force than had been achieved in any previous attack was an attempt to saturate the enemy defences, so it appeared likely that the target would be an important city within easy reach of the twin-engined bombers which still made up the larger part of any raid.

Once the preliminaries were completed and with further orders not yet received, but being confined to the airfield, we set about renewing acquaintances with those who had known the Thornaby of more than a year ago, and Vaux's Best Bitter reminded we Silloth brethren, forcibly weaned on State brew, of what we were missing. However, under the circumstances expected on the morrow, pints were restricted whilst anecdotes flowed.

Sadly, denial did not have its own reward: on the 30th we were 'stood down', and the force which had assembled at Thornaby was dispersed so back to Silloth we went, disappointed at not being able to add to the force of 1,046 aircraft which filled the news headlines the next day. Cologne had been the target successfully attacked, chosen because the meteorological experts forecast good weather over the Rhineland, whereas Hamburg, the alternative target was likely to be covered by thundery clouds. Two theories emerged as to the reason for our withdrawal – the first, the officially promulgated one, was that whereas Hamburg was comfortably within range of Hudson aircraft, Cologne was considered not to be; the second was that Bomber Command was able to provide all the aircraft needed, except four from Flying Training Command, and we presumed the latter must have had special crews or equipment. The middle of May had seen a period of bad weather which had prevented raids and therefore losses, and Bomber O.T.U. availability was enhanced by the bad-weather reduction in training. To us, the disappointed 'also-rans', the second seemed the more likely explanation, as Air Chief Marshal Harris was already strongly identified with the operational promotion of Bomber Command, and to go it alone would undoubtedly enhance the morale of the force he led, and the publicity it deservedly obtained.

Back, then, to the challenge of turning ungainly geese into competent swans, able to land gracefully whate'er may befall. Owing to the increasing number of pilots now coming through the training system whose use of English was at best hesitant, at worst inadequate – Poles, Czechs, Norwegians, Dutch – the experienced instructors to whom these fellows were allotted found communication more effective by gesticulation and "Good show!" – the exclamation of approval which was by now universal – than by the patter regarded as essential to the job. Whether because of a closer, often tragic, understanding of the consequences of war, or of more intense concentration because of the limitations of language, or because of a simple yearning for revenge, these pilots were excellent pupils and provided the little extra satisfaction which was all we could expect from the humdrum job we were doing.

The return of the Crown Film Unit gave Johnnie and me another welcome break. The gist of the storyline was going well, they said, and the 'sub-plot' would include the dive, the preparations for attack, and the stricken aircraft going down in flames. What was needed now was the actual attack on the pocket-battleship.

"Do we have one handy or shall we go and get one?" asked 'J'.

"No," came the reply with great satisfaction, "but we've got HMS Cardiff all dolled up to look like one. We've only got her for a couple of days, so we've got to get it right first time!"

The assistant director wanted shots of 'hits' on the ship, and plumes of water coming up from 'near-misses', to be filmed whilst 'Cardiff' was steaming off Ailsa Craig, near Girvan on the Scottish coast. The Squadron Leader decided he would make the dives and low passes over the ship, and I would have the camera mounted in the nose of my aircraft. We would each have a Wireless Operator to keep us in radio/telephonic contact with each other, so that I would know when the C.O. was starting his dive, then I would try to synchronize my low-level approach so that I would be very close to the ship as his Hudson passed over it. At this critical point the sailors would make flashes on deck and splashes in the sea, presumably using some kind of flare or smoke-bomb and small depth-charges. If fortune smiled, the camera would then capture the attacking aircraft diving over the ship, the explosions on deck and the plumes of water, before I too passed over it.

The navigator's table down in the nose of my aircraft had been removed, but even then the tripod and camera allowed little enough space for the intrepid cameraman. We were told that filming from the two positions they had used – one dangerous, the other cramped – was 'all in a day's work'; somewhat inferior to the more spacious conditions in a Sunderland flying boat, but certainly superior to the confines of a Beaufort torpedo bomber. We reckoned they had earned more than the few seconds' acknowledgement they would get as their names flashed on the screen when the film was shown in cinemas.

All set, we took off into a slight sea-haze over the Solway Firth, and found visibility further reduced as we approached Ailsa Craig, with the 'pocket battleship' nowhere to be seen. She appeared out of the haze a few miles to westward, and after exchanging signals we took up positions, whilst I ascertained from the cameraman that the light was adequate for filming. Flying low in hazy conditions reduces visibility when looking up or across through it, more than when looking down, and in the practice run, Johnnie, who was acting as my look-out, had difficulty in picking up the dive of the other Hudson after we had received the R/T message 'Diving now!' As it swooped near the warship, we watched the Hudson climb away again in readiness for the 'take', then suddenly the haze claimed it and we could only guess where it might be, when we heard "Are you ready?". We answered "Yes, but cannot see you!"

"I can see you; I'm at 4,000 feet," came the reply, as if that would help! "I'm starting my dive now!"

I turned my aircraft towards the ship.

"Can't see him yet!" yelled 'J'.

"Quarter way down!" called the Squadron Leader.

"Got him! – you'll have to approach faster!" 'J' pointed a finger up to the starboard rear quarter to help me find the diving Hudson through the haze. I opened the throttles.

"Half way down!" came over the R/T.

"Not too much throttle!" was 'J's next observation, "He's at a shallower angle and not so fast". I eased off the power.

The warship was coming up ahead pretty quickly now. Johnnie looked at the closing distance, up at the diving aircraft, then across at me.

"We're going to be there too early!" he yelled.

I moved the throttles back still further, and lowered the undercarriage so that the increased drag might slow us down. The airspeed dropped to 100 knots, and I wound hard on the trimming handle to help maintain this nose-up attitude.

"Still too early!" – I put down 30 degrees of flap to increase the drag still further, also to give a little extra lift to balance, working the trim and throttles to avoid losing height. Speed now 90 knots.

"Talk about hanging on the props!" mused the W/Op.

"I just hope the naval types don't think we're trying to land on their lovely ship, what with wheels and flaps down!" replied 'J'.

Suddenly, we appeared to have gone as far as we could without doing just that; and it all happened – the attacking Hudson flew over hardly above mast height, smoke billowed forth on the 'pocket battleship', the water spewed up in three or four places so that the spray caressed our aircraft.

With hands moving faster than I could remember them moving before, I opened the throttles and slid the variable pitch controls forward in the same movement, brought up the undercarriage and flaps, heaved back on the control column and trimmed like mad. We were over the ship and away; I brought the Hudson round for my personal farewell to our partners in these combined operations, and shot over the ship so that those on the open fo'c'sle bent low against the slipstream.

It could not have gone off better.

The cameraman and his cohorts started to dismantle the equipment as soon as we landed, and the tripods and mountings became again nothing more than tubes, angle pieces, plates and nuts and bolts. We did manage a short session with the film crew in the Mess, when they told us that the film would probably be on the cinema circuits later in the year, and if we couldn't see it then, a showing could probably be arranged at Pinewood Studios if we were in the vicinity. Away they went, to continue their exploits in the relative comfort of a 'Sunderland'.

When the aeronautical magazines appeared in the Mess, the usual perfunctory scanning of the lists would reveal the names of friends who had been posted as 'Missing' or worse, and the June issue gave notice of the loss of yet another of those colleagues whose comradeship I had valued highly, and with whom I had seriously 'joked' about a reunion at Manchester V.R. Centre after the war. It was Tom Mycock. I discovered he had not returned from a raid on Brest, the scene of previous exploits for which he was awarded the Distinguished Flying Cross. It was not difficult to imagine what could have happened over the most heavily defended target in Europe.

Such thoughts were perforce banished from the mind when the next interlude in the training routine was announced: the second 1,000-bomber raid. As on the previous aborted occasion, aircraft and crews were prepared for a move across to Thornaby, and once there we were busy with final preparations. During the afternoon of the 25th June, the Station Commander opened his remarks to the hundred or so aircrew assembled with the words:

"Gentlemen, tonight your task, along with many others, is to destroy the city of Bremen, and as members of Coastal Command which inevitably spends many fruitless hours searching for German U-boats, you will be particularly pleased to learn that your aiming point is to be the U-boat factory".

The Intelligence Officer then produced the usual maps and charts, identification points, the known anti-aircraft gun positions and night fighter stations, and the Senior Navigator elaborated on the tracks to be made good to reach the target area. The Met Officer forecast a clear night, a full moon to aid identification of landmarks, with perhaps broken cloud below 5,000 feet later.

When the admin details had been given – time at the Crew Room, drawing parachutes and Mae Wests for those based at Thornaby, transport to the aircraft by ubiquitous one-ton Bedford – we were dismissed, and I wandered to the perimeter track, smitten by nostalgia of the sheer enjoyment of being a fledgling ops sergeant pilot there.

Tonight would be different: all around, airmen were busy testing engines, bombing up, rotating turrets, pouring into the tanks 536 gallons of high-octane petrol, and, considerate 'beyond the call of duty', even cleaning windscreens! Such preparations, I thought, must be happening on at least fifty other airfields across the country.

Noel Coward's lines seem apt:

> *"Lie in the dark and listen,*
> *It's clear tonight so they're flying high,*
> *Hundreds of them, thousands perhaps,*
> *Riding the icy, moonlight sky...."*

And mindful of the fact that few of the airborne six thousand would be beyond the age of twenty-five:

> *"Lie in the dark and listen*
> *City magnates and steel contractors,*
> *Factory workers and politicians,*
> *Soft, hysterical little actors,*
> *Ballet dancers, 'reserved' musicians,*
> *Safe in your warm civilian beds."*

As the June sun made its hesitant disappearance amid the glow of twilight, we climbed aboard our aircraft, twenty-five small items in the terrible force being unleashed that night against the enemy, perhaps to those lying abed and listening a symbol of hope that eventual victory now beckoned more strongly than defeat.

We wondered if the enemy defences had learned any new tricks as a result of the thousand-bomber raid on Cologne and the 956 which had been over the Ruhr on 1st June? Our contingent would be among the 102 aircraft of Coastal Command inexperienced in this kind of operation which would be given an answer to that question.

Most of the pilots taking off from Thornaby that night had from experience developed their own additional tricks to add to the accepted methods of evading and warding-off enemy fighters in daylight. We had been reminded that it could be fatal to continue in straight-and-level flight when the 'night-hawks' were about, and that corkscrew rolling of the aircraft was the favourite tactic of the heavier aircraft of Bomber Command. Intelligence had passed on accumulated information that German night-fighters, mainly Ju 88's and Me llO's, were controlled from the ground and appeared to operate in pairs, one being directed by ground radar able to detect Allied aircraft, the other circling a radio beacon until called. If, however, a pilot had visual contact of a hostile bomber, he was to attack without further orders. The efficacy of German ground control over their night-fighters was regarded as not being entirely satisfactory, but this judgement was later shown to be a serious underestimate of the co-operation between the two.

Such were my thoughts as I waited for the take-off signal at 2200 hours that night. I was one of the few instructors to have a crew member who had completed a tour of operations; doubly fortunate in that he was Flight Sergeant Derbyshire who had served with distinction in 220 Squadron, and who was my rear-gunner on the occasion we encountered the F.W. Condor. The rear gunner on this raid, since Derbyshire took over as Wireless Operator, was a small quiet lad who was hardly familiar with the Hudson's twin-Browning rear turret and whose last real target firing had been at Gunnery School, whilst the Navigator was a Texan who had joined the RAF, had trained in Texas, and had never yet navigated any considerable distance over the sea. I turned to look at Derby, his hands over his earphones in the W/Op's typical 'getting interference' attitude, and gave him a 'thumbs-up' sign. He lowered his right hand and crossed his fingers in reply.

One after another the cohorts raised their deadly loads into the twilight-tinted June sky, the undulating roar of fifty engines from the procession of Hudsons giving audible signal to the citizens of Teesside that retribution was on its way eastwards. With navigation lights on to avert the danger of collision, a course to steer from the navigator, and a "Clear go!" from the W/Op, we started the long climb to our prescribed altitude. As the navigation lights were switched off, and the silvery-grey summer night closed in to remove any fleeting glance of the small armada around me, there returned a sense of the independence which had been customary during previous operations. It remained to be seen whether this hard-done-by training Hudson could achieve the desired altitude of 12,000 feet, and whether we would remain in total combat-readiness without oxygen.

All the twin-engined aircraft were to approach the target at that height, and attack between 0050 hours and 0110 – a twenty-minute period for hundreds of aircraft to go in and drop. This timing was essential, as the heavy bombers would be over Bremen before our allotted span and then immediately afterwards, releasing their bomb-loads from much higher altitudes. Woe betide anything underneath!

When we reached about half our desired altitude, the moon slowly rose from the far horizon, and within a few minutes the power of its light in the clear night air was as great as the sun's had been an hour before. A broad moonlit path along the surface of a smooth sea lay ahead of us. Lines from Alfred Noyes's "The Highwayman" seemed somewhat appropriate, and went through my mind in amended form as:

"The air was throbbing with danger for Bremen folk abed,
The moon was shining eastward where marauding craft had led;
The way was a ribbon of moonlight along the sea below,
And the highwaymen came riding, riding, riding,
The highwaymen came riding, with hundreds more to go!"

Apart from the occasional check between crew members at their different stations, the only sound came from the steady drone of the engines as the old Hudson slowly reached 12,000 feet. None of the crew had flown at this height before – child's play though it might be to the hardened and oxygenated crews of Bomber Command; our rear gunner in his unheated turret must have considered his introduction to operational flying less than heart-warming! Perhaps that was why he seemed strangely silent – most 'tail-end charlies' I had flown with were lively, chirpy types, whose language describing events which came to their sharp-eyed notice was usually descriptive if not decorous! At 12,000 feet I recalled that the only previous occasion on which I had flown as high was during the 15,000 feet height test at SFTS in an Anson, when reduced oxygen and thinner air was apparent both to me and to the aircraft; on this occasion neither of us seemed to be affected.

At the prescribed height, the navigator confirmed the compass course I was to steer, and we hoped the wind-speed and direction supplied by the Met people was reasonably accurate, for we had no means of checking it on such a night, nor did we have the navigational aids of Bomber Command. No doubt the planners reckoned that Bremen was an easy target for anyone who could get an aircraft into the air, to be approached from the wide mouth of the River Weser, where the flak would no doubt confirm a satisfactory arrival, whence the river would lead us up to the city.

I asked the navigator to give me our position in terms of nautical miles from the estuary turning-point. There was no reply. I peered down below as best I could to the navigator's seat and repeated the request. Again no reply! I left 'George', the automatic pilot, to fly the Hudson, went down below and leant over the plotting table.

"Can you put your finger on our position then?" I asked.

Within the dim light of the hooded lamp shining on the map, a pale face turned towards me with a shake of the head.

"Try sticking a pin in and let me know when you've worked it out!" I suggested, and returned to the controls. His forthcoming estimate concerned me little, for as I looked up from the plotting table before I left him I caught sight of faint intermittent flashes ahead – heavy flak! All I had to do now was to fly towards it, and when the guns around Wilhelmshaven were to starboard, and those at

Bremerhaven were ahead, I would know it was time to turn right to go up the river. The flashes became more frequent and more intense against the sweeping bands of searchlights as we – and no doubt others – approached.

For the first time, the rear gunner initiated a conversation.

"Hello pilot," he began, and after acknowledgement continued "I think I can see something behind us!"

With one bound, Derby was free of his seat, and up in the astrodome in the centre of the cabin.

"Night-fighter!" he yelled.

I slammed back the throttles, pushed the control column fully forward and in the same instant whipped the wheel over to the left, so that we were immediately in a steep, spiralling dive.

"Ye gods!" I heard Derby exclaim, and then as we regained some equilibrium "He fired just as we went over in our dive! Guess where we'd be now if we hadn't!"

We came out of the dive at 8,000-odd feet and looked around. A few fluffy cumulus clouds had appeared below at about 3,000 feet, casting an occasional dark shadow on an otherwise shimmering sea. I could see the flak barrage beyond the port wing and turned towards it, intending to return to the route to the target.

"Can you see any more trouble?" I called over the R/T to the crew in general and the rear-gunner in particular. There was no reply.

Then – "Jerry's still there!" from Derby "about five o'clock high, one mile, coming in!"

I reckoned it was not a one-to-one evens situation as I had a mute and apparently immobile rear gunner, in addition to the fact that .303 machine guns were no match for the night-fighter's cannon fire.

The clouds must hide us!

We got down there and were thankfully enveloped by the wispy entrails of the puffy water vapour, safely hidden for a few minutes whilst we took stock.

Wilhelmshaven was the secondary target if we couldn't get to Bremen within the twenty minutes between ten to one and ten past. I asked the navigator if there was any hope of a course to fly there, should we be delayed much longer.

"But where are we now?" was the answer. Good question!

"Probably about seventy miles northwest".

Silence-below; I was hoping it would be enough to get him started when the cloud suddenly thinned, then disappeared, and to any scanning eyes looking down from above we would be a silhouette moving across a moonlit sea. I continued on the westerly course which had become the only option, in the hope of taking any pursuer outside his range of action, and called Derby, still in the astrodome, on the R/T. "Have we shaken him off?"

"OK so far," he said, "He's certainly not up-moon, but...."

The navigator came up from his eyrie, with his finger firmly pressed to a spot on the chart he carried.

"If we're there" he tried to explain "I guess you need to steer one-three-five or so...." and he held the chart close for the hoped-for optimistic confirmation.

I shook my head, and jabbed a finger two or three times to indicate the need for his speedy return to his table. I certainly had no intention of switching on my cockpit spotlight now my eyes were adjusted to the night sky and what was out there, nor did I want him floundering around the cockpit should more violent manoeuvres be necessary.

Moving the compass ring round to 135 degrees, I had just started to turn the aircraft on to that heading, when Derby's voice burst through:

"Jerry's closing from seven o'clock high!"

Fortunately there was a larger mass of protective cloud about thirty degrees to starboard, and we flashed down towards it.

Time to think! In all probability there would by now be at least two night-fighters aware of our predicament, with one backing up the other nearer the target, taking a secondary interest in us and any other stragglers. So, one course of action, and certainly the more madly heroic, would be to turn round and cloud-hop as far as the cover allowed – which didn't seem to extend inland beyond the coast – then make a dash for the distant flak and searchlights which might indicate the secondary target. We certainly would not be able to carefully navigate our way there, or anywhere else, with the difficulties being experienced at the navigator's table.

The equation was a possible 4 x 250 lb bomb-drop against the near-certain loss of a Hudson and crew. Put like that, I was sure the choice would have been obvious even to the Commander-in-Chief. If one of the aims of an attack of this magnitude was to saturate the defences, there was no point in being shot down and thereby releasing a German night-fighter to attack other marauders, if the pilot or his controller was willing to play cat-and-mouse with me for as long as possible, whilst we moved inexorably westward and he moved away from the main battle area. Statistically, I thought, if we have 1,000 bombers and the enemy even an unlikely 500 fighters, if a one-to-one keeps one of them occupied it could be doing an unknown somebody a favour, and our journey would not have been in vain.

We came out of the cloud, and I decided it looked as if the cover would increase. The rate at which the clouds did so was a vital factor, for if the gaps between were too small or disappeared, the pursuer would regard his task as hopeless, and he would leave to try his luck elsewhere; if the clouds dispersed his task would be simple, and ours impossible.

Again Derby's warning came over the R/T, and again we dashed for the nearest white haven. There was no further response from either of the other two crew members, and I had several inhospitable thoughts not only regarding them and the inadequacies of training, but also about this example of the 'exigencies of war', in which the light cavalry were required, quite justifiably, to assist the heavy artillery.

Eventually, after more exposures to our pursuer followed by rapid returns to cover, the cloud became almost continuous, and our game was at an end. I was surprised that the German pilot persisted for so long; there must have been more worthwhile targets for him in the skies that night – perhaps a case of traditional Teutonic thoroughness. All we now had to do was to stay within this layer of cloud at 3,000 feet, and pay a visit on our way home to our third possible target – any shipping off, or military target on, the Frisian Islands. There was little benefit likely from further contact with the navigator, so on a mental E.T.A. I descended to 2,500 feet, below the cloud, and turned thirty degrees to port in the hope that this would lead to one of the islands.

A shoreline appeared, with a faint image of white surf on a moonlit beach, and I heard the first sound for some time from the rear – a sigh of relief. There was no shipping to be seen so I turned inland and soon came to the far coastline; I reckoned the island was about five miles wide, and flying along its length of twenty miles I assumed it to be Terschelling. I had no intention of dropping bombs on Dutch territory unless the target was clearly seen to be of a military nature and German. Solitary farmhouses, cultivated land, small groups of cottages, glasshouses – a tranquil scene in the diminishing moonlight. The next island, identified as Vlieland, offered no fairer target. "Home James!" I announced over the R/T.

So we returned with our bombs, and as soon as we had switched off and our feet touched the tarmac, Derby gave the rear gunner a piece of his mind, and I looked at the navigator in a way which suggested he could interpret similar thoughts from me.

"Why the hell didn't you give us more warning?" demanded Derby.

"Sorry, I wasn't sure and I didn't want to appear scared," was the sheepish reply. We sympathised; those sentiments must have been fairly frequent throughout the war. Perhaps we were too hard on the navigator; we discovered that there had been little need for navigation to the target for those pilots untroubled by the enemy's defensive interference, as the fires started by the earlier Bomber Command onslaught could be seen for miles. Harry mentioned the splendid view he had of

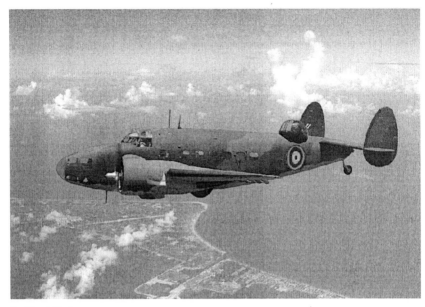

Lockheed Hudson

Navigator's nest

Filming: The Sqdn Ldr peels off in his dive, followed by self, then Johnnie Lane

The "flaming" dive, with the lines representing "film-tracer" firing

Sqdn Ldr Hodgkinson as he appeared in the film

The "attacking" aircraft seen through the warship's rigging

The warship's "reply"

The camera aircraft just before heaving over the warship

the U-boat yards, illuminated as in daylight. That he got there was not surprising – he never seemed to fail. With a half-guilty feeling we entered the Ops Room for de-briefing. "Better to bring bombs back than waste them in some pretence of finding a target" was the unexpectedly rational comment, although I was sure that the armourers would have been very unlikely saints to have held the same opinion. Their art of persuasion was to maintain that it was more difficult to take the bombs off than to put them on. Still, I slept the sleep of the just till lunchtime.

We left for the return to Silloth saddened by the news that our C.O., Sqdn Ldr Hodgkinson and his crew had not returned from the raid. We discovered later that, after dropping their bombs on the target at Bremen, they were crossing the Dutch coast at 8000ft on their way home, when they saw an aircraft on their port bow coming in the opposite direction at the same height. It was a bright clear night and Hodgkinson recognised it as a ME 110 night fighter. This was confirmed when the aircraft turned to get on his tail. Hodgkinson opened his throttles and dived for a cloud layer some 2000ft below. As he was about to enter the cloud he was hit by heavy cannon fire.

The Hudson immediately burst into flames and Hodgkinson headed for the sea to attempt to ditch the aircraft. He could not contemplate bailing out as he did not know what had happened to his crew. His intercom was out of action and there was smoke and flames everywhere. Terrifying as they were, the flames, in fact, played a part in his and his navigator's survival as they illuminated the surface of the sea allowing him to heave back on the control column just in time to make a successful ditching.

When the Squadron Leader came to, he saw a main wheel floating nearby in a heavy sea. He swam over to it and found his navigator, Flt Lt Cave clinging to it. Cave said he was badly shot up, and that the other two crew members had bailed out (their bodies were washed up on one of the Frisian Islands much later). After about an hour, when hope of survival was fading, they heard a great "whush" alongside them and up popped the main aircraft dinghy which must have worked itself loose from the wreckage. They managed to clamber in, and at dawn on the 26th, they were washed ashore on the Frisian island of Ameland and were taken prisoners of war. But Fate had apparently dealt the Queen of Hearts at this stage and passed the Ace of Spades to others. The Squadron Leader met the chap who had shot him down.

"I was lying on a stretcher" he recalled, "on the pavement outside a hospital in Amsterdam, waiting under guard for an ambulance to arrive and cart me away. A young Pilot Unteroffizier, wearing an Iron Cross, came up and, in perfect English, said he was sorry to have shot me down. I said words to the effect that I would have done the same to him if I had had the chance, and I thanked him for not putting another burst into me. He said that I was indeed lucky! Just as he was about to do so he was vectored on to a Halifax coming over at 20,000 feet. He saw that I had virtually had it, so he left me alone and climbed straight up and shot down the Halifax. He said I would meet the three survivors of the Halifax in the ambulance – which I did and they were very badly shot up."

It was not until the end of hostilities that Hodgkinson was able to see his Navigator again, as Cave had had to spend most of his time as a POW in various hospitals. When eventually they did meet, they discussed what had happened on the night they were shot down. Hodgkinson remarked that he was amazed that Tommy, his rear gunner, had remained silent when the ME 110 was getting on the Hudson's tail.

Cave replied: "What do you mean? We were attacked from head on, not from the rear!"

"Nonsense", said Hodgkinson, "I saw the aircraft turn to get on our tail – that was why I dived for the cloud."

"Well, I don't know what happened to *that* aircraft," commented Cave, "but I was sitting in the nose, and just as we were about to enter the cloud, another ME 110 came out of it head on, gave us a quick burst and hit us fair and square!"

To prove it, he rolled up his trouser leg and showed Hodgkinson his badly scarred leg. There was no doubt that he had been hit from the front!

For a few days, the return to the routine of dual instruction seemed very much an anti-climax, heightened by the loss of Hodge and the promotion of S/Ldr Holdway in his place. Charlie Holdway was an ex-Halton apprentice who had transferred in peacetime to flying duties, and was already a much-respected instructor when I first arrived at Silloth in the summer of 1940.

July soon showed itself willing to continue the pleasant interludes which the previous months had provided. An obsolescent 'Battle' single-engine light bomber which had been declared surplus to requirement was available for 'familiarisation flying'. It had a Merlin engine of the type used in the Spitfire, but was almost twice as large, so it was no surprise to find that spinning and aerobatics in it were forbidden. If a 'Spit' could be likened to a terrier, a 'Hudson' to a retriever, and a 'Lancaster' to a St. Bernard, a 'Battle' was an underfed lurcher. However, it didn't object to my handling, it came to heel as required, and we rolled along the runway safely after landing, without any desire for a repeat performance. I was sure the aircraft held similar sentiments.

The other aeroplane which was occasionally available was a Miles Magister of the species which had evoked a general lack of enthusiasm when threatened in 1939 with a posting to an E.F.T.S. using it for initial training. With 900 hours flying behind me, I had no qualms in putting it to the test now – an enjoyable experience, and although there was ample justification for confirming its inferiority to the Tiger Moth, it had to be admitted that rumour was its worst enemy.

The 'supernumerary' aircraft had to be flown for a certain number of hours to keep them airworthy, so, as there were flying-hours to spare from the minimum needed on the Magister, I planned a cross-country flight to Upavon on Salisbury Plain. I had recently discovered that Dorrie, the girl whose company I enjoyed in Thornaby days, had joined the W.A.A.F. and was serving in the Sick Quarters at Upavon. I decided I would visit her. Where possible, such flights were used for staff going on leave, and a colleague whose home was in the Midlands wanted a lift down to Wolverhampton airport. He left his helmet, goggles, flying-jacket and boots in the aircraft when we landed there, and after re-fuelling I flew on.

My assignation with Dorrie made no mention of the fact that there would be a spare seat in my Magister-made-for-two, and when I met her that afternoon she needed a little persuading that it was the duty of a W.A.A.F. Leading Aircraftwoman to take every opportunity of experiencing the ultimate purpose of the Service. To my disappointment she was on duty that night, but at least that meant she was free the following morning.

There was a "TOILET FEMALE" at the end of the hangars, to which by surreptitious means the flying clothing was delivered, and there, assisted by two amused but encouraging secret aides, she was transformed into an embryo aviator.

It was surprising that the figure which eventually emerged was allowed to plod across the tarmac without challenge – no hands were visible beyond the loose-hanging sleeves, the flying boots almost slipped off the feet with every step, and there was little more than a nose and a mouth to be seen below the enveloping flying helmet. In contrast, the trousers fitted perfectly and looked very smart – they were her own working issue. By the time she reached the aircraft, Dorrie decided that the flying boots were surplus to requirements and, screened from any watching eyes in the control tower, she daintily withdrew her feet and clambered up into the front cockpit. I stowed the boots, checked her parachute and secured the harness, climbed into the rear seat, and we were ready for start-up, check, and taxying.

I gave a running commentary over the intercom tube as we climbed and turned on the circuit, but there was no acknowledgement from the front cockpit; the head remained fixed, looking down, and I could only assume that the movement of the control column and rudder pedals had some hypnotic effect.

There was no reply to my query as to whether she was enjoying it, but suddenly she looked up and around, as if becoming aware of a different world. There was no stopping her enthusiasm now, as with a finger pointing first this way and then that, she turned as far as she could and gave me a beaming smile.

I circled round the objects down below indicated by the most extreme gestures, then suggested she should put her hands on the stick and feet on the rudder-pedals. For a time, this drew her attention back into the cockpit, and when her pressure on the controls suggested she had more confidence, I spoke into the intercom in my best 'Charles Boyer' voice:

"You've got what it takes, cherie! She's all yours!"

She almost jumped out of her seat, and with a half-turn of her head, the scared look was shared between the controls and me. I nodded encouragingly and said

"Go on, you're doing fine!"

After ten minutes of varied manoeuvres which must have surprised the Magister, I persuaded her to join the circuit, which she seemed loathe to do, making the most of one or two twists and turns first. We landed the aircraft together, thus sharing the two bounces between us.

As we taxied in I noticed the pilots of one or two aircraft nearby preparing to walk across to the control tower, so I told Dorrie I would stay by the front cockpit as an instructor elaborating a few points to his pupil, until the way was clear for her return to her 'changing room'. This formal relationship, however, would then have been suspect to any interested onlooker, for as soon as my pupil's feet touched the ground, she gave me a big hug, which left me in the air whilst she tripped back to the hide in her stockinged feet.

I was left to wonder what my reward might have been had I been able to stay longer, but the Magister was due back at Silloth that night, so I had to leave. It did, fortunately, lead to a meeting in London later that month.

Throughout August, the routine was seldom interrupted by such interesting diversions. The weather was the least predictable part of it, being more than typically seasonal in its extremes, which could have affected our output of trained crews but for the simulated night-landings we had been able to include for some time. The runways, like others on many airfields, had been equipped with sodium 'flare-path' lights, which glowed with bright orange luminosity, making the runway in use visible from a much greater distance in conditions of poor visibility. The lights were the only objects a pilot wearing dark goggles could see outside the aircraft, thus allowing simulated night-landings in daytime.

On a couple of mornings at the beginning of the month there was unseasonal ground frost, and throughout the middle days it was dull and wet with low cloud, so that no decision about the possibility of night-flying instruction could be taken until the cloud base had been checked at dusk by a quick whip round the circuit. Such ten-minute forays were sought after, as a brief release from the tedium! However, the weather made amends at the end of the month with three days of heatwave temperatures and good flying conditions, during which we got back on schedule by 'keeping up with the sun in the pursuit of daylight', as one instructor put it.

When Johnnie Lane and I learned we would shortly be posted back to an operational squadron, we were of one mind that we would prefer an anti-shipping strike squadron to one flying patrols against U-boats. Preferably, therefore, Beaufighters or Mosquitoes. We neither of us enthused at the possibility of flying what we then thought of as lumbering four-engined heavy stuff on very long patrols. The C.O. said we must put our requests in writing, then ask the Adjutant to do a little special pleading, but that was a kind of negative encouragement as we both knew how well-versed in protocol, desk-bound gentlemen could be. We thought of a direct approach to higher authority, but decided it would nought avail for two undistinguished Flying Officers.

A few days later we had to report back to the Adjutant, who briefly informed us that the first Beaufighter wing being formed at North Coates was not yet operational. To our suggestion that it was therefore not too late to join it, his asperic reply was that they had all the pilots they needed and obviously no replacements would be needed for some time. 'J' and I said we wouldn't mind waiting, but I fancy the Adj was looking forward to seeing the back of us, as his next words were:

"We'd never get any work done if everybody wanted the kind of individual attention you're hoping to get".

We had almost reached the door on our way out when he called us back:

"By the way, I almost forgot," he continued, "you're both posted to 269 Squadron in Iceland to fly Hudsons. Start your embarkation leave the day after tomorrow."

He passed the message with a straight face, but he was the sort of chap who would allow a smile to smirk his face once we were on the other side of the door.

"Hasn't this embarkation leave business happened before?" I reminded 'J'. "Perhaps there'll be another telegram like last time, changing the posting."

On the train to Carlisle, as the airfield slipped from view, we summarized our stay there as 'could have been worse'. We had been fortunate in having the monotony lifted by more exciting incidents, and we had neither of us had to fail any of the pilots we had trained. Bearing in mind A.V.M. Bennett's opinion of the Hudson when he evaluated it in preparation for Atlantic ferrying, there was some satisfaction in that modicum of success: 'tricky characteristics, could drop a wing if bounced, quite a nasty stall – a fine performer but a handful, which could be dangerous if one were careless'.

There was no telegram changing the posting this time, merely a message giving the date on which we had to report to Wick to collect a Hudson for delivery to Iceland. At least we were to be allowed the privilege of going by air, rather than by the sea-crossing in the much-despised ship known as "The Wallower".

Self and Pete outside Gladys Todd's house

CHAPTER 10

SHORT DAYS AND LONG NIGHTS

The nostalgia during our brief return to Thornaby in June was again evident on reaching the airfield at Wick, the more so because Johnnie and I were joined by Harry Ramsey, who had also been posted to 269 at the same time. Suitably celebrated that night, somewhat mystifying in its logic, Harry told us he also would have preferred an anti-shipping attack posting. Perhaps someone, somewhere, with greater 'nous' than we had could see the sense in posting a proven 'ship-buster' to an anti-U-boat patrol squadron equipped with aircraft which would be inadequate for the purpose before the end of the operational tour. Perhaps the squadron had a particular need for a trio of experienced pilots, we were conceited enough to suppose. We cherished our Hudsons, but we knew that their day was passing at least in the European theatre, for the enemy was now directing his operations to the middle reaches of the Atlantic, beyond Hudson range except when U-boats were in transit from Norwegian, Baltic or French ports.

We flew towards Iceland from the southeast on an overcast, windy day, with the grey Atlantic swell breaking into lines of foam-topped 'white horses'. To come upon our temporary home on such a day appeared to give unfair advantage to those who would question its virtues. As we approached the ungainly humps of the Vestmannaeyjar Islands a few miles off the mainland coast, we looked across to starboard for the imposing mass of Myrdals Jokull, one of the four areas of glacier-edged permanent ice and snow, and a small one compared with the vast expanse of Vatna Jokull away to the east.

We could see nothing beyond a coastline of black lava-sand, the swirling curtains of fine rain spasmodically covering the forbidding cliffs behind. As we passed the main offshore island of Heimaey, and now flying almost parallel to the shrouded coast, in the distance the lower lava-strewn land was slowly revealed, leading to the airfield at Kaldadarnes, 269 Squadron's base.

On the circuit we looked down on a collection of small Nissen huts, their ribbed semi-circular roofs giving a welcome touch of green to the dull grey surroundings, and the three larger Mess huts, the rectangular corrugated-iron hangar, the Operations block cocooned in protective covering, and the two square towers – runway control tower and electricity generating station.

It was obvious that the runway in use would grant no favours to a misjudged approach and landing – neither in its lack of length, and the quality of its lava-based asphalt surface. We agreed that any aircraft larger than a Hudson would not fit this environment. Harry produced a landing which was an effective demonstration of the skills the Squadron could expect from its new recruits, and the bleak chill of the day was ameliorated by the warmth of our reception in the Operations Room and later in the Mess. What better welcome than to find that the beer had the full flavour of its Scottish origin and did not come from Carlisle.

The Orderly Officer took the three of us and a Flying Officer named Johnson, who was to be 'J's navigator, to our quarters, one of the small Nissen huts which were shared by four officers. In each corner stood the usual iron-framed bedstead with its straw palliasse, a neatly folded pile of blankets and sheets topped by a bulky pillow, and beside it the ubiquitous small cupboard-cum-bookshelf-cum-table. Imposing in the majesty of its isolation in the centre of the hut stood the familiar round coke-burning stove, reacting to every opening of the door with a welcome roar and a surge in the ruddy glow on the concrete standing. Our first requirement would be a fork to sample its toast-making propensities!

Construction of various buildings was continuing throughout the camp, and within a few days we discovered a dump of surplus and discarded material, and a little melodramatic begging secured from the stores a quantity of nails and a loan of tools. After the usual flying familiarisation during daylight hours, by four o'clock and the descent of sub-Arctic night we began, and for three or four days continued, the conversion of our humble abode.

The structure of the hut dictated the form it would take: at each end a doorway, one of which we boarded-up and draught-proofed with layers of brown paper from parcels, and on each side of the doorways, a window. The stove in the middle had to be a shared necessity, so the plan was for the partitioning of the four quarters on a 2" by 3" wooden framework covered with plasterboard, with open access to the warmth emanating from the centre of the room. We even found enough assorted curtain material to cover the windows – not especially for privacy but to add another flimsy layer of insulation against the invading cold.

One of the tasks assigned to the squadron was to carry out sweeps, and escort convoys bound for Russia, and the weather forced upon us great admiration for those bound for even colder latitudes amid dangers beyond our range which we could do nothing to prevent, unless we were lucky enough to catch a U-boat en route. As many as three Russian convoys a month left Iceland to pass to the west of the island through the Denmark Straits for most of the year, until the winter threat of pack-ice necessitated passage along the east coast, which shortened air escort time, as the two air-bases were in the southwest corner at Reykjavik and Kaldadarnes.

My first task was to work up to operational standard with my crew – Warrant Officer Pugsley, navigator, and Flight Sergeants Jackie Noble and Jackie Hollis, W/Op- Air Gunners. Only on one previous sortie – the Bremen raid – had I flown with a navigator who was other than a co-pilot, and that particular experience left several questions unanswered, but Pug soon removed any doubts. He was a straightforward fellow of blunt but genuine opinions which hid some of his abilities from other people, but they were quickly revealed to me and we soon had great respect for each other. He had plenty of operational experience before joining 269, and the fact that some of this had been in a squadron flying 'Battle' aircraft was testimony in itself, bearing in mind my opinion of that aircraft when I flew it at Silloth. He said it was a joy to fly in a Hudson, and the other two were equally keen, so we became a confident crew.

The first days of November proved to be unfavourable harbingers of the real winter to come. On the best days daylight sufficient to read a newspaper only appeared between ten-thirty in the morning and about three in the afternoon, so seven-hour flights on patrol or escort either took-off or landed in varying degrees of darkness.

Once we had completed the refurbishment of our hutted domain, the two Johnnies, Harry and I spent many cheerful evenings in it, as the Mess was little more than an extra-large Nissen hut, although the relatively- cheap beer, whisky and Drambuie often ameliorated this fact. Breakfast in the Mess was the meal which most approached the food we would enjoy at a home-base, whereas the evening meal was always deficient in at least one respect – no fresh vegetables, therefore a lack of ascorbic acid. The M.O. reminded us in lurid detail of the days when lack of it led to scurvy – "swollen gums and livid spots" – and stressed the importance of taking one ascorbic acid tablet a day.

"Are they served in the vegetable tureens?" one wit asked.

"There'll be times when you may think they've been put in the gravy" came the reply. "Here's your supply; it's down to you".

On the 16th November 1942 we were allocated Hudson 'T' for an Ice Reconnaissance in the Denmark Straits between Iceland and Greenland. 'T-Tommy' had been equipped with extra fuel tanks to give an endurance of eleven-plus hours, and as a result carried no bombs or depth-charges; a special aircraft for reconnaissance only, and for which it was usual to take a second pilot. Pug was dismayed at not being able to crew this trip because of a minor illness; Warrant Officer Prince was his able replacement, as ready as Pug would have been to earn his 'Blue Nose' Certificate for crossing the Arctic Circle.

It was necessary to check the extent of the ice in the Denmark Straits not only to determine whether Russian convoys must now pass to the east of Iceland, but also to assess the likelihood of an attempted passage round the top of Iceland and through the Straits into the Atlantic by the German super-battleship "Tirpitz", and other strong forces known to be in Norwegian waters. The Admiralty was very mindful of the fact that this was the route the "Bismarck" followed when making a similar attempt. A repeat of that exploit had to be prevented at all costs, since the month's day by day repetition of bad news was later confirmed as the greatest monthly loss of Allied shipping throughout the entire war – 814,700 tons. The effect of a surface raider of the calibre of the "Tirpitz" being able to add to such a tally no doubt gave many an Admiralty planner restless sleep at night, and worried grimaces by day whenever P.R.U. Mosquitoes reported smoke from her funnels.

There was also the fear of a devastating attack on the Allied convoys which were carrying the Allied forces which were about to land in North Africa. So this reconnaissance was important, and Ops Room asked particularly for coverage of any open leads which might be safe for ships to follow. Three other aircraft were due off about the same time; two were on a standard 'Scat' patrol, the third as escort to an Atlantic convoy.

The darkness of early morning was softened by spots of light from buildings where early risers were crawling from their beds, and from the hangar and Ops Room whose occupants had risen even before we had been called. A strict enforcement of blackout was unnecessary, and in any event, being wartime 'guests', we could hardly expect to enforce it on the Icelanders. With the stars still twinkling in a clear sky, the Hudson's retractable lights which pivoted down from the leading edge of the wing were hardly needed. As I looked up after completing the pre-take-off check, the powerful beam of the runway floodlight shining down the greater part of its length reduced the line of 'glim' lamps to modest specks of orange, and made the impending take-off seem truly "per ardua ad astra".

Airborne at 0800 hours, we had chased our shadow down the runway until, as the wings took flight and bore us with them, the light and the shade disappeared, and the instrument-panel became my guiding star. We turned on to a northwesterly heading and were over the wide bay of Flaxafloi when the sun made a brief appearance behind us. No shadow before us now, however; the sun had neither the altitude nor the power to supply it. Heading for the 4,744 ft landmark of Snaefellsjokull, we started a slow descent which would take us down to observation height by the time we passed it by on our way into the Denmark Strait. As we headed out, the first traces of ice appeared below, and across to starboard we could see the imposing mass of Vestfirdhir, known as the 'claw' because of the several rocky fingers which were fierce pointers to the Strait. The narrow neck of land which joined this inhospitable tract to the rest of the island could be thought of as the wrist of a grasping hand.

The height we were to fly varied between getting as near to sea-level as safety considerations would allow, rising to whatever altitude best served the need to estimate the length of stretches of a particular ice formation or leads of open water. The overall track to be made good was roughly parallel to the east coast of Greenland, but W/O Prince called for several zig-zag excursions to plot the extent of varying conditions. As we reached 70 deg north where the ice was thick and fast, we checked his report together, and his diagrammatic representation on the chart:

"Observed occasional small detached ice floes and some skodser (small broken ice) at 66N 25W.
Plotted fast ice from posn 67.50N, 29.10W to 68.10N 28.10W and N. wards.
Drift ice was encountered in 67.10N 27.10W running up to 71.10N 19.40W and continuing north-eastwards.
There was one open lead running south from Scoresby Sound 20mls long by 40mls wide consisting of 1/10th brash.
A second open lead ran east from Scoresby 20mls long by 40mls wide of 3/10th brash.
Drift ice averaged 8/10th of floes of 20 to 200 feet.
Brash ice and skodser was plotted thro' 66N 26W to 66.48N 26.40W going S 6/10th.
Brash ice also seen in fields to north extending seawards from 70.40N 19.40W."

We decided to continue northwards from 70 deg north, as there was now solid shore ice stretching as far as the eye could see, and the clear beauty of the day tempted us to explore further our very own blue and white wilderness. The low-lying sun behind us now having reached its zenith for the day, we were again chasing a long pale shadow, whilst the sheer rocky crags of the coast a quarter mile away stood in dappled majesty. Passing Scoresby Sound and along the edge of Jameson Land, the scene changed to a snow-dusted landscape of less severe rock formations, and the Greenland Ice Cap receded beyond our view.

Inspired by the strong rumour that an English schoolmistress presided over the tiny classroom in the settlement nestling in a protective saucer at Scoresbysund, we decided we would show the flag in the shape of RAF roundels, so we turned and set course for the Sound – in summer a ten-mile wide channel of silvery water, but now a silken sheen of ice as smooth as any seen by Fenland skaters.

COASTAL COMMAND PILOT

We flew along it at 200 feet, and as we came to the haphazard collection of small buildings half- hidden in the snow' s embrace, the Danish flag could be seen at the top of a small mast, its rigging gently flapping in a zephyr breeze. By the time we turned at the point further inland where the inlet approached the ice-cap, to fly past the settlement again, there was a Union Jack flying beside the Danish flag, the few inhabitants were waving, and a small group assembled round the flag-pole responded to our fly-past with the exuberant reactions of children. We made a couple more low-level passes, took our leave with a dive and a roaring ascent into the blue, then set course for home.

Shortly afterwards, as we passed down the coast by Cape Dalton where a fringe of fearsome granite held back the ice-cap, I noticed a sudden flurry in the snow besides a protruding rock, and realised I was looking at a polar bear. He turned as if to query this intrusion to his domain, then acknowledged the mighty spread of this giant bird and scurried away behind the rock, just as the others responded to my exclamation. I strongly denied their suggestion that I had been day-dreaming – or worse!

At 2,000 feet on a southerly course towards the 'claw' of Iceland, with Smithy, my co-pilot, at the controls, I was in the cabin astrodome, watching the ice-speckled waters around us assume a grey chill as a layer of stratus cloud drifted across from the south, when Jackie Noble beckoned me as he finished writing out the radio message he had received:

"To aircraft K,F,Q,A,N,T. (Repeat till acknow'd)
RETURN TO BASE IMMEDIATELY. WEATHER CLOSING IN.
A/C S TO LAND AT HOFN. T.O.O. (Time of origin) 1100 HOURS.
KALDADARNES".

He acknowledged the signal, then said "There's more!"

"IMPERATIVE RETURN TO BASE BEFORE 1600 HOURS".

We both burst into laughter at this impossible command. The time was 1500 and we were more than 300 miles from base.

"Tell them we may be a little late" I said, "Get Jackie H out of the turret – you may need a break as you're going to be busy getting QDM's." (Magnetic courses to steer as directed from a direction-finding ground radio station).

We had obviously not received the recall signals because at the time they were transmitted we were at a low altitude, and not for the first time in my experience intervening mountains either bounced the waves to unknown destinations or swallowed them whole. Even during frequent repetition of the messages, we were probably scanning the ice floes, or paying our visit to Scoresbysund, screened by the mass of Jameson Land.

Ahead, as daylight rapidly waned and the overcast thickened, we could see the reason for the recall: a mass of ugly weather coming up from the south. Before darkness became an impenetrable curtain, we caught sight of the outermost finger of the 'claw' and headed out beyond it to begin our homing on the QDM's in the cloud and drizzle which now seemed to extend down to sea-level.

I took over the controls, thankful that I had taken the usual precaution of plotting safe bearings on my map, in this case not only to the airfield at Kalda, but also to the only direction-finding radio station, which was at Reykjanes on the southwest tip of Iceland, about 50 miles from Reykjavik and 70 to the west of Kaldadarnes.

Once we were well clear of the land, with the safety of the sea invisibly beneath us, I asked Smithy to place himself between Jackie and myself so that he could pass the QDM bearings to me immediately, then as I checked or adjusted the course, he could compare them with the safe bearings on the map, and finally hand them down to the navigator so that he could add distance to the plot. Our return now depended on three things – the skill of the operator at the ground station on his sensitive use of the direction-finding antenna; the perseverance and patience of Jackie in his constant request for bearings; and on myself.

The magnetic compass had to be used with a degree of caution in this part of the world, the magnetic Pole being in northern Canada, hundreds of miles from the True North Pole. It was therefore usual to keep to a course on the gyro-compass in the blind-flying panel, and on this occasion I needed to keep to a zero setting once we were on a safe QDM bearing. The 'Q' Code was also a speedy way of requesting barometric pressure at base, and from this we could decide what adjustment, if any, was necessary to the altimeter setting, and how the information could be related to the pressure chart we had seen at the Met briefing before leaving. This gave us a better idea of what the pressure was likely to be at sea-level, for although we had checked this during the last minutes of daylight, the rapid change in the weather was evidence of a rapid change in pressure.

About every 30 minutes, following any necessary re-setting of the altimeter, we slowly descended through the gloom and at about 100 feet reduced speed to 100 knots so that the landing lights could be switched on, still cautiously descending in the hope of catching a glimpse of the sea, and by that means discovering if the clouds had a base other than resting on it. With Smithy checking the barometric setting as I strained my eyes ahead, right hand ready on the throttles, we 'felt' for the base of the cloud. On only one of these descents did we catch the glimpse of the sea we were looking for, as the pale reflection of the landing- lights from the mist suddenly became a brief silvery glow. As we roared up and away from it, I knew I had a decision to make. If the cloud and fog were on the deck, we couldn't get into Reykjavik and certainly not into Kaldadarnes. We had no diversionary airfields within reach, such as would have been available in these circumstances in U.K. Furthermore, an incorrect 'blind' approach to either Reykjavik or Kalda might quickly lead to trouble with the higher land beyond.

I had known too many fatal crashes from trying to reach an objective from an uncertain position under low cloud, and I therefore decided we would have a much better chance of survival if we reached the radio D/F Station at Reykjanes. We would know immediately that we had passed it when the QDM bearing was 180 degrees from the previous one; we would also know that we had passed over hospitable land and were heading out to sea again. So I would then make a 180 degree climbing turn to port to take us back over land at a respectable height, the crew would leave by parachute, I would quickly point the aircraft back towards the sea, set the automatic pilot at a slow rate of descent, then follow the others. We might even land close enough to the D/F Station to pop in and congratulate the operator on a good night's work! I didn't see any point in sharing this plan with the others as yet, as minds were on other matters.

Ninety minutes had passed since cloud and darkness forced this forbidding return on us at the end of a memorable day, and Jackie had just obtained his 72nd QDM – a record then unsurpassed and one to be shared with the ground radio operator – when our second wireless operator tapped me on the shoulder. From time to time he had been looking into the A.S.V. radar screen as an ever optimistic but unlikely check against trouble ahead.

"They said the radar beacon at Reykjavik would be starting to transmit soon," he said "and I think I've got it on the A.S.V. set. It's on the port beam!" and he asked Jackie N. to check it with him.

They both turned to me in delight.

'That's it!" they yelled amidst enthusiastic whoops.

Giving them the thumbs-up, I nudged Smithy and pointed down below. "Can Prince tell us where we are?"

He came back with the answer I had hoped for: "About 40 miles from Reykjanes D/F Station, and 30 from Reykjavik airport."

"What does the A.S.V. make it?" – to the W/Op.

"Thirty miles to port" he replied, "I can probably give you distance about every five miles perhaps less when you turn directly on to it!"

I needed no second bidding. As I turned I was quite sure that the gremlins which had been dancing on the windscreen, fell off.

Jackie shook his tapping hand and flexed his fingers. After his long stint he was a passenger now, as were the others, apart from the A.S.V. operator, head to the viewing funnel, calling the tune in his unexpected role as the final saviour:

"25 miles, ahead" – silence in the cockpit as the crew watched, then looked ahead for any sign giving hope of a safe approach;

"22 miles, slightly to starboard" – I corrected;

"20, ahead....15, to starboard" – again I corrected and began to allow for an obvious drift; "12 ahead.......10 miles" – I started to descend from 700 feet at 100 feet a minute;

"8 miles....7....5....4" – we were down to 500 feet and still in cloud;

"3 miles!" then suddenly haloed lights appeared ahead, increasingly bright as we slowly sank through the last thin drizzly layers of clinging overcast. The runway floodlight went on, and on the far side of the airfield we could see the red warning light which was halfway up the local radio mast. The light on the top of it was somewhere up in the clouds.

The cheering on board subsided a little as I put the Hudson into a tight circuit which hardly extended beyond the aerodrome boundary, and there was little enough time to get the wheels down, flaps down, approach speed and landing lights down, before we and the aircraft were down, rolling along the runway at precisely 1744 hours, having responded promptly to the instruction to return to base (or Reykjavik) immediately upon receipt of the message.

The Squadron Commander rang through from Kaldadarnes with a "Well done! But why did it take so long?!"

After the legitimate explanation, I also gave him some idea of the terrific response of the crew when I said that they had decided that nothing, not even the Icelandic weather, should stop the award of our Blue Nose Certificates. After all, what was the point of enduring an Iceland posting without taking one home?

An endurance test it became, indeed, shortly afterwards in dark December. The patrols, occasionally cancelled and frequently hindered by the weather, yielded no sightings nor sinkings, and the conclusion was that rough seas and poor visibility were as much a hindrance to U-boats as they were to us. In fact, from the high total of shipping losses in November, in December they fell to less than half that amount. In the worst of December's gales, when the wind speed reached 120 m.p.h., the roof of the electricity generating station was blown off and the equipment damaged , leaving us without electricity during one of the shortest days of the year.

Only two patrols over the storm-tossed ocean yielded incidents worthy of note. The successful U-boat attacks on our shipping in November led to exhortations by the hierarchy that wherever possible, patrols and escorts should be extended to the very limit of endurance, and this need was keenly felt by Hudson squadrons, as the main scene of action against U-boats was now moving beyond our range.

On the occasion when the C.O. decided to fly with me, the weather was foul, with sudden rising air currents and equally unexpected falls, which made that part of one's anatomy resting on the seat seem to hesitate before following the jolting downward motion, leaving the stomach suspended in between. The C.O. was considerate enough to make it clear that he was with us only as an observer, an additional pair of eyes, and any extra vigilance was very welcome on such a day.

He positioned himself as look-out in the astrodome, which in itself required something of a balancing act, with frequent contact between his head and the top of the perspex dome. On several occasions he moved unsteadily to the various crew positions, and this was probably his undoing.

It was Jackie Hollis in the rear turret who first noticed his activity at the small toilet bowl, which had to serve all functional requirements of the human body. When the lid of this bowl was closed it formed a step into the rear turret, and was therefore very much within the rear gunner's range of vision. Jackie lacked none of the raucous Cockney humour, and on the C.O's repeated visits to the bowl, Jackie gave a running commentary over the intercom to the rest of us; owing to his frequent movement from one position to another, the C.O. was not wearing headphones.

The written word cannot convey the flavour of Jackie's monologue, but phrases such as:

"'e's got 'is 'ead well in!"
"oops, 'is cap's fallen orf!"
"'e di'n't expect to see that again!"
"it's not as green as 'e is!"
"get it all in the bowl" and
"there can't be any more left!" were imprinted on the memory.

Knowing that any one of us might have been affected had we not been in relatively stable positions, we sympathised, and sympathy turned to admiration when, half in jest, I asked if I should extend the patrol by 30 minutes out and 30 back, as we had the reserve of fuel necessary.

"Certainly!" replied the C.O. brightly, "Go ahead; we might be lucky!"

We were not; we saw nothing but angry sea and sullen sky, and when we landed we were met at dispersal by the usual Bedford pick-up lorry. Out stepped the Station Commander, an unexpected honour! We followed our C.O. on to the tarmac and lined up behind him. He came to attention and saluted.

"What sort of a trip did you have?" asked the Station Commander.

"Oh, very good, Sir!" replied the C.O.

"What is that – er, stuff – on your cap?"

The C.O. doffed his cap, and was embarrassed to discover that not all his outpourings had found the appropriate place in the aircraft. Laughter all round healed his pride.

The other incident could have had a much more unfortunate ending but for the airmanship of the pilot and the performance of the aircraft. Again in weather which left us in no doubt that it was Arctic midwinter, with temperatures well below freezing, we were in position 58.25N by 19.35 west when we intercepted an S.O.S. from Hudson X which gave its position and the cryptic message 'Engine failure'. We were due to return to base, and knew that the pilot of the distressed Hudson would also be on his way back, so we diverted to intercept, when Jack repeated a follow-up message he had just received: "X returning to base – assistance not required." The aircraft was now between us and the airfield, so we adjusted our course to follow his track. He arrived at base just before we did, having flown 268 miles on one engine.

Every effort was made to ensure that Christmas was a rousing occasion; after all, whilst people at home may be thinking of the infrequent event of a White Christmas, we were ninety-nine per cent certain of one. There was one possible deficiency – the Mess Committee discerned an impending lack of beer. I was detailed to take an aircraft down to Edzell, near Aberdeen, for a full overhaul, and return with a replacement – and two extra barrels of beer. They were but empty casks by Boxing Day, and for some time afterwards it was almost like being on a 'dry' station, but the festivities lubricated relationships throughout the Squadron. The 'family feeling' was heightened, as one imagined it would have been on a peacetime station – though not perhaps in such an abandoned manner – as the tradition of officers waiting on airmen at Christmas Dinner, and inter-Mess visits proceeded merrily on a fine day which the Met people claimed they had kept specially for the occasion. There was an obvious advantage in the fact that Kalda was only big enough for one Squadron.

I was now in the habit of a brief reminiscence at the end of a year, and on the last day of 1942, Johnnie, Harry and I summed up the score. The optimism generated by success in North Africa and by the Russians at Stalingrad was tempered by the sense of personal loss. I thought about Tom Mycock; it seemed ironic that after SFTS we had gone our separate ways in different Commands, yet he apparently spent much of his operational flying against German warships in Brest whilst, having had a brief interlude of the same, I had been engaged on a similar mission in the North Atlantic. Neither Harry, Johnnie, nor I wished to dwell on the sad consequences of war, but those with whom we had trained and were lost – now half of those I knew at Rissington – were not forgotten.

The first escort of 1943 produced what Pug aptly described as fireworks. It was a convoy which, as we learned later, had been attacked by long-range German aircraft, and as a result one of the Naval escorts remained 'trigger happy'. As we approached the convoy I was discussing some navigational detail with Pug when Jackie drew my attention to the flashes which were appearing round the aircraft. This was our first experience of being the subject of 'friendly fire', and perhaps our own fault in that we were late in sending the identifying letter of the day by Aldis lamp; it was very quickly rectified, and Pug left the SNO in no doubt of our identity by firing off the colour of the day from our Verey pistol as additional aid.

Flashes of a different kind surrounded the Hudson on our way back to base. As we left the convoy we could see several large cumulo-nimbus (thunder) clouds on the darkening horizon, and we set course on the shortest return route, which meant flying across a strip of relatively high land. I checked with the W/Op that he had wound in the trailing aerial, a favourite path for the passage of lightning to the body of the aircraft.

Whilst in this cu-nim mass of heaving cloud, forked lightning seemed to merge into sheet lightning as it spread around us, briefly lighting up the cabin in a lurid glow. Occasionally it appeared to rattle down the fuselage, and the propellers became whirling discs of St Elmo's Fire. Whenever there was a momentary lull in the illuminations, the pelting rain continued the fusillade with such force that we subconsciously cringed from it; we were tossed about like a feather above a herd of stampeding cattle.

The memory of meteorological lectures briefly returned – it requires an upward current of at least 1600ft/min to tear rain drops apart, leaving a positive charge on the drops, and a negative charge carried to higher levels in the rising current. The lift we were in gave every sign of being out of control and we would certainly not dispute those figures! I expected to see some sign of the aircraft's ordeal when I examined it after landing, but there was nothing to show for its battering, except stowable equipment very much unstowed!

On 16th January, co-ordinated attacks on a U-boat by Squadron aircraft 'F' and 'K' offered some reward for the long hours flown without a sighting. The Operational Record Book explains:

"A/c F (Capt W/O V.D.Croft DFM) sighted suspicious swirl at 1239 hours in posn 59.45N 24.23W. A/c circled position after which swirl disappeared. In posn 58.32N 25.15W at 1317 hrs, Capt decided to return on reciprocal track, for he was convinced it was a U-boat swirl being very experienced in U-boat attacks.

At 1351 hrs flying at 800 feet and emerging from heavy rain, aircraft sighted a fully-surfaced U-boat in slightly brighter patch on a bearing of 015 degrees/ 3 miles, and on a course of 275deg/4 knots. A/c dived immediately to attack, turning slightly to port; U-boat disappeared when a/c was about 500 yards distant. The attack on the swirl was carried out at an angle of 70 degs to the track, dropping 4 depth-charges which were seen to explode dead on track and 40 yards dead ahead, and gave the impression of going off together in a big upheaval.

A/c R (Capt P/O Lane) intercepted U-boat sighting report and proceeded immediately to position given and at 59.59N 24.15W sighted U-boat on a bearing of 170deg/¾ mile distant, on surface on a course of 220/10knots. A/c carried out tight turn to port and attacked with 4 DC's. At instant of attack extreme top of conning tower was visible and the stern protruding from the water at an angle of 35/40 degrees....After the attack, a/c saw explosions subsiding, but no part of the U-boat was visible."

At least, a shaking; at most, serious damage. A 'Possible kill!'

Self and crew: from left: Jackie Hollis, 'Pug', Jackie Noble, Self

CHAPTER 11

GREENLAND AND THE "GAP"

In the latter part of 1942, the 'happy time' for the German U-boats which had followed American entry into the war was over. By that time, air cover had been provided along the American seaboard, and though there were still easy targets in the Caribbean and Brazilian waters, Admiral Dönitz, the German U-boat chief, decided to concentrate his forces in mid-Atlantic. There was now greatly increased danger to any U-boat within 500 miles of Allied air bases, but beyond that distance there were only escort vessels to contend with, and even those had been seriously depleted by the need for safe passage of the fourteen convoys to North Africa for the 'Torch' landings. The U-boats in the N.Atlantic attacked in areas lacking air cover; in areas covered by regular air patrols their one aim was to disappear.

Dönitz's diary was succinct in expressing the alarm he felt:

"In the Atlantic the enemy's daily reconnaissance covers out as far as 30 degrees west, which forces U-boat dispositions far out into the centre of the Atlantic with consequent higher fuel consumption, shorter operational periods, and greater difficulty in finding the enemy convoys."

The inhospitable sea area south of Greenland – the gap in air cover – thus became the next 'happy hunting ground' for U-boats, and a graveyard for many a merchant ship. The effect of air escort was seen in one of the earliest 'Wolf-pack' encounters.

During the morning a convoy was attacked by nine U-boats towards the edge of the 'gap'. Later in the day, the convoy came within range of aircraft from Iceland. One U-boat was sunk, the rest dived. In his War Diary, Admiral Dönitz explained that he decided to break off the action, as experience had shown that further pursuit in an area under constant air patrol would be useless.

The Allied authorities assumed that, until the Very Long Range Liberator aircraft were operational, and able to cover the Atlantic westward from bases in Iceland/U.K., and eastward from bases in Canada, defence against U-boats in the Gap could only be supplied by surface escort vessels. The experience of four aircrews of 269 Squadron provided evidence to dispute that assumption, and showed that it was a grievous oversight which led to many more casualties among sailors

---

and seamen than would have resulted from better co-operation and a more thorough research of the possibilities.

There was little surprise in the Squadron when, towards the end of January 1943, we were told that a detachment of four Hudsons would be leaving shortly for Greenland. For months the hours of painstaking patrol and escort yielded little action; we knew where the U-boats were but we couldn't get at them. Any crew on the Squadron would have jumped at the chance to get closer to them, and that could be done by operating from Greenland. In the event, the four crews, all on their second tour of operations, were:

F/Lt Jimmy Haigh; W/O Prince; F/S Baker; F/S Wharry;

F/O Harry Ramsey; F/S's Williams, Beardman, Goudie;

F/O Johnnie Lane; F/O Johnson; F/S's Arnott, Garredus;

Myself; W/O Pugsley: Sgts Hollis, Haffner, with Jimmy Haigh i/c Detachment, which would include four Corporals as ground crew, one to be carried in each aircraft.

As midwinter was likely to have more severe effects on aircraft and personnel in Greenland than in Iceland, the Medical Officer had some advice:

"In very cold conditions, your nose will give you the first warning that your body doesn't particularly like it, and this will be followed by fingers and toes. To protect the vital functions, blood will be centralised; your skin will soon know about it and lose its healthy colour. You will be feeling very cold before your temperature actually drops, and that's a warning point. Spasms of shivering will start, but as you get colder still you won't be able to, as confusion and lethargy begin to affect you. When your body temperature has dropped to freezing point you pass out, and at anything below that your heart will cease to function. If you have a forced landing in bad conditions and you manage to survive, let's say on the Greenland Ice Cap, it's essential to stay with, and preferably in, the aircraft until help arrives". Dog-sledge, or St Bernard with Brandy bottle? Thanks for the warning!

We needed no reminder to pack all the aircrew underclothing we had, which even Iceland hadn't so far seen, as Hudson aircraft had a very efficient flightdeck heating system. The warm air, quickly generated once the engines had warmed up, passed through small adjustable grills, one of which was located near the pilot's left foot. However, we knew nothing of the living conditions on the ground, so items of insulating clothing were de rigeur.

We had no qualms about the Hudsons because, although superseded by militarily more up-to-date aircraft, in ability to fly in any weather Hudsons were never bettered. To prevent icing on the wings they were equipped along the leading-edge with adjacent strips of pneumatic 'boots', the lengths of which, when switched on, inflated in a prescribed order, producing a corrugated effect sufficient to crack any thin layer of ice which might form, before it had the strength to become thick enough to affect the lift supplied by the wing. The carburettors could be heated as necessary, and it was possible to cover the propellers with a fine spray of oil from the constant-speed hub cover. Add to this formidable protection a coating of 'Kilfrost' de-icing paste on important parts (of the aircraft!) and we would be ready for anything.

Information about Greenland was pitifully inadequate, considering that it had a strategic value equal to that of Iceland, which British forces had entered almost three years earlier. This missed opportunity was made to seem the more unfortunate when it became known that in the Spring of 1941, Captain D.C.T.Bennett (as he

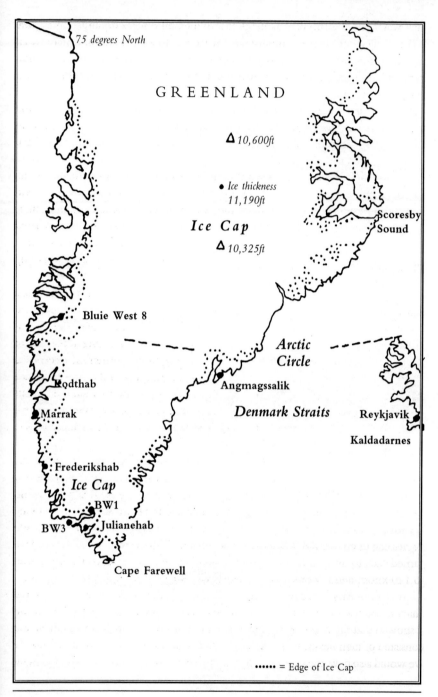

75 degrees North

GREENLAND

△ 10,600ft

• Ice thickness
11,190ft

Ice Cap

△ 10,325ft

Scoresby
Sound

Bluie West 8

Arctic
Circle

Godthab

Angmagssalik

Marrak

Denmark Straits

Reykjavik

Kaldadarnes

Frederikshab

Ice Cap

BW1

BW3

Julianehab

Cape Farewell

•••••• = Edge of Ice Cap

then was, later A.V.M.) had taken the first of the B24 (Liberator) aircraft on a long flight from Gander in Newfoundland to Greenland to look for a suitable site for an airfield. He discovered one of the very few reasonably flat areas on the west coast large enough to allow aircraft to land; it became the American Army base known as Bluie West One.

Equally disturbing to someone well aware of the inadequacies of operating from Greenland, the Public Record Office at Kew contains a Coastal Command file of many memoranda covering a lengthy period in the middle of the war regarding British/American discussions on the setting up of adequate Meteorological reporting stations in Greenland. Scoresby Sound and Angmagssalik had been instructed to stop broadcasting weather reports in plain language, and letters galore passed between Air Ministry/ Command/United States about possible codes to be used, and the dropping of information about them to the isolated weather stations. If such a matter took so long to agree at such a level, procrastination certainly became the thief of vital time. Another quotation from Edward Young came to mind: "Be wise today; 'tis madness to defer!"

The four crews due to leave were certainly not aware of any meteorological assistance which came from any place other than RAF Iceland, and we soon had reason to query forecasts which did not originate from there. The Met Report was of vital importance during briefing in the Ops Room that morning at the end of January 1943, as we prepared to leave for Bluie West One. When the overriding factor is endurance – the length of time an aircraft can stay in the air – there is a point on the route, known as the point of no return, beyond which the aircraft cannot go if it is to retain the option of returning to base, or a suitable alternative within the same range. You either go on, hoping to reach your destination, or you turn back.

At the briefing, allowing for the expected wind direction and speed at the height we were to fly, and bearing in mind the fuel reserve which might be needed to cope with unexpected circumstances at the receiving end, this point of no return was less than halfway to BWI. If we decided to return we would be flying against the northeasterly wind for which we had waited a day, and which would be helping us on our way to southwest Greenland. If its speed was 30 knots and we turned back to fly at 150 knots against it, our speed over the sea would be reduced to 120 knots, and it would take us longer to get back than it had to come out.

It was not easy to recognise Bluie West One on the black and white hachured chart which was the only location map we had at the briefing. The spot heights on it showed that the ring of rock surrounding the island of ice which was Greenland consisted of high peaks, which made a direct flight to BWI a hazardous course, as we would also have the southern edge of the ice-cap to cross followed by a difficult descent on the far side. Cape Farewell is a high, rocky promontory at the southern tip of Greenland, just below the 60 degree North line of latitude – considerably further south than Iceland but with a much colder climate dominated by the effects of the ice-cap, 11,000 feet thick near the middle.

We were to set a course to take us to Cape Farewell, 750 nautical miles, with the point of no-return near our crossing of longitude 35 deg west. From the Cape we would then fly along the west coast for about 80 n.miles until we reached Bluie West Three, the island of Simiutak, on which was based a radio station operating on an unknown frequency, but, more importantly as far as we were concerned, which pointed the way up the 50-mile long fjord at the head of which was the airfield.

Pug and I decided that it could be unwise to fly a course aimed directly at Cape Farewell. If our navigation was faulty or the wind played tricks and we drifted south, and/or if the visibility was affected by the sea fog common in those areas, we could pass beyond Farewell (Farewell in fact!) and perhaps not realise the mistake for some time. Pug pointed out that Labrador was the next stop! We would aim to make landfall along the east coast, sufficiently north of the Cape to allow for any error. The wind was unlikely to change direction, only to strengthen, according to the forecast. The briefing ended with a pointed reminder that we needed to land at BWl in daylight, as a landing after dusk would be a very hazardous operation on a first acquaintance with the approach.

So, at 1044 hours on a bright morning we left Kaldadarnes and the cosy abode which for two months had provided the four of us with very pleasant accommodation and which, unknown to us then, we were never to see again. The flight was uneventful, but the early morning sparkle disappeared from the day the further west we went. However, the wind continued to help us on our way, and we had no hesitation in passing the point of no return. Greenland, here we come!

Greenland gave us a chilly, foggy welcome. About ten miles from the coast we met the ice we had been expecting; a patch of coagulated skodser here and there, with a thin overhanging mist indicating the cold East Greenland Current beneath, then runs of firmer ice and thicker mist, until we reached continuous ice and the mist became a dull, threatening fog which almost eclipsed what meagre daylight the day had managed to produce.

Suddenly, the coastal cliffs appeared, truncated into columns of rocky pillars by the levelling effect of reduced upward visibility. We made a sharp turn to port, continuing at a height of 100 feet parallel to the coastline. Pug's navigation had brought us to the intended landfall, and after ten minutes of flying through the tunnel of gloom, the fog thinned and gradually disappeared, the cliff face veered away to the west, and we knew that just round the corner we would see the imposing mass of Kap Farvel. The transformation was reminiscent of a theatrical scene change from the villain's dark cave to the Prince's lake by the Ice Palace.

The sky was now clear and the ice reaching down behind the ledges of rock had a pale blue aura which deepened to aquamarine in the crevices. Sheet ice which covered the water for some distance from the shore had been sprinkled with a thin layer of gleaming snow. There was no problem in recognising the island turning point: it was the only one with a radio mast! We turned to fly up the fjord and saw before us a channel which in its grandeur and precision looked like some gigantic scheme of human engineering, a cavern with steep sides infiltrated with fingers of ice, a pale blue ceiling canopied over the still waters beneath.

The sun was slowly disappearing behind us as the corridor ahead narrowed, casting long shadows from projecting rocks on the cliff faces, which ranged up to 3,000 feet within a short distance of each side, making any future need for a turnaround in the fjord seem a tricky task. The ice-cap, as yet invisible, signalled its presence by the heavy pale-grey sky beyond the far horizon.

We faced a wall of rock as we approached the head of the fjord, but within two hundred yards of it we could see we needed a turn to port, and another wall of rock came into view a quarter mile ahead. Then, to starboard, there was the airfield, in what at first glance and in declining daylight seemed to be a replica of Shangri La from the film 'Lost Horizon', on the only area of reasonably level ground we had seen since leaving Iceland. Even then, on a tight circuit, it was obvious that the long runway sloped from the end nearest the ice-cap down to the waters of the fjord, so it would be necessary to land up it.

This we did at 1715 hours local time surprised at the much-shortened landing-run the upward gradient caused, and with what looked like a mile of unused runway ahead. Probably the only landing ground which could be described as a direct link 'twixt deep lagoon and truncated glacier, it owed its existence to a freak of nature many years ago when the ice which had gouged its way down to the sea for some reason then stopped short, leaving a levelled area strewn with debris, which in one or two corners could still be seen, collected into mounds of rock.

The other three aircraft landed shortly afterwards, and we were guided by a Corporal in a Jeep to a parking area near the top of the runway, where our Hudsons joined a cluster of United States Air Force machines, including Marauders, Mitchells, Bostons, and Dakotas. Lights began to appear beyond the landing and parking areas, revealing the wide extent of the base, vehicles of many shapes and sizes passed to and fro, and giant snow-clearing machines were being moved into position, presumably in case they were needed next morning. Our briefing at

Kaldadarnes had not led us to expect anything as big and bustling as this, and already questions were forming in our minds as to why this base offered nothing, so far, to our war against U-boats?

Two Dodge pick-ups arrived, and we were taken to a long wooden hut near the Mess Hall, whilst Jimmy reported to the Control Officer, Major Lindsay of the U.S.Army Air Force. We were all to be billeted together, as the Mess buildings for officers and NCO's were not yet completed; this turned out to be fortuitous, as we became a very cohesive unit which helped us to face the tribulations which lay ahead.

The food we had at BWl was lavish in both amount and variety, surpassing anything we had seen in Iceland, or in England since 1940, and it was obvious the inner man was going to be well supplied throughout our stay. The barrack-room was spacious, well-lit, and adequately heated, its relaxing ambience spoilt only by late-night incursions from revellers, and occasional vocal explosions from groups of poker players. Breakfast next morning continued to broaden the menu – gammon, bacon, sausages, eggs, tomatoes, and then some. Ah, forgot the grapefruit! We seemed a long way from front-line action, but it was waiting just round the corner.

It was suggested we should visit the Admiral (very much 'Rear') in charge of the Naval Section. We were uncertain as to what this included as there was no obvious sign of Naval activity, and the Admiral gave every indication of being uncertain himself. We later saw one or two sloops and a few aircraft bearing Naval insignia, although there was little indication in his small office of an organisation requiring subordinate staff. An officer of the Royal Navy would have considered himself lucky to command such a post in the rank of Lieut-Commander, but he would equally have thought himself unlucky to find his war effort relegated to being of little importance against what was emerging as the primary task of BWl – the ferrying of U.S.A.A.F. aeroplanes to Britain.

That much became clear during our first meeting with the Admiral, together with the fact that neither he, nor apparently the aircrew who from time to time came under his command, had much idea of tactics against U-boats. He was concerned that two troop-carrying ships bringing American servicemen to Greenland had recently been sunk, with many men lost from their ordeal in the icy water. We visited some of the survivors later in the Base Hospital, and the plight of those suffering severe frostbite was pitiful to see. They said there had been no air cover. If the Admiral was hoping to avoid a similar catastrophe we would certainly do all we could to help. One of the reasons why air escort had apparently been absent, we discovered when talking to a pilot who had been flying 'anti-sub', was because patrols were flown at heights up to 10,000 feet. This certainly gave a broader view of the ocean on a fine day, but how many such days were there, and how long would it take to attack a target which would be well aware of the aircraft, or to direct the meagre escort vessels to it? However, efforts to pass on suggestions gleaned from hard-won experience were not eagerly accepted, and we discerned a lack of real interest in helping to protect the convoys now being forced ever nearer Greenland's frozen shores.

Jimmy, as Detachment Commander, obviously knew the state of play better than we did, and was quite likely to be even more frustrated by the lack of operational integration and co-operation than we others were. We were still under the control of Headquarters Iceland, which seemed less than sensible when they knew so little about local circumstances; but it wasn't long before we realised that, equally seriously, there was a local lack of information about convoys, their routes, and their tactics.

In the Mess, however, we were overwhelmed by the camaraderie and hospitality. The alcoholic beverages were not entirely to our taste, but this became less noticeable as the evening wore on! An Army Air Force lieutenant jumped on a bar stool and called "The Kee Bird", there was an echoing roar "The Kee Bird!", he took from his pocket a creased piece of paper and started to recite the following verses. Those in the know joined in the 'Kee' verses, and before long we were noisy participants:

THE SONG OF THE KEE-BIRD

You have heard the wail of the siren
As an ambulance sped down the street,
And mayhap you've heard the lion's deep roar
Down in Africa's grim desert heat.

Or the piercing cry of the tiger
At night, as he stalks his prey;
Or the locomotive's high shrill whistle
As it sped, through the night, on its way.

But these sounds are no more than a whisper –
You've heard nought, I assure, till I've told
Of the blood-curdling cry of the Kee-bird,
In the Arctic's cruel, frigid cold.

This bird looks just like a buzzard,
It's large, it's hideous, it's bold,
In the night, as it circles o'er Greenland
Crying "Kee Kee Keerist but it's cold!"

The Eskimos tucked in their igloo
Toss fretfully while in their sleep,
And their huskies asleep in a snow-bank
Start burrowing way down deep.

For this cry is so awe-inspiring
It freezes the blood I am told,
As the Kee-bird flies in the Arctic
Crying "Kee Kee Keerist but it's cold!"

The Mounties abroad on their dog-sleds,
Visiting these wards of the Crown
Oft hear this cry and stare skyward
With a fierce and desperate frown.

For odd things happen in the Arctic
And many weird tales they have told;
But their voices drop to a whisper
Hearing "Kee Kee Keerist but it's cold!"

And many a brave man on base site
Strong and bold but now in a state,
Will be taking the first ship back homewards
To forget this bird's song of hate.

They can 'take it' it seems in the daytime,
But when midnight's hour is tolled
They cover their heads in protection
Against "Kee Kee Keerist but it's cold!"

So back to the States they are going,
To sleep in a real bed as of old,
To slip strong arms round a loved one
Her fair slender form to enfold.

Then off to sleep in warm comfort,
And wifey's soft hand they will hold,
To wake, terrorised by a "Kee" nightmare
And the cry "Kee Kee Keerist but it's cold!"

In the daytime the camp was a hive of activity, not only on the airfield but also among the many wooden buildings, some going up, some being worked on inside, others being wired or painted, and the daddy of them all, the new Officers' Mess, being fitted with a stone-walled chimney. A stone-walled chimney? Seemed rather incongruous in a land with no wood or coal! Marvel as we might at the rapid rise and the relative splendour of the pine-clad buildings, there yet remained one basic facility back at RAF Kaldadarnes which was superior to the one at BWl.

After landing on the first day, we needed to respond to the call of nature and were directed to a building which contained only the facility for that particular kind of minor relief. The fact that the facility for the other kind of relief was missing was not apparent until later, when the need was pressing, and a hurried search of that particular building yielded no comfort. I asked an American airman where the number two building might be.

"Oh, you want the 'arsenal'" he replied, "this is only the urinal," and he pointed to a block across the way. I entered and it was immediately obvious that about half the thirty-odd seats were occupied. Obvious because there was a complete lack of privacy; seating was arranged on the four sides of a square, each side being a continuous length of wooden planks with a number of holes about the size of a normal toilet seat cut in the surface. The open space in the middle of the 'box' left no one in any doubt about its contents! There was no artificial heating in the room, although there was considerable warmth generated from natural sources! Indeed, from the number of occupants blissfully sitting there reading newspapers and magazines during working hours, one could only assume that it was much preferred to the task in the frigid air outside which had to be temporarily abandoned in order to let nature take its course.

During the brief period we were obliged to use the latrines before the opening of the new Officers' Mess, there were one or two tricks we learnt from the experienced incumbents: firstly, to keep a close watch on the toilet paper which had to be taken to the chosen seat, because it was more than likely that the fellow on the next seat would have forgotten his; secondly, should digestive problems tend to produce audible evidence of the natural act, sit next to someone and look at him in surprise when the audible act occurred; and try to avoid patronage during the busy time just after breakfast, because you may find that all the occupants are sadistic people who enjoy watching you pacing up and down waiting for a vacancy.

Keeping the Hudsons ready for operations quickly became a problem, and the four-man ground crew team worked wonders, with, at first, little help from our hosts. It was obvious that one aim to them was paramount: ensuring that the passage of aircraft to the U.K. for the American operations against enemy-held Europe continued unabated whenever the weather permitted. In February and March of 1943, however, there were many occasions when conditions at BW1, or Reykjavik, or the area in between, were unsuitable, and the delays caused congestion. USAAF ground crews were well equipped, they also had the assistance of civilian engineers from the engine and airframe makers, but they had little spare capacity to help our hard-pressed corporals.

There was no doubt that the civilians came to this frozen outpost fully prepared, as a notice on the Mess message-board indicated: "Remington 'Remette' portable typewriter for sale. $20. Perfect condition, little used. Contact Jake Gromlek, Engineer, Wright Aeroengine Corp in 'B' hangar." I did so, and managed to get my English money changed at $4 to £1, so the machine cost me £5. I thought it was a bargain; Jake was non-committal, he had just got the latest model 'on the firm'.

Throughout our stay at the base, the runway was always serviceable in spite of ice, snow and blizzards which caused large drifts elsewhere, but never on the runway – in bad weather it was constantly patrolled by huge blowing and sweeping machines. Hot-air machines removed ice from the wings of the aircraft, but on only one occasion could they be spared for use on our Hudsons. So in preparation for my first patrol from BW1, after briefing and an uncertain weather report which did at least forecast reasonable conditions in the fjord and at base, we had to spend almost an hour helping the ground-crew to chip and scrape ice off the wings and control surfaces. A delay of more than an hour might lead to problems when returning in fading daylight along the narrow fjord, and in the landing, until we were more familiar with the tricky approach.

Ready at last, I taxied through the serried ranks of transit aircraft, carried out the cockpit check, and turned on to the runway. In the full light of day it was even more impressive than at dusk on our arrival. It appeared to be almost as wide as the runway at Kalda was long, and the slope down to the fjord and the bluff beyond was quite pronounced. As soon as I released the brake and before I had opened the throttles, the Hudson started to move, and in the shortest run I had experienced in the aircraft, even when on some past occasion I had opened the throttle against the brakes, we were airborne and up to a height of 300 feet before we passed over the end of the runway and turned to negotiate the dog-leg into the fjord. The effect of the morning sunlight coming from behind the high ground on our left appeared to divide the fjord into two parts – deep shadow to port stretching more than halfway across the water, and bright sunlight on the rocky cliff to starboard, which turned grey into shining silver.

There were ominous signs of a different sort of weather as we turned south over BW3, the island at the bottom of the fjord, looking towards Cape Farewell, and by the time we reached there large flakes of snow began to impair visibility. It soon became obvious that this was the edge of a continuous belt of wet snow, moving up from the south, and ice was beginning to form on the wings. I switched on the de-icing 'boots', and turned to return to base; there was no useful purpose served in patrolling in conditions which would obscure visibility to any U-boat as much as it did to us. The snow followed us at its own steady pace, and an hour after landing there was a heavy fall at BW1. So we had not deserted our post unnecessarily.

On the 4th February, a week after our arrival, Jimmy returned from the Control Office with the surprising news that we had been instructed by H.Q.Iceland to return forthwith. We busied ourselves with the necessary arrangements, getting aircraft serviceable and packing, all with mixed feelings. We had begun to realise what could have been achieved from BW1, but had been unable to achieve it so far, whilst at the same time not relishing the circumstances under which we operated – and missing the Squadron 'nous'. The next day the weather was unfit for the departure, and on the 6th a signal was received cancelling the instructions to return.

This volte face became the subject of speculation. Was the order initiated by one source, then countermanded by another, higher level of command? One Jackie reckoned that the Yanks had bitched about our 'insouciant expertise'; the other Jackie that Jimmy Haigh had complained to Iceland about the latrines!

We managed to keep all aircraft serviceable until the 10th, when, in the absence of instructions from H.Q.Iceland, Jimmy's diplomatic contact with the U.S. Navy led to all our four crews being airborne, together with U.S.Navy aircraft, to carry out an anti-U-boat sweep ahead of an American convoy. On the 14th, after a delayed take-off caused by rundown batteries on the starter-trolleys, I continued to sweep for a convoy proceeding towards BW1. Poor engine-starting was one of the symptoms of strain on the system – we relied on the American starter-trolleys, and if they had previously been used that morning to start their own engines, they had lost their zip by the time we had the use of them.

By this time, we were regular users of the PX, the American (much superior) equivalent of the British NAAFI. It was an Aladdin's cave! Not only were there very plentiful supplies of everything which the isolated serviceman could want, from off-duty clothing to toilet and hygiene requisites, but there were items of certain appeal to the girls back home, such as nylon stockings, hair curlers and perfume. It made one wonder whether all PX's had the same inventory – all-male, or mixed; torpid or tropical! Jackie made two pertinent points on seeing all this,

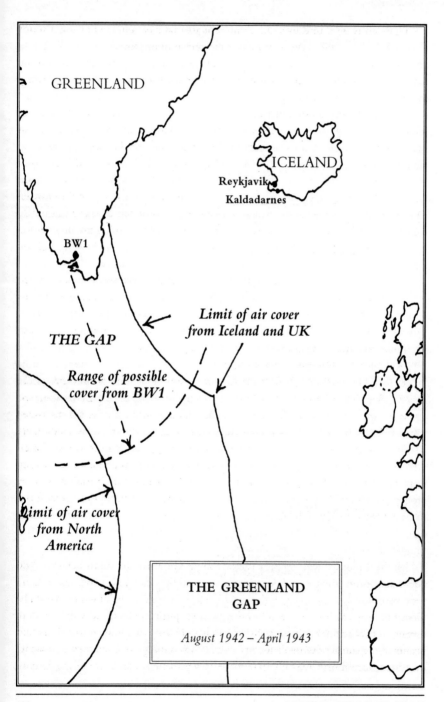

GREENLAND

ICELAND

Reykjavik
Kaldadarnes

BW1

*Limit of air cover
from Iceland and UK*

THE GAP

*Range of possible
cover from BW1*

*Limit of air cover
from North
America*

**THE GREENLAND
GAP**

August 1942 – April 1943

having recently been told by a U.S.Army private that a Greenland posting was not subject to a time limit, unlike our one-year Iceland posting:

"If I had to be stationed here, I'd rather they used the shipping space on me than on the baubles. In any case one of my letters'll curl more hair than those things!"

Being domiciled all together at one end of a large hut with American airmen at the other end led to an amusing incident. The frustration caused by a lack of operational activity enlarged a trivial incident between Jackie and me late one night into a bout of all-in wrestling. The others gathered round shouting bloodthirsty encouragement, and the Yanks couldn't resist such an attraction, seeing an opportunity to wager the outcome. The odds were being shouted when an American Military Policeman came through the door at the far end, and quickly tried to intervene. As he pushed his way through, ordering us to break it up, he saw two battling figures clad only in vest and long underpants surrounded by others in similar garb.

"Break it up, or you'll be on a charge!" he thundered, to no apparent effect, except that it gave the American onlookers the opportunity to speedily return to their quarters, whilst the M.P. physically separated the two of us.

"I.D! I.D!" he shouted, "I.D. Ho" someone replied, whereupon he took out his notebook and licked his pencil.

"I.D!" he called again, "Identification!"

He grabbed the RAF name-and-number tag which hung around my neck. For one statuesque second he looked at it, then looked at me. An embarrassed grimace flitted across his face, and he sprang to attention, a fine, smart, knife-edged trouser-creased white-armbanded figure, said "Sorry Sir", produced a truly American salute, and turned to march back down the hut. All the USAAF men were quietly reading or already in bed, but as soon as the door closed they surrounded the G.I. who had taken their bets and demanded their money back. A request to continue the bout was refused – Jackie and I couldn't even remember what we were arguing about.

My next flight was an escort to a convoy passing through the top edge of 'the Gap'. After the usual pre-flight preparations of briefing and de-icing, and the promise by the Met people that the 2,000 ft cloudbase in the fjord which would be hiding the tops of the cliffs was 'itinerant', we again picked our way through the throng of parked aircraft, wondering why, if a convoy was obliged to risk the icy waters to the south of Greenland, our aircraft was the only one detailed to assist it? The Americans must have known that the very presence of air cover near a convoy was a deterrent to U-boats, and would be so even if the aircraft carried no depth charges or bombs, for the enemy would be unaware of this fact, and would not wait to find out.

We had orders to meet the convoy, then sweep ahead, then behind. Suppose that three of all those serviceable aircraft, thwarted in attempts to cross to Reykjavik and U.K. by the weather there, had accompanied us. We could have supplied simultaneous cover ahead, astern, and on both sides of the convoy. We knew that transit crews were not trained for anti-U-boat work and did most of their navigation along radio beams, but they could have followed a leading aircraft, carried out the sweep, re-formed at a rendezvous near the convoy if they wished, or returned by using the radio beacon exactly as they did when crossing from Canada.

With these thoughts uppermost as we went down the fjord, Jackie H. reported for the first time on the strength of the radio beacon at BW3, as he had only recently been able to adapt the receiver to that particular frequency. But as a reminder of the tricks radio waves could play, as we passed Cape Farewell and he switched to the listening watch frequency, he picked up a 'local' message from Gibraltar!

En route to the convoy the weather deteriorated. The cloud base remained at 2,000 feet, but the wind strengthened from the northeast, whipping up plumes of spray from the wind-lanes across the turbulent sea. We approached the convoy, flashing the identification code letter on the Aldis lamp, but received no reply; nor could we identify the Senior Naval Officer's vessel. A heavy freezing mist reduced visibility so that we couldn't see the foremost ships in the convoy, and as we passed ahead along the lines we noticed ice floes and even mini-icebergs floating past as the ships plunged slowly forward. It was as if some giant hand had wound them up, set the rudders, and put them into the water on one side of the Atlantic pond, and there they were, with no evidence of life aboard and not a soul to be seen, moving inexorably towards the other side. It was not a day to be up in the Crow's Nest!

Again we voiced our great admiration for those who had the courage to sail in those conditions, facing the dangers we could do so little to avert. A U-boat sighting was most unlikely on such a day, and true to form we returned to BW1 without the luck needed to make a 'kill'.

The opening of the new Officers' Mess was quite an occasion. When we five Englishmen moved in with the American officers, its opulence amazed us; we wondered what their reaction would be when they reached England, perhaps to be based on an airfield with the now customary 'bare necessity' buildings. The entrance to this Officers' Club, as it was to be known, could be equally described as an imposing foyer, and the central feature on entering the Club Room was the huge stone-clad chimney-piece, below which logs glowed cheerfully in the wrought-iron basket of an open hearth. As if the splendid heat from this was insufficient , there were smart convector heaters at intervals around the walls. The bar offered Scotch whisky as well as Bourbon, and many other varieties of alcohol to assuage discerning tastes. After a couple of hours there was no surprise in being referred to as 'intrepid RAF aviators', embarrassing accolades which were accompanied by hand-around-the-shoulder confessions that the speaker was just aching to get at 'them durn Nazis'. Lieutenant Miller, a B26 pilot, went further: "You know what's stopping me?" he explained, "I'll tell you! It's this durn weather! Last week you heard 'The Kee-bird', now listen to this!" So saying, he drew a paper from his pocket and launched into

PHOOEY ON BLUIE

You've read of the brave Russian Stalingrad stand,
How the Axis was chased through North African sand,
But speaking of battles we know there is none
To compare with our winter at Bluie West One!

The mountains of Greenland rise into the sky
At a field on the fjord where the ice drifts by.
The worst of it is, with its infinite trials
There isn't a woman in one thousand miles.

No! someone has mentioned it isn't quite so!
Don't forget Henrietta, the coy Eskimo!
But wait just a moment, it's not as it sounds,
For the Bluie C.O. says she lives out of bounds.

So what to do for excitement and thrills?
We hunt for live glaciers, roll boulders down hills,
We listen to records and read books galore,
We sit through old movies we've seen twice before.

We circulate rumours mass-produced as of late,
And argue that Texas is an abnormal State,
Says one guy 'Seattle's a place unsurpassed',
Another looks forward to life in the past!

Halfway to London in late '42
Wait eighteen Marauders for skies to turn blue.
It's said they serve who just sit and wait,
Yet a war's lost with too little, too late!

Then who do we blame for causing this mess?
Not Adolf, not Hermann, you might never guess –
It's the man who charts weather, drawing rings on a map
Bringing lows into Greenland, high winds from the cap

Each night he craftily traces his lines,
He says 'It looks good, Reykjavik's sending 'nines'',
So when we get up it's supposed to be clear,
But what do you know, it's closing in here!

Then get out the cards, boys, and shake up the dice,
You're better off here than up on the ice.
When you're down on the ice-cap they say 'Sit tight'!
Yet some guys still sit for their fortieth night!

Perhaps we're too critical, there's good features too,
But rule out the Mess with its eternal stew,
And cross off the permanent officers here,
The brief fleeting daylight, the shortage of beer.

Only hermits and lamas can do without sex,
So give us good weather and we'll fly on to 'X',
To us just one place in this world really rates,
So let's finish this war and get back to the States!

A very adequate summary, and a suitable reminder that however good the facilities, which included billiard and table tennis tables, a juke-box and piped-music, they could not alleviate the boredom implicit in waiting on the weather. An equal frustration to those of us used to the detail of RAF briefing was the lack of information about the purpose of sorties. The picture of Atlantic action which we saw in the Admiral's office was contained on a small chart showing minimum information about convoys, and even less about U-boat dispositions. It seemed that most of it was gleaned from the brief operating signals from Iceland. The folly of a missed opportunity of a Combined Command became increasingly evident.

CHAPTER 12

THE BLIZZARD

With no sign of improvement, we felt there were two 'gaps' – the one lacking air cover in mid-Atlantic, and the one lacking maximum use of Allied resources here. The only enemy sighting and operational 'reward' the detachment had was when Johnnie saw a U-boat at intermediate distance, went to attack as it dived, and, hopefully by that means protected the convoy.

On the 1st March 1943, a signal was received from Iceland requiring anti-U-boat escort to convoy ON 168. Whilst at BWl, the four crews had been rotated in turn; Jimmy's crew and mine had been the last to fly, and as two Hudsons were unserviceable and maximum effort was required, it was now down to Harry and Johnnie. The Detachment Report in 269 Squadron's Operational Record Book unfolds the drama which followed:

1st March 1943 269 Squadron Detachment, BWl Greenland
AIRCRAFT
M – Serviceable   G – Bomb doors u/s
O – Ditto   N – Engine change

M F/O Ramsey	F/Sgt Williams	**Orders**
(FH 363)	F/Sgt Beardman	To provide anti-U-boat
	Sgt Goudie	escort to convoy ON
O F/O Lane	F/O Johnson	168.
(FM 423)	F/Sgt Arnott	Signal FC 1, 7375.
	Sgt Garredus	March 1st 1943.

Weather forecast in area:
Marrak (Teague Field) 63.26deg N 51.15 W, to provide a good alternative landing; visibility 30mls, ceiling 5,000 feet. Pilots were instructed to return to base with endurance to reach Marrak in case of possible diversion through conditions in the fjord. Pilots stated that they would fly out to BW3 at the base of the fjord and consider conditions before carrying out patrol.

Forecaster stated that the weather conditions in the fjord would probably remain the same throughout the day.

1200Z	(Local time) Aircraft M airborne.
1252	Aircraft O airborne.
1300	Weather conditions deteriorated at base. Visibility one mile in snow. Consulted weather forecaster who stated that occasional snow showers would temporarily reduce visibility at base. *Control Officer not in Operations Room.* F/Lt Haigh decided to recall aircraft in view of bad conditions at base. Signalled to both aircraft: 'Return to base'.
1345	Signal acknowledged by a/c O.
1349	Signal acknowledged by a/c M.
1400	From a/c M: E.T.A. 1515Z.
	Weather conditions at base remained poor, with continuous snow and visibility occasionally clearing from 500 yards to 2/3 mls. Conditions at BW3 (Simiutak, at base of fjord) were rather better: Vis 10mls., ceiling 2,000ft.
1405	*Sent signal: 'Return to base or to Marrak' to both aircraft.* Acknowledged immediately by M, but no reply from O. Continued to call a/c O, but no further wireless communication was established. Last contact made at 1345.
1410	Checked on weather at Marrak. Information received in last broadcast (1230Z) was vis 30mls ceiling 5000. Marrak broadcasts weather every six hours, *so requested base forecaster to radio Marrak for present weather there.*
1441	Sent base weather (vis 2mls, ceiling 600 ft) to a/c M which was immediately acknowledged. 'Wireless difficulties' made it impossible to obtain present weather from Marrak until 1750.
1530	A/c M requested position of Marrak.
1541	Position of Marrak sent to M, and acknowledged.
1545	*For some time a/c M had been requesting present weather at Marrak, but due to 'lack of communication' the desired information was still unavailable.* The base forecaster could not supply an accurate estimate of the present weather at Marrak, but expected to receive this special information by radio 'at any moment'. The Army station had been *trying to contact Marrak since 1400hrs but received no reply until 1730.* In

view of the above circumstances *the information re Marrak weather desired by M could not at that time be given* and the a/c was asked to wait. N.B. The a/c had the weather forecast for Marrak, and there was no way of knowing if any change had occurred.

1630	Weather reports from Godthaab and other stations on the coast indicated that *the whole of the west coast up to Cruncher Island* (at the base of the South Stromfjord leading to Bluie West 8) *was closing down, and the forecaster stated that BW8 was the only landing ground with fit conditions.*
1637	Sent signal: 'Proceed to BW8 – field open' to a/c M, immediately acknowledged.
1640	Aircraft M requested posn of Bluie West 8.
1655	Position of BW8 sent to M; acknowledged. A/c M requested weather at BW8.
1700	Replied: 'Ceiling 10,000ft, vis 30mls' N.B. Weather at Cruncher: Ceiling 5,000ft vis 10mls.
1710	To a/c M: Request position.
1712	M replied: North of Marrak.
1712	Sent position, frequency and call letters of radio beam at Cruncher to M. Acknowledged immediately.
1740	Sent instructions to a/c M to enable contact to be made with BW8 on that station's frequencies. No reply from a/c M. By this time the 1730 weather report on Cruncher had been received: *Visibility 1 mile with snow and gale winds 50 m.p.h. from north-east.* No further contact established with either aircraft in spite of repeated calls. Arrangements were made with Naval Communications Officer to keep a continuous watch all night on Frequency 6666 kcs. Arrangements were made witll Major Lindsay, Control Officer, to carry out maximum search with all available aircraft (including transit) as soon as possible. Lieut Commander Soule, U.S.Navy, instructed the two Navy ships in Tungdliarfik Fjord to carry out a search immediately, and one ship in the vicinity of Godthab, to search the coast north of Marrak as far as possible.

DIARY OF SEARCHES FOR MISSING AIRCRAFT
2nd to 22nd MARCH 1943

March 2nd   Weather unfit for flying. Snow and fog in fjord prevented U.S.N. ships from going out to search. Bomb doors on a/c G repaired. Aircraft serviceable. Search co-operatively organised by Colonel Sweeney, U.S.Army Air Corps Commander. Permission sought for RAF Ferry Command to use its aircraft for search. (Later granted).

3rd   Weather unfit for flying. The Danish Governor of Greenland was requested to contact native settlers and discover if any aircraft had been seen or heard on March 1st.

4th   Weather fit for flying morning only; field unfit after midday – therefore area searched very limited. Aircraft G u/s: port engine cutting out on one magneto. Four a/c airborne; searched from Cape Desolation to 40mls south of Julianehab. Tungdliarfik & Brede fjords thoroughly searched. No results.

5th   Weather unfit for flying. Heavy snowfall & strong winds.

6th   Weather unfit for flying. Lt Commander Soule instructed U.S.N. ship 'North Starr' to search northern part of area, but snow, poor visibility and gale winds delayed this operation. Signal from Iceland: 'Detachment being withdrawn. List requirements'. Arranged to send excess baggage & personnel (Sgts Hollis and Haffner) by Ferry Command aircraft.

7th   Weather fit for flying. Due to extreme cold and difficulties in starting pre-heaters there were only two aircraft airborne. These carried out local search in nearby fjords. No results. (A/c G u/s until 1400 hrs due to plug change; by then, weather unfit).

8th   Weather unfit for flying. Village 20mls south of Godthab reported seeing an aircraft circling during the afternoon of 1st March, exact time unknown. Village of Kangamuit, north of Sukkertappen, reported hearing aircraft engines at approx midday 1st March. Natives instructed to carry out searches in fjords adjacent to their villages when weather fit for kayaks.

9th   Weather unfit for flying. Frequent strong winds caused drifting snow, with *visibility often zero on most days since the two aircraft were missing.*

10th   Weather fit; area searched limited by bad weather south of Godthab. G carried out search from 40 miles north of Cape Desolation to 20mls south of Julianehab. Airborne 5hrs 40mins. All fjords covered thoroughly. Three Ferry Command Hudsons and one U.S. B25 also carried out search. Total area covered 40mls north of Cape Desolation to Cape Farewell.

11th	Weather unfit. Work carried out on aircraft.
12th	Weather fit. Area searched limited by bad weather south of Godthab, A/C G airborne 4 hrs, searched area Cape Desolation to Julianehab and 40mls inland over ice-cap. 4 Ferry Command Bostons, 3 Hudsons and 1 B25 carried out local searches in same area. USN ship 'North Starr' calling at Godthab for the most experienced pilot in fjord navigation. Two USN ships searching Tungdliarfik, Brede, and Ivigtut fjords.
13th	Weather fit for flying. Area searched limited by bad weather north of Godthab. A/c G searched area Cape Desolation to Godthab. Bad weather prevented passage to BW8. One Hudson, 4 B25's, and 1 Ventura also carried out searches.
14th	Weather fit for flying. A/c G searched area north of Godthab to Cruncher, South Stromfjord, and landed at BW8. One Hudson, 3 B25's and 1 Catalina also carried out searches. A/c G now detached at BW8 to search locally. Crew: F/Lt Haigh, W/O Prince, F/Sgt Baker, F/S Wharry. At BWl: F/O Rayner, W/O Pugsley, and ground staff. Sgts Hollis and Haffner instructed to return to Iceland with Ferry Command as soon as possible.
15th	Weather fit for flying at BW8 but a/c u/s. Aircraft wreckage reported from Danish Governor at Julianehab. Posn of wreckage 4 mls N. of Julianehab.
16th	Weather fit for flying at BW8 but a/c still u/s. Sgts Haffner & Hollis departed for Iceland on Ferry a/c.
17th	W/O Pugsley despatched to Julianehab in USN cutter, along with USN & US Army personnel to identify wreckage. A/c G airborne for search & return to BWl but due to engine trouble returned to BW8 after 30 mins.
18th	Weather at BW8 fit; A/c G airborne for search & return to BWl. Requested BWl weather en route – deteriorating, instructed a/c G to land by 1700Z. E.T.A. G at BWl – 1800Z, therefore returned to BW8, searching from Godthab to Cruncher. W/O Pugsley returned from Julianehab. Wreckage identified as missing Catalina of U.S.Navy.

	F/O Rayner required to identify cap and boot marks found in vicinity of wreckage. Not of our missing crews.
19th	Weather unfit at BW8 & BW1. Too bad for further work on a/c N at BW1.
20th	Weather unfit at BW8.
21st	-ditto- A/c N tested & serviceable.
22nd	Weather fit for flying at BW8. A/c G returned to BW1 carrying out search on journey. Searches by all aircraft now discontinued. Requested Post Commander that all aircraft flying from this station be informed of necessity to apprehend any wreckage or signals, especially en route to BW8.

The lack of radio contact after 1345 hours on 1st March with Johnnie Lane's crew in a/c 'O' suggested that the blizzard had claimed them, and we who were waiting anxiously, having flown in such conditions but in areas where high ground was less in evidence, were depressingly aware of what could have happened.

Johnnie and I had served in the same units since October 1940, and in the long hours of waiting for the news that never came, I despaired at the loss in such a way of so splendid a person and so skilled a pilot.

In this barren place, where German targets seemed beyond our reach, we knew that Harry, on his long journey north into the unknown, would press on as he had on so many occasions, not now against the dangers of enemy fire, but of clinging snow and ice which would be trying to drag the aircraft down.

Extracts from 220 Squadron records exemplified his bravery and outstanding skill as a pilot when the enemy was within reach of his determined strike:

(F/O Ramsey – actions within Norwegian coast & fjords)

19th July 1941	Attacked MV 6,000 tons & 1 escort vessel. Dived from 6000 to 1500'; Dropped 4 250lb fused 11 seconds G.P. Bombs. Heavy anti-aircraft fire from escort vessel – pom pom, tracer, light H.E.
9th October 1941	2,000 ton MV attacked. 4 250lb G.P.'s explosion amidships. Attacked 3,000 ton MV with incendiaries. 1 hit.
13th October 1941	Nordfjord. MV 1,300 tons attacked. 4 250lb semi-armour-piercing bombs. Scored hit.
29th October 1941	Attacked MV entrance to Nordfjord – violent explosions and portions of deck & s/structure thrown in air. Clouds of steam & smoke.

6th November 1941	Sighted Ju88, Me 110 on tail – evasive action into cloud.
11th November 1941	F/Sgt Ramsey awarded the Distinguished Flying Medal.
28th November 1941	MV sunk near Stavanger – hits, ablaze from stem to stern as though filled with oil, then sunk within two minutes.

Two of eight airmen whose loss the Squadron could ill-afford.

Towards the end of March, to me the most miserable of all months during the war, the remaining ten members of the detachment had no hesitation in agreeing wholeheartedly with the decision to withdraw. Even then, Greenland seemed reluctant to relax its icy grip, as the Detachment Report in the Record Book states:

March 24-29th	Between these dates, a/c ready to return to Iceland. Awaiting suitable weather.
March 30th	A/c G F/Lt Haigh, W/O Prince, F/S Baker 2 Corporals (ground crew) Airborne 0830. Landed Reykjavik Iceland 1330. A/c N F/O Rayner, W/O Pugsley,F/S Wharry 2 Corporals. Airborne 0835. Landed Reykjavik 1340.

BLUIE WEST ONE IN RETROSPECT (1)

In planning the return flight we had decided that if the weather was suitable, we would track directly from BW1 to Reykjavik, which meant crossing the southern end of the ice-cap at a height of 10,000 feet or more. We would climb as we went down the fjord and turn across the rocky fringe towards the ice-cap when we had sufficient height, saving perhaps two hours compared with the alternative of down the west coast to Cape Farewell, then across to Iceland from there. The flight went as planned, with only a few anxious minutes when the starboard engine faltered as we reached 10,000ft, but then the rocky pinnacles on the far side fell away steeply below, and the engine recovered as the demand on it was reduced and we descended to more familiar levels.

As I looked to the north at the slowly ascending height of the ice-cap, I was reminded of that part of our search on the 12th which had taken us 40 miles over the ice-cap. It had been a cloudless day, but the sky was a faint grey rather than a positive blue, and when the coastline and all other features were lost to view, there was no horizon, because the lower levels of the sky took up the hazy reflection of the unbroken white of the ice-cap, merging snow and sky. The slope towards the highest part further north was insignificant and immeasurable, and the need to increase altitude from time to time would suddenly become apparent as the tiny ripples on the snow-covered surface became visible a few score feet below the aircraft wing.

Other thoughts then intruded as we continued on our long-awaited return flight. For the first time during my Service career I had been miserably alone at BW1 when aircraft 'N' became unserviceable and Jimmy and his crew left for BW8 on the 14th, until 'N' was ready for Air Test on the 21st. The fact that I was the only RAF officer in the crowded Mess, and the rather overpowering geniality of sympathetic Americans, heightened the feeling of useless isolation. As the blizzard kept Pug and the rest in their small corner and I in mine, I saw them only on the rare occasions when they were able to work outdoors on the aircraft, or when Pug and I made our way through the thick snow to the Control Room for the news of the day.

On the 10th the search had taken us over the edge of the ice-cap to where a narrow but deep glacier meets the sea beyond Avigait. A few large icebergs and several smaller pieces had already broken away from the edge of the glacier, forming a floating line of stately white pinnacles on their voyage to infinity. As we circled overhead, spellbound but not silent, we watched a long crack about 50 yds in from the seaward edge of the swath of ice slowly widen, so that we could see down the gap to the pure clear blue of the water below. That is what I saw; but I heard the chill chords of Vaughn Williams's "Euphonia Antarctica" as the majestic island of ice left its birthplace for ever.

Music of a different kind had become obligatory listening in the Mess during my waiting sojourn there. The new building had been lavishly equipped throughout with loudspeakers, and there were few times during the day, and certainly none between 6p.m. and 11p.m., when they were silent. Various kinds of popular dance music filled every part of the Mess, none more so than Glenn Miller's – then at the height of his popularity – and much as I enjoyed it, the constant repetition of 'Moonlight Serenade', 'String of Pearls', 'At last', and the whole repertoire of his and several other bands began to pall as a result of over-indulgence, and were to become irrevocably associated with the sudden ending of treasured friendship.

As we approached the point of no-return on our way home, and Pug came up from below to ask me to check the fuel, I was reminded of an incident during an Air Test, when we were flying over the waters of the fjord. He had suggested it was an appropriate place to test the bomb-doors, as they had been giving trouble again after being exposed to the extreme cold of the night, in case we had the good fortune to have the opportunity to use them during the anti-U-boat sweep which the journey home would provide. I opened them over a stretch of clear water, and one of the depth-charges dropped out. If Pug hadn't said "Sorry, but never mind

– it'll make us that much lighter for the journey home, and we can still deal with anything we see", I could have believed it was nothing more than an accident.

Another thought as I adjusted the control-knobs of the auto-pilot as we crossed the Denmark Strait: why had we been told to land at Reykjavik and not at the Squadron base at Kaldadarnes? At least on this flight the weather forecast was correct in every detail, which led me into more thought about the forecasting on that fateful 1st of March. They must have had experience of the effects on local conditions of a northeasterly wind off the ice-cap, and even to a rule-of-thumb Met person such as myself, once a very cold wind started blowing towards a warmer area it would be likely to persist, and probably intensify.

Yet even when the weather had deteriorated at 1330 to a visibility of one mile in snow, the forecaster referred to 'temporary snow showers'. Strengthening of the wind from the northeast was verified by the report from Cruncher at 1730 of a northeasterly blizzard. The reason for the lack of contact with Marrak weather station until 1750 had not been explained, whilst the aircraft seen circling by villagers 20 miles south of Godthab during the afternoon was almost certainly Harry trying to find Marrak.

I felt strongly, now we were two Hudsons returning instead of four – and from a relatively fruitless mission – that the lack of adequate co-operation was exemplified by the absence of the Control Officer at the vital time, when Jimmy had to take over. Yet a fair assessment must recognize the co-operation and concern shown during the period of searching and waiting. Now, as the never-so-attractive coastline of Iceland came into view, I decided that further analysis would be better left for a less emotive time.

Landing at Reykjavik provided the answer to one of the questions: the Squadron was now based there, as during our absence the whole airfield at Kaldadarnes had been put out of action by flooding, owing to the bursting of a natural barrier which held back melt-water from the snow and ice on high land behind. Strange though it would have seemed when leaving for Greenland, I did not now regret the loss of our cosily-quartered Nissen hut, for I would have been the only one returning to it. The Record Book states: "6th March 1943. The river overflowed its banks and was soon over the runways, and within a few hours hangars and camp were seriously flooded".

We were granted immediate leave, taking an aircraft to U.K. for overhaul. We agreed that Jimmy would visit Johnnie's widowed mother in Bournemouth, and I would see Harry's wife and his mother and father in Whitley Bay, whilst other crew members would arrange visits among themselves to the relatives of Johnnie's crew. Unfortunately, relatives of the three members of Harry's crew could not be visited as they were Australian. His crew were all married; Johnnie's were all single. Both Harry and Johnnie were each an only child. Jimmy and I felt that face-to-face explanations of the circumstances might make the customary telegram which would have arrived with no explanation of the dreaded word 'missing' a little easier to bear.

Harry's parents and I arranged that I would visit them, and Harry's wife would join us. As I knocked on the door of their neat house my mind was a blank; a release from emotion but troubled by an unavailing search for the measured words which would be needed. Mr Ramsey opened the door, stood for a moment looking at me as if gathering courage, then quietly took my hand in greeting. He was older than I had expected, hair turning grey, small in stature, precise in speech.

"This is Mr Rayner, Harry's friend," he said as we went into the living room to meet Harry's mother.

"It's so good of you to come" was her greeting, trying hard to add a smile to the words. "Do please sit down and have a cup of tea; we've been so looking forward to meeting you. You've known Harry for such a long time haven't you?"

"Since October 1940" I confirmed.

"He had a lot to say about you and Henry when the three of you were together on 220 Squadron" Mr Ramsey recalled.

"Henry is a prisoner of war, isn't he?" added Mrs Ramsey.

Again my mind was a blank as one of the difficulties became apparent. It was common knowledge by now that 'missing' was not the end of hope, and the unfailing optimism of many recipients of that awful message was justified by the arrival of a second telegram bearing better news such as 'Prisoner of war' or 'returned to unit'. Even 'believed killed in action' demanded adjustment to new circumstances by grieving next-of-kin. It was more than a month since Harry had not returned, and it needed no imagination on my part to realise the trauma suffered by these two genuine people as they waited hopefully for further news of their only son. If they still hoped that by some miracle Harry might return, wouldn't it be better to encourage them to face the brutal truth that even in the most optimistic circumstances of landing somewhere, somehow, without a crash, survival in blizzard conditions of extreme cold was impossible unless rescued within 24 hours? Or would they be so shattered at being deprived of a slender thread of hope that life would have no meaning for them?

At this point Harry's wife arrived, and the preliminaries were repeated. The warmth and understanding I had felt was less in evidence, and I had the impression that she could not long delay a return to her employment. I explained the circumstances in detail, and left her in no doubt of the extensive searches carried out, and the co-operation which made them possible. When she asked what would happen next, I felt the question had more relevance for her future than for the routine associated with missing personnel, and I saw a shadow of doubt flicker across Mr Ramsey's face. Then, rather abruptly, she left, and I hoped it had been nothing more than a very brave act.

Mr and Mrs Ramsey asked for more detail, as if they also wanted to live the hours of Harry's last flight as we knew it. I was encouraged to describe the conditions we had all met, both in the camp and beyond it, the ferocity of the weather, and the efforts we had made to defy it in flights attempting to reduce the "Greenland Gap". Gradually, and thankfully, I could see that these details were resolving the matter, as telling glances passed between them and they realised that if a second telegram should arrive it would confirm the inevitable. Mrs Ramsey's face betrayed the deep emotion; Mr Ramsey's was a mask.

As if I had become another departing link, they wished me to stay longer. I had to resort to the old 'train to catch', leaving them hand in hand at the door, eyes not dry nor yet filled with tears, waving a brave farewell.

BLUIE WEST ONE IN RETROSPECT (2)

I spent some time during the remainder of that leave attempting a perspective of the failure which I felt was not only ours, but which emanated from higher command and perhaps from flawed strategic thinking. One thought was uppermost in my mind: of all the times to attempt to start anti-U-boat operations from Greenland, the month of January was the worst possible choice. The weather affected not only our operations, but inevitably led to a build-up of American transit aircraft unable to fly the next stage on their way to U.K. Pragmatists might argue that it was a response to dire need, perhaps a cri de coeur from the U.S. Command which had lost troopships to U-boats in those waters. Strategists would counter that it showed a fatal lack of foresight.

Again I thought of the dichotomy apparent in the use of BW1 airfield, the importance given to passing transit aircraft along the chain, compared with using it for direct action against the enemy. I also recalled the different attitude of the U.S.Navy in providing air escort for their own convoys compared with their apparent lack of concern for British convoys. How different it could have been if the RAF, with its experience of running a base for different types of operations, had been in control, for at BW1 we were seeing the problems which could arise when air power was divided between Army and Navy.

I realised I had begun a purely academic exercise for two reasons: Firstly, even if the time had been more propitious for ideas to be implemented, it would have been necessary to find a higher-ranking mouthpiece than myself; and secondly, it would have been essential to overcome the lethargic approach to the problem of the

Greenland Gap consequent upon the belief that Very Long Range Liberator aircraft would shortly be able to cover the whole of the Atlantic from bases on both sides of it. This belief was encouraged by the promise of getting VLR aircraft operational in sufficient numbers at a faster rate than proved possible, and was accepted in the expectation of full co-operation between the Allied Commands. This took longer than expected to materialize; meanwhile unnecessary additions were being made to the tragic loss of Merchant Navy personnel, which were to total 33,000 men lost by the end of the war.

In Vol. II of "Royal Air Force 1939-45", Richards and Saunders state that "the prime need was simply to abolish the gaps....from August to October 1942 an average or nearly half-a-million tons went down each month in the North Atlantic alone. Worse still, new U-boats continued to come into operation very much faster than the old ones could be destroyed."

Although this focus came some years after the events, it was painfully self-evident at the time, not least on the Operations Board of Headquarters Coastal Command. Someone there would certainly have been wrestling with the problem, as I was in my lowly state, trying to justify criticism of the operations we had been ordered to abandon.

If BWl could have been used as an anti-U-boat base a the start of U-boat 'Wolf Pack' tactics in the summer of 1942, what aircraft did the RAF have which could have been used beyond their accepted limits in an emergency operation until the Very Long Range Liberators actually became available?

(1) THE HUDSON, with its range and endurance enhanced by greater flexibility of use. Knowing the aircraft well, and having completed a 10-hour flight in one, with a further two hours' fuel supply unused in the extra tank which replaced the bomb load, I was prompted to refer to the Air Ministry's Pilot's Notes for the Hudson, which had only become available to me during my second tour. This showed that at a true airspeed of 130 knots, fuel consumption would be 44 gallons per hour, which with the normal fuel capacity of 536 gallons would give a theoretical endurance of over 11 hours. Theory such as that was rightly regarded by the practising pilot with suspicion, but my own experience suggested that with careful navigation and nursing of the engines, it was possible to extend the accepted endurance. Moreover, although the heaviest fuel consumption was during take-off, the slope of the BWl runway, and its length, would allow a greater all-up weight, as well as some saving in fuel.

Any suggestions aircrew might make usually took some time to be ratified from on high, but some flexibility was surely permissible at lower levels? Methods and procedures came to be generally, even thoughtlessly, accepted, and I found it surprising that a more independent line of thought by some commanders was not in evidence. Extra fuel capacity could be provided by reducing the weight of armament, equipment, or even bodies. Two depth-charges could be carried instead of four, with fewer rounds of ammunition as there were no German aircraft in the area; one W/Op-Air Gunner would be sufficient instead of the usual two, and even the rear turret could be dispensed with as only the front guns were essential during an attack on a U-boat.

Indeed, Hudsons from the production line in California, without rear gun turrets, could have been crewed by an experienced pilot and others trained in Canada, to operate from BWl as necessary during their eventual passage to U.K., once alternative air cover for convoys had been provided. Ancillary equipment such as front guns and depth-charge systems could have been fitted at BWl. During the long summer days the need for diversion to another base was unlikely, and not beset by the problems of winter. With flexibility an endurance of 12 hours should have been possible, and would have brought Goose Bay airfield in Labrador within emergency range. Risky perhaps, but most pilots would have felt that no more was being asked of them than was constantly asked of the men in the ships below. Perhaps the greatest advantage of being able to tackle the U-boats as soon as they started their 'Wolfpack' depredations in the summer of 1942 would have been to persuade them that it was not a viable operation. Such suggestions may have been ridiculed by the planners and armchair specialists, but they would have been acceptable at operating levels.

(2) WELLINGTON AIRCRAFT had already proved their flexibility in a number of operating roles. I had no experience of them, but many of my acquaintances were flying them, and had complimentary tales to tell when we met. There was no difficulty in reaching an endurance of 12 hours with a bomb-load reduced from 2,000 to 1,000 lbs i.e. Four 250 lb depth-charges, the normal load for a Hudson.

(3) WHITLEYS, which were being superseded in Bomber Command, had a greater endurance than Wellingtons, but at a slower speed; and the performance of both aircraft in the role needed could be enhanced by judicious reductions in ancillary weight, particularly in armament and gunnery personnel consequent upon the absence of German aircraft from the operational area.

These three types of aircraft would have had no difficulty in using the long, wide runway at BWl, a fact well proven by the number of larger 4-engined aircraft such as the Lockheed Constellation which we saw during our stay.

(4) AMERICAN AIRCRAFT. There were many such aircraft crowded into the parking area at BWl. In particular the

MITCHELL twin-engined bomber of the type flown off an aircraft-carrier to bomb Tokyo on 18th April 1942 proved its suitability by that act. Its published range was stated as 1,635 mls with a 4,000 lbs bomb-load – greater than the Wellington's at equivalent load – giving probably another 600 miles, or a total endurance of 12 hours, with a bomb-load reduced to 2,000 lbs to allow for increased fuel capacity.

THE BOEING FLYING FORTRESS, entering the American and Royal Air Force in rapidly increasing numbers, would have had no difficulty flying from BWl, again with an endurance of 12 hours.

Why then, I wondered, was an attempt to cover the Gap not made by one of these means in the summer of 1942 when the U-boat packs started to create havoc in the area? Indeed why was an airfield so strategically placed not used by anti-U-boat aircraft as soon as the site was made into a landing-ground? The overriding importance was simply to get aircraft, even inadequately armed, into the air around the convoys. There had been several instances of U-boats crash-diving when approached by aircraft which had already dropped their depth-charges elsewhere, no doubt because their commanders were unaware of the aircraft's lack of them, but were aware that aircraft could bring Naval vessels to the scene. Dönitz's diary confided that "experience had shown that further pursuit in an area under constant air patrol would be useless".

Furthermore, Captain Bennett's discovery in Spring 1941 of the site which the Americans colonised as BWl could have been no secret to the Air Ministry, burdened with the ever-increasing task of countering U-boat depredations. The Royal Navy and the RAF had by far the greater share of responsibility for getting British and American supplies across the Atlantic.

Iceland 1940 – Foresight! Greenland 1941 – Foredoomed?

BLUIE WEST ONE IN RETROSPECT (3)

That a political dimension existed in relation to the Greenland Gap was not in doubt once the relevant facts had been considered. The release of official papers after the war showed that it emanated from the highest level. The 'man-in-the-bombed-street' might have the impression of wholehearted co-operation between the Allies, but this was not always the case, as several War Historians discovered. In "RAF 1939-45 Volume III" which was written with full access to official documents, the late Hilary St George Saunders, sometime Librarian of the House of Commons, outlined the procedures designed to put Allied aircraft over and around the Atlantic convoys for which the Royal Navy was responsible.

There was the Anti-U-boat Sub-Committee of the British War Cabinet, which handled all matters of policy and which could take the decisions which any Ministry or H.Q. would be obliged to carry out. American leaders, including Naval representatives, received its papers and could share its decisions.

"In fact," states Saunders, "wholly efficient Anglo-American control was never achieved."

From the U.S. entry into the war, Coastal Command pressed for a unified command in the North Atlantic. The U.S. Naval Staff in London agreed, the Chief of the United States Navy did not.

Air Marshal Slessor, on taking over Coastal Command, again emphasised that the North Atlantic was "one battlefield in which the Allies had to counter the flexibility of enemy forces, possible only by equally flexible defence and an integrated system of control".

"The Allies came near to falling into an error as old and hoary as war itself," Saunders suggests, "to have great strength available at what to each separately were important points" leading to "too many anti-submarine craft at some places (e.g. the sea-coast of the U.S.), too few at others".

An Atlantic Convoys Conference held in Washington agreed procedures which were never adopted, its offspring, the combined Procedures Board produced a combined scheme, then the American Navy Department stepped in and prevented its implementation.

An Allied Anti-submarine Board – two British and two American officers – produced a number of recommendations as a result of touring Anti-submarine Commands. They were ignored.

"The probable explanation of this state of affairs" suggests Saunders, was that the U.S.Navy was "far more concerned with the great sea-and-air campaign in the Pacific" and they kept "unnecessarily powerful anti-submarine forces in the areas close to their own Atlantic seaboard." A cynical U.S.Navy officer remarked that to get the U.S.Navy as interested in the Atlantic as they were in the Pacific, it would have been necessary for Hitler to devastate the Atlantic fleet, caught unprepared in their base at Newport News, as the Japanese did at Pearl Harbour in their surprise attack on the U.S. Pacific Fleet. It was a matter of pride emerging from the humiliation that the Japs should be plastered, he added. No comparable feeling against the Germans existed at the time.

The minor events, in the context of the World War, consequent upon the strategic misuse of the Greenland base is summarised in the Vol. III mentioned in "the conclusion that Admiral King (U.S.Navy) and his staff did not view the Battle of the Atlantic in the same light as General Marshall (U.S.Army) viewed the invasion of Europe in 1944".

Hence BW1: *Major role* – Army aircraft to Europe.

Minor role – Navy, for U.S. convoys.

Servicemen actually in contact with the enemy often wondered why, given the ready co-operation one with another, those who directed their operations seemed less inclined to overcome their differences, their pride, and their purely national loyalties. The wholehearted co-operation of all concerned in the search for the missing aircraft at BW1 exemplified what could be achieved, and impelled me to look for an answer to the abiding question of what prevented the Greenland base from alleviating the perils of the Atlantic from mid–1942 onwards.

I was satisfied that there was something more than the odd icy gremlin responsible for the disasters in the waters and in the air associated with the Greenland Gap.

During the month of May 1943, U-boat losses reached a peak. The Germans analysed the causes of these losses, and found that 35 per cent occurred when in transit to and from the operational area, and all these sinkings were by aircraft. In the operational area – the open Atlantic – total losses were 26 per cent, due in equal part to air attack and naval attack. When in action against a convoy, losses rose to 38%, the majority of the sinkings being by escort vessels. By proper use of the Greenland base, U-boat losses around convoys in that area would have been greater, and Allied shipping losses fewer.

As a consequence of waging total war, the essentially friendly population of enemy-held ports such as Lorient, St Nazaire, and Brest suffered heavy air bombardment, for the huge shipping losses in mid-Atlantic at the end of 1942 caused the Allied leaders at the Casablanca Conference of January 1943 to order retaliation in force against the source of U-boat patrols. One more result of failure to minimise the opportunities for U-boat attack in the Atlantic; failure to make the most of Bluie West One.

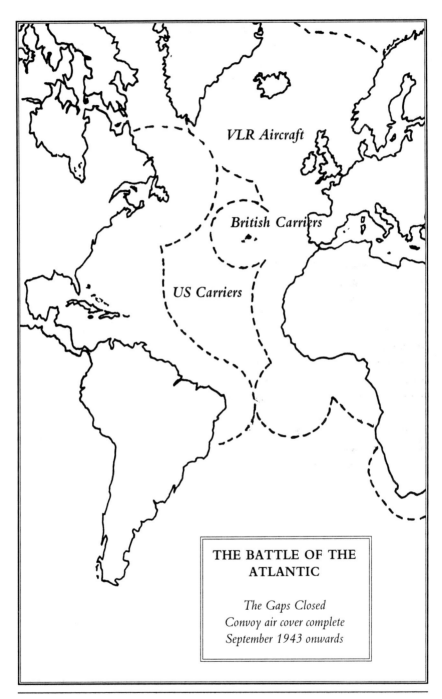

VLR Aircraft

British Carriers

US Carriers

**THE BATTLE OF THE
ATLANTIC**

*The Gaps Closed
Convoy air cover complete
September 1943 onwards*

CHAPTER 13

THE GREMLINS CAME TOO!

Realising they were losing the battle as the opposing forces then stood, the Germans began to fit the Schnorkel breathing tube to existing U-boats, and then to re-arm with larger and faster boats. The schnorkel allowed a U-boat to charge its batteries at periscope depth whilst being driven at 'dead-slow' by its diesel engines, so that during the vital manoeuvre only a few feet of tube showed above the water.

Schnorkels could be fitted in the safety of the U-boat pens in the Brittany ports; the new larger U-boats had to come from German ports, reaching the operational areas by passing between U.K. and Iceland. These were the sectors where the battle of aircraft against U-boat was most intense during the spring and summer of 1943.

269 Squadron helped to cover the northern transit route, and patrolled the northwest Atlantic as far as the range of the Hudsons allowed. The deterrent effect of the sorties was in their frequency during the long summer days, but it was obvious that Hudsons would be obsolete for the purpose during the winter nights to come, as the new A.S.V. and Leigh Light equipment was needed for the long-range four-engined aircraft coming into service. Nevertheless, the Squadron still had a job to do in helping to impede the passage of U-boats into the Atlantic, and by virtue of their perpetual presence to make the U-boat captains prefer to keep beyond Hudson range after running the gauntlet.

Admiral Dönitz to U-boat Commanders, message 1769, 17th May 1943: "The situation in the North Atlantic now forces a temporary shift of operations to areas less endangered by aircraft".

Even when lacking the satisfaction of a sighting and strike, patrols were seldom without interest or entertainment. There was still the pleasure of meeting a convoy 'spot-on', the exchange of greetings and the idiosyncratic form of language used by some Naval officers in the messages flashed by Aldis lamp. We were not yet equipped to be in radio/telephonic communication with them, and the signallers must have had quite a task in rough weather, swivelling the lamp to keep us in the sighting-line whilst sending 'Greetings, humming-bird' or 'Lost sheep' when contact with a straying merchant ship had been lost. There was the delight of watching the changing pattern and flickering colours of the Aurora Borealis against a sprinkling of stars in the isolated darkness of the aircraft's cabin; or the daytime passage over a small bay of shallow water teeming with the rippling silver of countless fish.

Pleasures of life on the ground were more prosaic. The Squadron had been allocated a section of the airfield nearest the sea, and the Mess was situated at the head of a tiny inlet, giving ready access to a rocky foreshore where one might sit, but certainly not bask, in comfort during off-duty summer afternoons. The town of Reykjavik was beyond the far side, and a rough asphalt road led to it through a grey-green open space. Walking across after the evening-meal, in the slowly fading twilight, the lights of houses appeared one by one like stars in the arc above, but in the streets they were lost in the wide beams of floodlights shining on trenches excavated along the side. Huge pipes were being welded and lain as part of a system throughout the town for providing domestic hot water from the hot springs to be found in many parts of the island. The intention was to extend this perpetual gift of nature to commercial use also, particularly in horticulture. We were told that the enterprise was contracted to a German firm, which made even more certain the supposition that, Iceland having retained neutral status, the enemy was aware of the military units on the island, including numbers and types of aircraft, Squadrons, and the routine of operations.

Whether they knew that the Squadron had acquired a Sports Officer is unlikely to be told. The gentle advent of summer inevitably led to a stretching of muscles which had been over-cocooned in winter, whilst simultaneously there emerged a hierarchical desire to appoint junior officers to posts of minor responsibility. If the intention was to help alleviate off-duty boredom in out-of-the-way places, it succeeded. Having a premonition that this was about to occur, I volunteered as Sports Officer, preferring to stretch my legs rather than my mind – or my patience!

Over a period of a week or two I arranged a number of activities which met with a good – even hearty – response. We then organised a soccer match between two nebulous sides which somehow managed to exhibit amazing enthusiasm. A pitch had been laid out on a patch of reasonably level ground and the surface was typical of the area – black lava soil with several indentations and little grass. The supporters, though few, were vociferous, and their exhortations to 'get it in the net' made more sense than those passing between the players on the pitch. At last we appeared to have a chance to follow the supporters' instructions when I received the ball with a clear run towards the opposing goal. A defender came across and I went past him on the outside. From the left wing I prepared to cross the ball to the centre, but as my left foot sent it on its way, my right knee felt painfully detached and I collapsed to the ground amid cheers: the ball had been put in the net as I was put out of action. The necessary swivel of my right leg had only partially been achieved because my right foot had been held in a shallow hole of a size which made a perfect clamp, whilst my body above the knee rotated. My embarrassing removal to hospital was followed by the news that my side had won. "They really put their backs into it after you left!" Player-managers take note of how Sports Officers achieve their objectives!

The large spongey swelling around the knee was aspirated the next day, and the next day, and the treatment was ameliorated by the attentions of a pretty nurse, who, in the course of conversations more concerned with meditation than medication, confided that she enjoyed ballroom dancing. As such pleasures were not included in the sparse programme of Mess activities, she accepted my offer to escort her to whatever substitute the town had to offer, as soon as I was mobile again. This caused some surprise in my frequent requests for electrotherapy, to avoid wastage of the knee-muscles, an amusing process causing regular involuntary spasms of the thigh. Such treatment, together with the determination I showed in frequent hobbling across the room when I was able to hold on to the nurse for support, led to a rapid recovery. The M.O. warned against a hasty return to athletic pursuits, and I became a restrained sports person, for which most members of the Squadron heaved a sigh of relief.

At the first opportunity when we were both off-duty, I accompanied the nurse into Reykjavik in an attempt to find a place to dance. My supposition that this would not be easy was confirmed – let joy be unconfined was not the motto of the capital at that time – but we found a barn-looking cafe which played recorded dance-music through a hidden source. Fortunately the quality of the music was better than the quality of the establishment and the food it offered, which encouraged us to make the most of the dance floor. This was also the intention of most of the other patrons, so that we could hardly move; thus were the limitations of my ballroom-dancing technique saved from exposure, but I put the maximum effort into the minimum movement permitted, and enjoyed a close relationship. She was posted before it could be enhanced, and I haven't needed to suffer a really bad knee since.

During most of the 1943 summer the weather in the low levels in which we operated was varied but never hazardous; the escorts and patrols continued in unending sequence, and there was a general yearning for them to be enlivened by a little sharp action. That, however, seemed to be happening at the other end of the spectrum down in the Bay of Biscay. In July, out of 115 U-boats sighted in the Atlantic area, 88 were in transit through the Bay. We had only one sighting and sinking in 'our water' throughout the period, the consolation being that it probably indicated a delayed build-up of the new U-boats which would have to traverse our area when moving to join the Atlantic battle. We became quite vicious in our treatment of any pieces of flotsam large enough to invite a practice attack and imaginary dropping of depth-charges – always on target; the rear-gunner was well-trained! – and occasionally we caused startled dives among the seal fraternity. In one instance, Jackie was using the half-submerged remains of a dinghy as a target for turret-firing practise when from a different angle it seemed it might be occupied, but on closer inspection it was nothing more than some navy blue material resembling human shape, floating on the water. With two cockneys in the crew, life aloft was seldom dull.

"Let's go down and count the bullet-holes!" one 'J' would request after firing. "Forty five!" might well be the figurative conclusion.

"You only b***** well fired 35 of the ruddy-things!" the other would reply. I merely expressed amazement at their high sensitivity in the matter of seeing and hearing.

On a bright midsummer day I was detailed to take a Hudson which 'had only got one-and-a-half engines' down to U.K. for overhaul, and the fact that we would carry passengers going on leave was of little concern as I had complete faith in the aircraft's single-engine flying capability. However, a request from the Navy for a Naval Officer with a broken neck to be taken to a U.K. hospital caused some misgiving, as a single-engine landing was likely to be less than perfect, and a sudden jolt would certainly not improve his condition. Whilst we were preparing for departure a message came through cancelling the arrangement, to my relief, whether because of improvement or deterioration in the officer's condition, I knew not.

For my return to Iceland I was instructed to collect an Anson aircraft and fly it there in three stages, so that it could be used for communication duties throughout the island. Before I could depart for Iceland, I had to collect items needed for minor modifications which would be carried out at Wick, and it was agreed that on my journey to Maintenance Units in England, I would take various passengers on leave. It was a pleasant change crossing the summer-hued landscape of home after the barren areas over which I had recently flown. After half-a-dozen take-offs and landings, some involving much taxying, I was finally airborne for the return journey to Wick in the early evening, and crossed the mountains of Scotland whilst shadows began to creep along the rocky crags as I looked towards the setting sun.

It was ten o'clock by the time I arrived, and the runway lights were already on in the half-light which enhances pale outline but diminishes detail, and I taxied carefully along the perimeter track, as the lead-in lights were not yet showing. As I passed the Control Tower towards the hangars, with my hand on the brake-lever below the throttle-quadrant, I could feel that the air pressure which operated the brakes was insufficient unless the lever was almost at the top of its travel. I now became very much aware of one of the deficiencies of the Anson aircraft, which I knew about but which had not previously caused any concern: the fact that the air bottle from which the brakes were pneumatically operated (as the Pilot's Notes explain) "has to be inflated by external means as there is no engine-driven compressor". In other prophetic words, one couldn't replace what one had used. Yet a glance at the gauge down to my left showed the needle registering a quarter full. Perhaps I should have been a pessimist, and thought of it as three-quarters empty!

As I turned towards the hangars, the dim figure of a guiding airman appeared in the gloom, and after moving a few yards in his direction, he waved his arm vigorously towards the hangar on my right. The doors were open and the lights inside shone out powerfully so that the figure in front of me was nothing more than a silhouette. It was obvious that this was the hangar where the modifications were to be done.

"Poor chap!" I thought, "waiting for me to turn up at this time of night. I'll get as far as I dare, so that it'll be easier to put the Anson in".

With engines hardly ticking over and with the brake lever now at the top of its travel giving faint, but so far just adequate, pressure on the brakes, the aircraft slowly approached the hangar. Then the snail's pace gradually started to increase, so I immediately cut the engines, and again applied fully what remained of the brake pressure, but this time there was no response. I had a desperate look at the gauge – still the same – then realised that, although still moving very slowly, the pace was inexorably increasing, and it suddenly occurred to me that there was a slight slope from taxi-track to hangar which had been indiscernible in the twilight against the blinding flood of light from the hangar.

As the Anson's remorseless trundling continued, I could see that a space had been prepared beyond the open doorway for the aircraft's reception, which had hardly been expected in this particular way! Further inside, various aircraft were parked in tight formation, and by now the shepherding airman had become an amazed bystander as the inevitable drama unfolded.

Throughout what seemed an age I tried to think how I might help those determined wheels to stop revolving, first putting the flap lever in the down position in the forlorn hope that they might be lowered by rapid use of the hand pump in time to cause additional drag. Meanwhile I was holding the control column as far back as possible in an attempt to add still more.

By this time, however, although now on level ground, the beast had been given enough impetus to show a smooth-running accomplishment, so I sat completely immobilised with both hands pressing the wheel against my stomach, awaiting the inevitable. For a moment I was filled with hope as we moved so slowly that I felt a hand against the nose would be sufficient to stop the rolling, and I half-expected the airman to do the obvious and grab the tailplane, but he was dumbfoundedly statuesque. I wondered whether I should dash down to the door, fling it open and jump out or drag my foot to provide the necessary brake. No time! And thus, gently but full of purpose, the gremlins completed their task – I knew they were behind the aircraft, straining their wiry little bodies to complete our apocalypse!

The Anson met the next aeroplane with a quite subdued collapse of wood and canvas, and the receiving aircraft passed an even more subdued rendering on to the next. Compared with the horrendous images which flashed through my mind during the traumatic aeon of time in which we moved ever inwards, the damage was minimal. There followed the customary reporting of the incident to the Duty Officer, investigation, and Court of Inquiry, all procedures which made no allowance for the possibility of a faulty gauge, a leaking or incompletely-filled air bottle, and the effect of the slope: all, I had to agree, excuses rather than reasons for stupid airmanship.

There was no excuse for taxying so close to the hangar under the circumstances, and I was therefore reprimanded. That was nothing more than I expected or deserved, but I was annoyed at the offhand remark of one of the officers that this "blotting of my copybook" would affect "past good deeds". I thought the punishment in itself adequately fitted the crime.

By the time the inquiry came to its conclusion, the aircraft had been repaired and the modifications fitted, and I was ready to take it to its strange new habitat, being, so far as I knew, the first Anson to visit the frozen wastes. No further risks were to be taken with this aircraft! It had by then been stressed more than once that it was intended for use by the hierarchy, so I agreed to a three-stage journey: Faeroe Islands to refuel, and at Hofn on the east coast of Iceland if necessary, then across to Reykjavik. I was given a map of the Faeroes, with the additional information that the population was about 42,000, but as I didn't expect a welcoming party of quite that size, it seemed irrelevant. No alcohol was allowed on the islands; staying overnight was out, however strong the invitation!

On a bright day, the flight was uneventful, but the refuelling stop certainly added to the interest. This was on the small landing strip on the island of Vaago, the most westerly island of the group. They had been surveyed in the early years of the war in a search for a flying-boat or seaplane base, and for a landplane airstrip. The Sorvags Vatn lake which met the sea over a 90ft high waterfall at its southerly end was mentioned as a possible site, with a likely strip on the left of the lake, length 253 metres, or on the right almost 400. It was this one, extended a little perhaps but not by much, which I approached very low over the waterfall. With a surprising length of airstrip to spare – it was another 'land-up, take-off down' runway – I looked for the usual arm-waving airman and taxied towards him.

I could not say whether he had left a kettle about to boil, but in a time reminiscent of a pit-stop refuel, he had emptied half-a-dozen large square cans of petrol into the tanks, obtained my signature for it, given me the thumbs up, and disappeared into the flimsy hut which presumably served as watchtower, orderly room, workshop, and dormitory. I taxied up to the head of the airstrip, turned and carried out the pre-take-off check. It was an unusual sight to see the land ahead end in a rocky ledge beyond which was the open sea, with the narrow end of the lake disappearing over the right-hand shoulder of rock.

Applying power against the brake, the Anson was airborne in a matter of yards, and I was high enough to turn to starboard over the waterfall as I climbed away, one of very few people, I thought, able to look vertically down through the spray to the seething cauldron below. Much to be preferred to going over the edge in a barrel!

The landing-strip at Hofn, on the southeast coast of Iceland, was on a spit of land which tidal currents had thrown up to almost enclose Hofnafjord from the sea. Approaching it at 2,000 feet I could see the white back drop of the Vatnajokull ice-cap ahead, one of the largest glaciers in Europe, which occupied about one-twelfth of the land mass of the country, creating its own unpredictable weather, even in summer. In the higher parts it reaches well over 5,000 feet. I descended to 500 feet to take a closer look at the airstrip, and was amazed at the grandeur of the Hornafjord lake, where grounded masses of ice appeared as large as mini-glaciers, and vied with sheer rock faces reflected in the clear water. Welcomed by a solitary wind-sock, which fortunately indicated a wind in the general but fluctuating direction down the landing-strip, I turned towards the petrol-bowser after landing, and looked for a repeat of the performance given at Vaago. No such luck, but, I thought, who is to criticise the keepers of lonely outposts? The village of Hofn was across the other side of the fjord, if he should feel the effort of getting there socially worthwhile. His tardy appearance might well have been due to a restless night in a storm-tossed hut and a failed alarm clock! If so, he made a remarkable recovery as he suddenly appeared, and with a cheery wave and broad grin he beckoned me closer.

"Oh, I don't mind it here, though I haven't had a winter here yet! It's peaceful!" he replied to my question.

"Boring?" I asked.

"Takes all sorts! I'm no battling Briton, and I'd rather be bored than spend the rest of my life dead!" he added with the kind of smile which justified the statement.

It occurred to me that the personnel section had selected well for this particular posting.

With a notable lack of urgency, the refuelling was completed, and I prepared for take-off along the rough strip. As speed increased and the wheels reacted to the frequent undulations, it was rather difficult to avoid a premature departure from the ground, but give-and-take use of the control-column got us safely airborne, and I headed down the coast. Rather than risk an increase in the cloud which drifted across the top of the Vatnajokull ice-cap, I intended to round the 6,952ft peak of Hvannadalshnukur at the southern edge, then fly direct from there to Reykjavik.

If Hekla, at 4,892ft, and the surrounding area was visible as I approached, I could continue direct, otherwise I would turn out to sea and fly round the coast. The mountain duly appeared as a lava-streaked carbuncle, rising from the serried lines of lava-fields to the west, whilst beyond it were the billowy puffs of water vapour which were erupting from the hot springs below. After a nostalgic flight across the area where our previous base of Kaldadarnes once stood, the faithful Anson had the satisfaction of an excellent landing at Reykjavik. We then parted company, and I never had the pleasure of seeing her again.

Next day, it was back to the old routine, interspersed with giving instruction to pilots experienced on other aircraft, and who were joining this or other Hudson units in a senior capacity. Now we were looking for U-boats which positively refused to appear in this part of the Ocean. At least, during the long summer days! When flying at night, during the brief five hours when semi-darkness prevailed and the only visual indication of a vessel on the surface might be its long white wake – and then only in rare calm waters – we had to rely on the A.S.V. radar for contacts. The possibility that this might lead to a target was slight, since U-boats had been equipped with counter-measures which detected the aircraft radar, giving sufficient warning for them to dive out of harm's way. The new A.S.V. equipment and the Leigh Lights to illuminate the targets were, understandably, not for our obsolescent Hudsons but for the new V.L.R. machines which were ultimately to win the Battle of the Atlantic.

For these reasons I had no regrets about leaving the Squadron when I became 'time-expired' at the end of my year in Iceland. The friendships and enthusiasm of the period before Greenland's debacle had not resumed afterwards, and apart from the wrench of leaving the dependable Pug and the two Jackies, parting was less than 'sweet sorrow'. Neither was joy unconfined when the posting came through, requiring me after leave to report to No.5 Coastal Operational Training Unit at Long Kesh in Northern Ireland.

I was fortunate in being able again to take a Hudson to U.K., and the wind direction determined that I should use a runway which took the aircraft over Reykjavik. With the increased acuity which comes with a parting observation, I looked down at this northernmost capital of any nation, a well-ordered city the size of an English County Town, where the inventive use of thermal springs had created a clean-air environment, so that the gaily-painted roofs of the houses made a corrugated patchwork below, glowing in the clear morning sunshine. It sat as if in the palm of a giant hand with fingers of sparkling blue water reaching out to the sea.

But in winter? .... Perhaps Northern Ireland would be better.

CHAPTER 14

CAUGHT IN THE ACT!

There was little sign of a better winter to come when I crossed by ferry from Stranraer to Larne on a dull October day, surprised at the swell in the North Channel which treated the ship like a cork. There was a delay before disembarking, caused by what appeared to be, in my innocence of the hidden circumstances in the province, an abnormal scrutiny of passengers. Could these officials be looking for enemy agents? One man was asked to accompany an official through a door marked 'N.I.Constabulary', but if he was German he had taken remarkable trouble to speak with an Irish accent.

The train into Belfast was crowded, and the compartment in which I joined two Army officers and another Flying Officer was soon filled with local people, most of whom appeared to be returning from visits to relatives in England and Scotland, making the main topic of conversation a comparison between conditions 'across the Channel' and those at home. The consensus of opinion was that things were slightly better 'on this side of the water', with enthusiastic assent when a woman who had been to East Anglia told of the "hundreds of big aeroplanes bombing Germany." My own satisfaction came when my colleague told me that he was one of the pilots operating Long-range Liberators from the airfields in the northwest of the province, and they were meeting others from Iceland and the far side of 'the pond'. The Greenland Gap was at last being closed.

After a heartening account of the success they were having, we parted in Belfast, he to join the train to Londonderry, I to go south to Lisburn. Long Kesh was a perfect example of the type of airfield planned when German bombs had exposed the serious disadvantages of a compact grouping of buildings on a convenient side of an airfield. The traditional 1930's pattern was for a group of three large hangars in line by the perimeter track, backed by the administrative block and the three Messes, with married quarters not far away. If a bomb missed one building it was likely to hit another. The Long Kesh type was at the other extreme; even the different sections of administration were physically separated, the Officers', Sergeants', and Airmen's Messes apart beyond bomb-blast range, hard-standings for aircraft at various points hundreds of yards from the runways, and hutted dormitories at distances from the respective Messes and offices which meant cycling was preferred to walking. Bicycles were issued to all ranks, and those unable to ride a bike quickly took the trouble to learn.

The Officers' Mess was a "structure, wooden demountable, large, officers for the use of", as were all the other buildings for their different uses, apart from the corrugated-iron covered hangars and aircraft dispersal shelters. The airfield had been sited in undulating pastoral countryside, with a network of truncated lanes abutting the boundary. One of the first discussions I had with an ex-269 colleague was on the need for such a dispersed Unit so far removed, at this stage of the war, from the firing-line. Our first conclusion was that a blueprint perhaps prepared during the bombings of 1940 would take more than a year to become reality on the ground and was a prudent analysis of need at the time. Then I remembered a remark made in 1940 by Paddy, a pilot I had known whilst serving with 220 Squadron. His home was in Ulster, and his prophetic words in discussing the film "The Informer" were "The Troubles aren't over yet!" Perhaps dispersal was a sound stratagem: the fact that we were ordered never to violate the air space beyond the Six Counties emphasised an uneasy neutrality. Again I was reminded of how the tragedies of our losses at sea could have been mitigated, this time by the difference it would have made if the west coast of Ireland had been available for use as air bases for anti-U-boat squadrons.

The aircraft I was to train pilots to fly was the Ventura, made by the American Lockheed Company which produced the Hudson, and mainly used in Coastal Command for Meteorological flights. It was an enlarged version of the Hudson, with two powerful Pratt and Whitney Twin Wasp engines with two-stage 'blowers', a similar arrangement of controls and instruments, equally adequate de-icing, and a roomy cabin entirely suitable for packing with the equipment needed for meteorological readings. For all that, after the hundreds of hours I had spent piloting Hudsons with such confidence that to me they were very flexible aeroplanes (remembering mock 'dog-fights' I occasionally had with USAAF 'Lightnings' in Iceland), the Ventura gave nothing like the same enjoyment. It seemed to be more difficult to instil the necessary confidence into the trainee pilots; it was generally agreed that the atmosphere of a station pervades the personnel and the tasks they undertake, and Long Kesh was a depressing place at this time of year.

The weather interfered with much of the scheduled flying, as part of the training programme consisted of climbing in a prescribed way to permit a Met Observer to take instrument readings up to a height of 10,000 feet, and the minimal descent and landing conditions required upon return were seldom achieved in the month of November. When day after day was unfit and the pleasures and comradeship of a Squadron Mess were noticeable by their absence, and when transport to and from Belfast involved a lucky hitch to the nearest railway station and a probable walk back from it, the journey was seldom made. I spent many hours in my room in the little group of dispersed huts, reading and drawing.

I found that frustration floated free when I was running along the lanes and paths bordering the airfield, and one dark night I jogged along to the Mess and waved a hand at some vague figure at the door as I passed by. Then I took the path past the sentry post at a side entrance, and out on to the lane. After I had gone about fifty yards, I heard a distant pad-pad, pad-pad behind me, fluctuating in volume, now almost too faint to hear, then increasing. A few yards more, then silence.

Soon I was on my way back, and as I approached the spot where the footsteps had ceased, I could dimly see two figures sitting on a low wall by the side of the lane. One was the portly Engineer Officer mopping his brow, the other his Flight Sergeant. Between great gulps of air, the former explained that they had arranged to run together, the Flight Sergeant having promised a reasonably slow pace, and that when I waved as I passed the Mess door he assumed that I was his pacemaker. My reconstruction from the garbled account I heard, was that the Engineer Officer followed me, and as the Flight Sergeant appeared just in time to see the E.O. set off with obvious determination, he thought it might be unwise to impose his own idea of pace on his master, so he trotted along behind. When I had stopped, apparently for a breather, the E.O. was desperate for one also, and when the pace dropped further along the lane, amid the snorts of his efforts the E.O. became aware of a steady tread behind, and, thinking there must be a third jogger vying with him, he tried to find the energy for a spurt, but failed, and stopped. Along came Flighty, full of congratulations for the valiant effort made by his superior in his assumed role of pacemaker, but it took a couple of minutes for the grimace of pain to give way to unholy mutterings! We walked back to the Mess and I stood him a well-deserved pint.

Two types of flight were common during the prolonged period of bad weather when the clouds hung low: the everlasting circuits with landings ordinaire, landings precautionary, landings full flap (in all senses!), or landings 'go-round-again'; and occasional flights taking aircraft to the mainland for overhaul, or bodies on official business, perhaps staying overnight at a 'live' station if the weather could by any stretch of the imagination be termed doubtful or worse. I had managed two or three of these when, on a day to be remembered, such a flight had been allocated to another pilot. It was Security Exercise Day!

Everyone on the station, except those with vital functions such as cooks, had orders to take part, either as Defenders or Infiltrators. (Some said there should be three "i's" in that word!). Their aim was to cause 'damage' to vital parts – but not to the cookhouse, nor yet to human bodies – by placing 'home-made bombs' in or on suitable buildings, machines or aircraft. Success in achieving such a mission without being apprehended by the patrolling Defenders was to be shown by placing a chalked cross on the item concerned. I was surprised that during a briefing which exhorted the Infiltrators to think of and practise every kind of ruse and dirty deed, the briefing officer didn't mention that a concerted attack on all the bicycles would be the surest way of bringing the station to a standstill! Merely to let down all those tyres would enliven the proceedings, but we were reminded that the type of target was strictly allocated to avoid duplication. One budding secret agent asked if this was a dry run, could we do the job properly if there was nothing more interesting to do and the camp reverted to its usual state of boredom.

Presumably we had spies in the Defenders' briefing room, because we were told that they would be organised in three sections: an outer patrol round the boundary of the airfield, a roving patrol inside, and patrols near certain vital areas such as hangars. We climbed into the back of a Bedford 3-tonner, meandered around the lanes in the vicinity to try to confound the Defenders, and had the chap with the map desperately looking for a landmark. Then the driver began a series of stops and starts, and when this was queried he replied, with all the wisdom of past experience, that such manoeuvres would fox the Defenders because they could probably just see the top of the lorry and they would think that the stops were in fact 'drops'!

When we reached the area of the real 'drops', another instructor, Tony, and I were the third pair to leave the lorry. We felt very exposed in the middle of the road, two figures in dungarees looking lost, whilst the remaining Infiltrators shouted as the lorry drove away "Hey! You've forgotten your bucket and chammy leather!"

We crouched low as we ran along behind the hedge, occasionally popping up for a quick scan, feeling and looking like villains in an amateur melodrama. The hedge then became post-and-rail fencing, our cover was gone, and from this point it was obviously necessary to move in towards the airfield. We surveyed the scene from the end of the hedge. The first obstacle was a deep ditch, with open space beyond which was being patrolled by two Defenders who met, then turned about and marched away from each other. It might be possible, we thought, to slip across whilst they were looking away, but another quick look showed the idea to be impracticable when we saw two other Defenders moving towards the original two, facing the gap through which we had intended to make a dash. This seemed to be stalemate, so Tony and I decided to separate and act independently, on the assumption that two singles stood a better chance than one double.

Timing my run when the two Defenders met and lingered for a chat, I dropped into the ditch and managed to straddle it with a foot on each side. Although a deep cutting, it didn't give quite the cover I had hoped for, and I could only move forward slowly in a crouching position. This was very tiring, and I was considering which of two options would be preferable – to climb out, or to wade through the muddy water – when I saw that, at a T-junction, the ditch was joined by another which ran beside a disused farm building.

On reaching the junction, I discovered it was more of a trench than a ditch, lacking a foothold, but fortunately the water was only inches deep. My hopes of soon reaching a resting place in the old building were dashed when a quick look over the top revealed a Defender coming my way, and I considered it likely that his area of search included the ditch. I scampered through the water as best I could towards the building, hoping that the guard would ignore the stirred-up mud which darkened the water, and when I reached it I could see that an old farm track crossed the ditch over a large pipe. If I could avoid being seen behind the building, I could dash to the far side of the track when the Defender moved away on his return patrol.

It became obvious, however, that this particular airman was of the bulldog breed, and from my spy-hole in the dilapidated wall, I watched him look into the ditch, then move towards the building. By now having entered fully into this splendid sport, with a determination to play the Scarlet Pimpernel which surprised me, I decided the tunnelled pipe was wide enough to take me. Retaining a modicum of common-sense and propriety, I had no intention of traversing the whole length of the tunnel, so I went in feet first, pushing myself out of sight, then drawing in my arms to support my head out of the water. I heard the crunch of cycle tyres on the gravel overhead, then a moment's silence before the muffled sound of voices, and I assumed that the cyclist was a supervising corporal seeking a report from the Defender. After a few minutes of wondering how intensive their search of immediate surroundings might be, the voices faded, which I hoped was an indication that they were moving in the direction of the perimeter track.

Now or never! I dragged my numbed body out of the pipe, then scampered across the track to the ditch on the far side and slid into it. As I plodded along I could see the banks were getting lower and I looked desperately for cover. I was approaching a point opposite the half-open doorway of a hangar, where airmen were working, presumably on some vital task which excused their participation in this charade. The cyclist had gone, and the Defender was still marching away from the ditch and being approached by his link-man. Whilst I watched, fate was on my side, for they stopped to have a brief chat and gave every indication of sharing a cigarette.

I leapt out of the ditch and was across the intervening space to the hangar as quickly as any other rabbit. Inside there were several other dungareed figures, and I casually passed among them, causing one or two quizzical glances at my damp condition, to which I replied with a grimace which I hope suggested I had been unfortunate in a washing-down task. Lady Luck stayed with me until I was half-way through the hangar, when I saw a Defender in the doorway at the far end, the end to which I was moving. I tried to merge with the other airmen, and picked up an engine-cowling as though I knew what I was going to do with it. This was almost my undoing, as a corporal was just coming for the very piece I had picked up. He gave me a suspicious look, I thrust the item at him, and dashed through the door into the office at the side of the hangar from which he had appeared. There was a startled yell as I went out on to the perimeter track beyond, and as I stood for an instant looking left and right for signs of the 'enemy', I saw a group of eight aircraft in front of the next hangar. This was it – a final dash!

As I reached the first one, I heard a call from the airman standing sentry at the end of the hangar, and an answering yell from behind me. I managed to place white chalk marks on six of the aircraft before I was threatened with retribution from the spout of a rifle, though whether I could have planted six bombs in the same time was a moot point which didn't concern me. I had been caught in the act, but not quite quickly enough!

After a shower and clean-up, we had a merry old time in the Mess recounting the 'damage' we had done. Whatever the organisation, group, force, or clandestine army which was seen by higher authority as possible intruders, it had given me the best day I was to spend on the station.

There was a serious side to it. We heard later of the consequences of actual intrusion in 1942. A Spitfire of 152 Squadron, flying near Londonderry, suffered an explosion which blew off the elevators. After baling out, the pilot reported that he had not been shot down, and it was found that the aircraft had been sabotaged.

Only three flights that December were interesting beyond the routine of instruction. The first was an opportunity to pilot a Bristol Beaufort torpedo bomber. Being tall, I felt the cockpit canopy was resting on my head, and I missed the comfort and space which, from my experience of Hudsons and Venturas, and examining Bostons, B 26's etc in Greenland, seemed to be an integral part of the design of American aircraft. British designs of the period seemed to suffer from so many afterthoughts – instruments or minor controls – and it was some time before British-built aircraft achieved the internal symmetry befitting their superior external characteristics. The five or six-hour flights across the North Sea which we used to make in Hudsons must have been very much more comfortable for the crew than the comparable flights made by the Beauforts.

It was an entirely different and delightful experience to be able to make a short flight in a Mew Gull when a friend from Rissington days, then in Ferry Command, arrived with some V.I.P. If ever an aircraft of that era was created as the epitome of comfort, control, convenience and cost-effectiveness, this was it! It contradicted my feelings about British interiors!

A less enjoyable experience was in a Ventura which developed a fault in the port engine shortly after take-off at a height of 800 feet with a cloud base not much higher. The undercarriage was up, we had reached a safe speed, and as a quick check of switches, dials, and fuel tank selectors showed no apparent cause, I closed the throttle and feathered the propeller to reduce drag. As there was a cross-wind from starboard, which would widen the circuit if I turned to port as usual, I decided to make a righthand circuit instead. A quick winding of the rudder-trim handle countered the yawing effect; I then closed the cowl flaps on the failed engine, and turned off the petrol supply to it.

It was on the cross-wind leg on the down-wind side of the runway that I suddenly noticed another Ventura approaching in a similar way from a left-hand circuit. I remembered that a trainee pilot was on the detail for a solo circuit and landing, and if this was the chap, in the poor visibility most of his concentration might well be on his approach to the runway. I had lowered the undercarriage, and intended to make the final approach at a steeper angle of descent than would be normal using both engines, as it was advisable to 'have height in hand' on a single-engined approach, since it was easier to lose height than to gain it if the angle of descent had been misjudged. This meant that as the other pilot was looking down and my path would take me above him as we both moved towards the point of turning in to the runway, it was my last chance to attract his attention. He could abort his present approach and climb to make another circuit much more easily than I could.

I flicked on all the light switches I could put my fingers on – landing lights, navigation lights, identification light, even interior lights, and, thankfully, a wobble of the other Ventura's wings showed that the pilot had been startled and alerted. In an exemplary demonstration of 'going round again', he put on power, upped his wheels, and climbed away. I steadied on the approach, put down flap, came in on a steep half-glide, and landed. I waited for the pupil pilot to land, gave him a brief reminder of the need to use both eyes – "one here, one there, and the other...." and congratulated him on his performance thereafter.

Apart from the traditional bonhomie between ranks, and the opportunity to pay tribute without embarrassment which festive cheer encourages, Christmas celebrations on the station gave little joy, and New Year's Eve 1943 even less.

Inevitably, as had somehow become my custom, my thoughts were with those I had known who would not be with us to enter 1944 with the hope which was beginning to overcome the war weariness. Especially, I thought of Johnnie and Harry, their crews and their people, and the pervading uncertainty surrounding their loss.

Though lacking interesting activity in the air around Long Kesh, the early weeks of the New Year provided it in other ways. Since returning from Iceland my romantic inclinations had been with a girl who was a student at a Physical Training College in the Midlands. I had managed to save enough of the petrol coupons available to operational aircrew to drive down there whilst on home leave, and I booked into the Beechwood Hotel nearby. She was domiciled in a large house, detached at some distance from the main block, and when we met at the end of the day's lectures, mindful of the fact that 'our young ladies require an official pass to leave the premises other than on off-days', she brought an illicit invitation from her house friends to visit their Common Room.

Although they dined in the main building, they had facilities to boil an egg and make a cup of cocoa, and I was promised clandestine scrambled egg and baked beans on toast – and cocoa. Who could refuse? The service was excellent, apart from the lack of tables, the company embarrassingly thoughtful and charming, the fare excited the appetite, and the whole made the evening too short. It was an unexpected and excellent way to celebrate my birthday!

Arriving to take my leave at 8.45 the next morning, prior to the young ladies departing for the Morning Service held fifteen minutes later, I was persuaded to wait in the room she shared with her friend, so that, after she returned from the Service, she and I could spend half-an-hour together before her first lecture. A few minutes after they left to walk along the drive to the Hall, I was subjected to an increasingly persistent call of nature. Could I resist it for the time it would take to walk, or even run, back to the hotel? Even if I could, I would be unable to return before she arrived back from the assembly, and she wasn't the kind of girl to suffer the indignity of an unannounced departure, in her room in silence. More likely she would go straight to the gym to work off her feelings.

I knew there was a toilet along the passage, on the landing at the top of the stairs, but on my previous visit to it I had only used it for a lesser need than the one which was now filling my consciousness. I hurried along to it, bolted the door, and found blessed relief. I felt obliged to flush the toilet, as there was undoubted evidence that a healthy young male had been there.

Just as the sound of a cascade of water filled the pungent air, the slamming of a door downstairs warned of another intruder, quite possibly a member of staff.

Footsteps along the downstairs passage were followed by more on the stairs. With a hand on the bolt of the toilet door, the briefest of pauses was sufficient for me to realise I had to choose one of a possible two courses of action. I could open the door as quietly as the squeak would allow and hope to flee across the landing to some safer haven before the intruder reached the turn at the top of the stairs. I couldn't emerge and rush down past him or her on the stairs because I had left my uniform jacket in the room. Perhaps I should stay, momentarily secure in my lair, hopeful that the unknown person was hard of hearing. But if the sound of the flushing, rushing water had aroused suspicions, would not the ensuing conversation go something like this, I wondered:

"Who is in there?" (Mature lady's voice; rattling of door handle).

No reply.

"I know you're in there! Who is it?" (More rattling).

No reply.

"Are you feeling ill?" (A little more sympathetically).

Still no reply.

"Is it er a young lady's problem?" (More sympathy).

"M'mm?" (Very faint reply).

"Why aren't you at morning service?" (Demanding).

By this time, it would obviously be necessary to try to imitate one of the young ladies I had met, and with a little luck the response might be:

"Oh, it's you, Penelope!"

"Yes, m'm"

"Now open this door!" (Patience exhausted).

"Please fetch the matron." (Suggesting distress).

Then, whilst the enquiring lady was responding to my request for the matron, I would hear her descending the stairs, collect my jacket, leave a hurried explanatory note in some hidden corner, and exit to freedom. Would the situation resolve itself so conveniently? Unlikely; but one option remained.

Dreams are said to be brief, but this fantasy was more so, and my hand was still on the bolt. I drew it back, opened the door as silently as I could, and fled in tiptoed steps along the corridor to the door opposite. Inside the room, I picked up my jacket, dashed to the window and had my hand on the catch, but there was no means of escape, no tree, no drainpipe. And no available space under the bed. The wardrobe! It was a sturdy utilitarian type, with a large door and an easy latch. I was inside and behind the hanging clothes as if primed by a magician, but had my disappearing act served any purpose other than merely to delay the inevitable? I heard the rattle of the room door handle, then silence, followed by the sound of a few hesitant paces across the room, then another silence. The process of elimination would take no more than a few seconds – window, closed; bed, too low; chest of drawers, small table, chair? Conclusion – wardrobe! I heard an apprehensive but demanding "Who is it?" and the wardrobe door opened a couple of inches. Between the lines of clothes, I saw one eye and half a stern face, then the door opened fully and the hanging clothes parted.

We looked at each other for a second or two – an RAF officer suffering deserved humiliation for having fled from an enemy patrol, and an avowed custodian of integrity, perhaps torn between generosity and duty, assessing whether the result of this particular reconnaissance was worthy of a report to higher authority.

"You will come with me!" she said, and I knew that in her eyes I was one of those airmen who painted lascivious bathing belles on the nose of his aircraft. As I walked behind her along the path to the main building I hoped that my meek acquiescence would be a point in my favour when I came face to face with Authority. After all, it was the decent thing to do; had I forcibly ignored any objections to my leaving the scene of the crime, the plight of the young lady in question would have been much worse.

No such generosity was forthcoming and my plea of innocent intent was received with frosty amusement. Had there been a firing squad in attendance, or even a hockey team with sticks at the ready, I had a feeling they would have been called for duty. Thankfully the inquisition was brief, accompanied by disdain on the one hand and relief on the other, and I was escorted to the road. With not a word, my chaperone simply turned on her heel and began to walk back along the drive. I watched with a growing sense of disbelief in the events of the last twelve hours, and in due course the retribution suffered by the young lady suggested a fear that the world outside the College gates was beginning to intrude. How fortunate, I thought, for the young ladies of the W.A.A.F. – and for us! – that they do not have to live under a similar regime.

Two days later, I was again a passenger on the Stranraer to Larne ferry, and returned to find Long Kesh in lethargic mood. There was evidence that we were producing more Ventura pilots than were needed, and after a few more days adding to the apparent surplus, I was called to the Adjutant to be told that I was to be posted to RAF Leuchars in Scotland. There had been rumours that Leuchars was, or was to be, a base for aircraft flying shipping strikes, so perhaps my request for such a posting had been heeded at last! The Adjutant could tell me no more; the detail of the posting would presumably be revealed on arrival.

An aircraft was due to go for overhaul to the M.U. at Edzell in two days' time, so I claimed the right to fly it across, then made a leisurely tour of Long K, taking pleasure in the routine of leaving, handing in equipment, getting clearance forms signed, paying Mess bills, and bidding farewell to those whose company I had found congenial.

From the Edzell motor pool I hitched a lift into Aberdeen with a Scottish WAAF driver who gave a continuous commentary in what seemed to be a foreign tongue, although she pronounced precisely the time of the next train south, then gave a hair-raising demonstration of high-speed driving to make sure I caught it. Travelling south through Montrose, Arbroath, the Tay Bridge, was reminiscent of the coastline panorama seen from the air in 1941, and I found myself passing the time by looking for familiar landmarks. It was early evening when I left the train at a desolate and windswept Leuchars station, but good fortune was again on hand when a Bedford pick-up arrived for a group of airman due to arrive on the 'down' train.

After breakfast next morning, I hurried across to the Station Adjutant's Office hoping to confirm my optimism, which had already suffered some disillusionment because I saw little evidence of strike squadrons on the station. They were mostly detached, he said, and I was in fact posted as an instructor to No 1510 B.A.B.S. Flight.

"BABS?" I asked.

"Blind Approach Beam System," he replied, "Ansons"

Rather disconsolate at reverting to the 'plane on which I had been taught to fly twin-engined aircraft, I sought to justify the posting as a penalty for one of my misdemeanours, but then pride took a hand and I remembered I had a good instrument-flying rating, and returned from the Watchfield Lorenz Blind Approach Course in 1941 with an above average assessment. I was content to think that was the probable reason, and in any event my greatest wish had been to get away from Long Kesh.

1510 Flight just before I arrived. S/Ldr Sunnucks is 6th from right, front row.

CHAPTER 15

A DIFFERENT OCEAN SWELL

I soon felt at home at Leuchars, and quickly forgot my disappointment. The station had a blessed compactness which Long Kesh had lacked, and was ringed only by dispersal points for aircraft. The main buildings were of brick and in the style associated with pre-war rearmament, the Mess was pleasantly appointed and staffed, whilst during my time on the station there was a lull in operational use, so space was not at its usual premium. Three years ago it had been one of the east coast bases, as had been Thornaby and Wick, from which the Hudson North Sea patrols and Scandinavian strikes had been made; similar activities were now being flown by squadrons based at Leuchars, but whose sorties usually started from airfields which had been constructed in northeast Scotland since those early days. During April 1944 the Beaufighters and Hampdens of these squadrons were moved to Langham in Norfolk in preparation for D-Day, leaving only a Photographic Reconnaissance Squadron requiring occasional use of the runways at Leuchars for one of their Mosquitoes, Spitfires, or – do my eyes deceive me! – a Hudson in sky-blue livery! So, for the second quarter of 1944, No 1510 BABS Flight was able to virtually monopolize the runways, until Liberator aircraft of 206 Squadron began to arrive in late July for offensive work in the Skagerrak/Kattegat area of the Baltic Sea.

As soon as I reported to the Flight Commander, S/Ldr 'Tubby' Sunnucks, I sensed that it was a happy, efficient unit. He was a rather rotund, warm-hearted ex-World War One Submarine Commander who had indulged in peacetime aviation, and he had the knack of exercising his authority in the pleasantest possible way. He looked on his unit as his own brood, and he reserved the few caustic remarks he occasionally made for the 'faceless people with carpet on the floor'. This phrase referred to the fact that whenever he visited Air Ministry or a similar distant arm of the body politic, all but the most senior RAF personnel had no carpet on the linoleum-covered floor, but the civil servants' floors were graded, as were the occupants, from small rugs, to larger square, to extensive and expensive spreads. As one might expect, with such a man in charge, a genial atmosphere pervaded the Flight, and all ranks worked happily together.

The reliable easy-to-fly Anson with dual controls was the ideal machine for this kind of instrument-flying, allowing the trainee pilot to concentrate on relating the position and attitude of the aircraft to the information he was receiving from his radar operator. The purpose of the Flight was to put into practice the experiments which had been made in using radar beams to assist landings in minimum visibility, the forerunner of systems which would add safe landings to safe navigation. The Ansons were equipped with a radar set which recorded distance from the radar beam transmitted from an antenna at the far end of the runway, which also sent out 'dots' on one side of the runway, 'dashes' on the other, and a steady beam along it and beyond. It was a radar interpretation of the Lorenz system, which used radio beams in a similar way, but which was subject to more interference and lacked the precision in recording distance which the radar system provided. Also, as radar beacons for homing were being set up on operational airfields, there was an obvious advantage in using radar for both homing and landing.

The beam approach could be used by the experienced pilot in conditions when one end of the runway could not be seen from the other, and in conjunction with the homing beacon which could be picked up at a distance of twenty miles or more, I soon found it possible to land on the runway beam in conditions which 'had the birds walking'.

Needless to say, at this stage of development, the pilot was entirely dependent on the skill and clear thinking of the radar operator. He called "Left, left" or "Right, right", or "Stea-dy!" as needed, reading off the distance as the runway was approached. The pilot carried out the normal routines on the approach, adjusting height and speed accordingly, aiming to cross the down-wind end of the runway at 50 feet, less if the runway was very short, or more if the conditions were turbulent.

The radar operator's expertise became apparent in the finer interpretations of the aircraft's position, such as correct estimates of fractions of a mile, and the point at which the position of the aircraft within the beam was close to the adjoining zone. He would be the first to recognize the effect of unexpected drift, giving graded instructions to counter it. I teamed up with such a radar operator, Flying Officer Wally Bagnall, and we quickly developed an empathy.

As the only unit giving this type of instruction, the pilots and radar operators we took came from various Squadrons and Groups, Coastal, Bomber, Night Fighters, some Fortress and Liberator crews, and Dutch, Norwegian, and Dominion personnel. The Mess became very cosmopolitan.

Most came from O.T.U's and Squadrons, and many a 'line' was 'shot' in the Mess over a pint of beer, with tales of the round-the-clock pounding of the enemy, which was now commonplace by the heavy bombers. As was to be expected, such pilots often found some difficulty in readjusting to the relatively light-as-a-feather Anson, particularly in landing, but this was of little consequence so long as the pilot and his radar operator developed a mutual understanding. One or two of the day-bombing boys of the USAAF were uncertain in their use of the six dials in the instrument-flying panel, and we found it necessary to familiarise the doubting pilot with our type of instrument-flying in three stages: 'Up and away'; 'Finding the beam'; and 'Down to hold-off':

The Ansons were equipped with a hood over the pilot's seat, which could be pulled forward to detach him from all but the instruments and controls. The best instrument-flying revision was achieved without the use of the hood in layer cloud with a base above 2,000 feet, when he would be instructed to go 'up' into it, and 'away' from the airfield – and other aircraft. Even in the thickest cloud, the awareness of a dim external shape made I/F flying, for some pilots, less claustrophobic and therefore more relaxed. Then, still without the hood, flying on instruments and in co-operation with the radar operator, they would work together from the instructor's predetermined position, in finding the beam – perhaps starting in the 'dash' sector, recognising which way to turn to approach the full beam – the steady sector – then flying along it and at prescribed distances adjusting to the heights needed at those points. If the approach to the runway made in this way was satisfactory, at a height of about 200 feet the pilot would be told to climb away along the beam until he passed beyond the transmitter at the upwind end of the runway, to add to his knowledge of the whole of the radar layout.

Then he would be asked to repeat the approach procedure, adjusting to the information being given by the radar operator, down to 100 feet at a distance of a quarter of a mile from the landing end of the runway. From that point he would make a normal visual landing. I considered this routine important in helping the pilot to appreciate the need to interpret the effect of drift as soon as possible, in the approach down the steady sector of the beam. In the initial stages of training, pilots when in the air tended to discount the explanations previously given on the ground, and, having been led by the radar operator into the steady sector, they liked to set the gyro compass on zero and keep the aircraft on that heading. Correct! But only in calm conditions, or with the wind directly down the runway. Allow for drift before flying a heading!

A cross-wind would cause the aircraft to move to either the dot or the dash sector, and the pilot's ability to appreciate the need for a correction upon hearing "Steady fading, approaching dot sector" from the radar operator, was usually a fair indication of his overall ability. His mental calculations would be based on an image of the beam which increased in width with distance from the source, and would include an estimate of wind strength and direction calculated by noting the time taken to move from the steady sector to the edge of the dot sector. A good pilot would quickly make a satisfactory adjustment, reset the gyro-compass, and give every indication that he knew what he was doing; the less-able pilot would make a half-hearted turn to try to keep within the steady sector, and be forced to follow that turn with others, so that his machine virtually wriggled its way down the edge of the steady sector. In actual conditions of very low cloud or fog, such an approach could lead to an unfavourable position for landing, particularly with heavy four-engined aircraft which most of the pilots we trained would be flying when they needed to use the system under operational conditions.

I was surprised that, three and a half years after my own debacle owing to the lack of cross-wind landing instruction, there were still some pilots who did not appear to understand the fundamentals, and I wondered whether, as a consequence of basic flying training now being overseas, the training airfields in Canada and Rhodesia were minus runways with landings always made into wind? Experience had shown me that certain assumptions were made by one unit or Command in relation to another, and one of them was that cross-wind landings were taught during basic training. I knew that several pilots who were now instructing pupils to 'wings' standard had never used a runway, and when I thought of the number of accidents, including fatalities, caused by inadequate landings, it seemed a heavy and unnecessary toll to pay for someone's oversight.

The third stage, as the pilots increased in competence and confidence, involved about an hour's sustained concentration under the hood, and needed reasonable weather conditions so that the instructor could keep a check on other aircraft. The pilot would be told to fly wherever he pleased downwind of the airfield, then the hood would come down, and the instructor would take the controls, making quite sure that although the pilot may have known the position before being hooded, he would no longer know it by the time he was told to 'home' on the beacon, then find the runway beam, and put the aircraft into a position for landing. With the better pilots, on the final approach one could let them take the aircraft across the end of the runway and talk them through to the throttling back and hold-off, before taking over to put the 'plane down, to the astonishment of the pilot as he pushed back the hood and found the Anson rolling along after landing. On one or two occasions, with the very best of the pupils, and if it had been possible to establish a perfect rapport, I had the satisfaction of talking him through the landing routine from a good approach at 50 feet so that he actually landed the aircraft whilst under the hood. My left hand would be hovering near the throttle quadrant, and my right almost touching the control column on my side of the cockpit. I would take over merely to keep straight as we rolled along the runway. As the pilot emerged from the hood, the sense of achievement was invariably reflected in his face, which alleviated the tension of the final few moments and made the risk worthwhile.

The weather had to be very severe to bring flying to a complete halt, and that did not happen often that Spring, which we found to be true across the country as a whole on those occasions when we had to fly to other far-flung airfields. Again

I could fly over attractive landscapes at a chosen altitude, rather than at heights where the countryside loses its detail. The area around Leuchars itself was an idyllic panorama – the Firth of Tay and the Tay Bridge to the north, the coastal area of Fife and the Firth of Forth to the south, and on most days an approach for landing or take-off climb across the renowned Royal and Ancient Golf Club links of St Andrews, where the sea lapped the dunes surrounding the green oases.

We became in effect a minor Communications Flight as well as a BABS Flight, especially for V.I.P's who had reason to expedite their movement around the country, but we managed to balance this duty with concern for our own personnel by combining, where possible, the need to test radar beacons up and down the country with air transport for airmen and women going on leave.

The first of such 'comm' flights allocated to me was on the 28th February when I had the pleasure of taking Wing Commander Barron DFC & Bar to Predannack, on the Lizard Peninsula in Cornwall. He and S/Ldr Hodgkinson, both born leaders, had been Flight Commanders when I was with 220 Squadron at Thornaby, and he was now on his way to take command of a strike squadron.

He had started the war on Ansons, so we shared the flying en route – across the Southern Uplands, Dumfries, St Bee's Head, the Irish Sea to St Orme's Head by Llandudno, across to Carmarthen Bay, the long bleak finger of rocky Lundy Island, and across the strip of Cornwall where derelict mining engine-sheds dotted the landscape. Before we parted at the airfield, I tried the direct approach regarding my wish to join such a squadron, and left with some hope of it being fulfilled, but before long came the news that the Wing Commander had been posted missing. I feared that any further message about him would lack the report of safety which had followed Hodge's demise in the Bremen raid, for the Cornish-based strike squadrons operated over the Bay of Biscay. Thus the sad loss of both the Flight Commanders whose leadership permeated 220 Squadron in my fledgling days.

We learned later that Jimmy Barron's fateful day had been the 11th April 1944, on a strike with 248 Squadron.

Life at Leuchars soon became a pleasant mixture of teaching the BABS routine, and itinerant journeys around Britain, testing radar beacons and delivering personnel. If I had kept detailed notes on 'the best approach for the discerning pilot using radar to land at....', I could have published a guide for the airfields at Ballykelly, Banff, Beccles, Blackpool, Downham Market, Drem, Fairwood Common, Findo Gask, Hooton Park, Ipswich, Leavesden, Montrose, Newmarket, Northolt, Ouston, St Athan, Salmesbury, Sealand, Tain, Turnhouse, Wick, York, et al. Of these, some were associated with evocative circumstances.

The flight to Ipswich enabled me to call at Beccles on the return journey, where I had arranged to meet Pug, my navigator on 269 Squadron. He had been posted to a strike squadron which was very active in attacking shipping and port installations across the Channel prior to D-Day. He seemed very much on edge, not at all like the cool, straightforward chap I had flown with on ops. I could see that he was dissatisfied with the rest of his crew, and could only surmise that they did not have his experience. Older means wiser was a truism which reflected operational experience in terms of what could happen to threaten one's safety, and being ready for it if it did.

The only reasonable supposition to explain the need to retain on operations navigators who had already completed three tours, was that there was some imbalance between the supply of trained pilots, and that of trained navigators, at least in Coastal Command. There was I, being told that the supply of pilots had exceeded the expected losses, and there was Pug, making it very clear that he had not volunteered for this further tour of operations. However, I realised that whereas there were other jobs for pilots who had survived operations, such as one-to-one instructing in the various stages of pilot-training, or in helping develop new techniques as I was, there was a limit to the ways in which other members of aircrew could be employed when not 'flying against the enemy'. There had been several occasions when I was thankful that I was not 'other aircrew', obliged to put my survival in someone else's hands, and this feeling was reinforced as I talked to Pug and could feel the depth of his concern. I felt then that it was the navigators, wireless operators and air gunners who deserved the greater tribute for air operations; theirs was the greater need for courage to place their destinies largely in the hands of others. I flew back to Leuchars counting my blessings. A short time later, I had a letter from Pug's widow, telling me that he had been killed on operations with 524 Squadron.

Throughout the Spring of 1944 and until it finally capsized after a raid by RAF Lancasters on the 12th November, the German battleship 'Tirpitz', sister-ship of the 'Bismarck' which had been sunk in 1941, was a threat to Atlantic shipping from its shelter in the Norwegian fjords. In fact, the 'Tirpitz' had been a prime target when circumstances allowed, since April 1942, when Wing Commander (later AVM Pathfinder Force) Bennett was shot down leading an attack, thence to escape via Sweden. Photographic Reconnaissance aircraft kept a constant watch on the battleship, flying many sorties from Leuchars, and on one of these in April, after an attack on the ship by Fleet Air Arm 'Barracudas', a thick sea fog on return made it necessary for the P.R.U. aircraft to land at Wick. I was despatched with Wally to collect the film from Wick and return with it for interpretation at Leuchars.

We couldn't see the far end of the runway as we took off, but the lights were on and we had no problem in climbing away across the coast. The light wind from the east was the cause of the fog, and we eventually emerged into clear skies over a calm sea, on course for Wick. It was on such flights that the presence of the radar operator was doubly welcome: firstly, of course, for their expert assistance in getting from A to B, and secondly for their sympathetic (?) response to the physical needs of the undercarriage, for they were thoughtful chaps responding to a reminder that the Anson flew better with the undercarriage up rather than down, and that it was very necessary for the pilot to concentrate on flying the machine in adverse weather conditions! When the flying was merely local, both pilot and operator were spared the 160 turns on the cranking handle to lift the undercarriage, but on longer flights failure to raise it resulted in slower speed, increased fuel consumption, and on occasions a bumpier ride. Wally seemed to enjoy a brief respite from the radar set when asked to share the cranking, and we gave the procedure a competitive edge by each counting the number of turns we could achieve in one minute. The effort persuaded us that even a hydraulically-operated undercarriage would be hard pressed to better our best performance.

On the return from Wick, we decided to home on the Leuchars beacon, and went up to 4,500 feet over the Grampian Mountains, now covered in cloud which had come in above the fog. We had descended to 2,000 feet by the time Wally called "Over the beacon now!", and I turned out to sea, quickly losing height to 1,000 feet followed by a wide turn down to 500 to line up on the runway beam. The fog seemed thinner, yet we saw little more than the nearest runway lights on the final approach, but Wally had put me spot on the middle of the beam and he was still reading distance as we crossed the end of the runway. Whether he was still at the radar set or looking over my shoulder when he said "Should be touching down now", was not for me to question. Once again, he had done his job perfectly; the P.R.U. film was duly delivered.

At this time, we who were trying to make a success of the general use of the BABS system for landing in poor visibility had little indication of how well it was being integrated into operational use. We wondered, in fact, whether it was to be used in conjunction with, or in competition with, F.I.D.O.

'Fido' was a means of lifting fog sufficiently for landing by heating the air around a runway using scores of petrol-burners along its length. It was available at three airfields with emergency facilities. Carnaby, Manston, and Woodbridge each had runways about 3,000 yards in length and were 250 yards wide, equipped with navigational aids. Before the end of the war, thousands of emergency landings were made at these 'Fido' airfields. In handling so many landings, it was obvious that an efficient system of control must be operative, and in the absence of any feedback, we wondered how effective the BABS system might be at ordinary airfields not equipped with Fido. The only way to find out was to question pilots sent to us from operational stations, and in many instances they could not say whether their stations were, or were to be, equipped with BABS.

Another instructor and I decided we would prove to ourselves how effective BABS could be. The aim was to approach in the usual way to a height of 50 feet, on the beam and on instruments, then locate and land visually, one aircraft to follow the other at an interval so that the first would be ahead on the runway at the time the second one touched down on it. The risk was not so much on the runway, as the second aircraft would be prepared to fly off if necessary, and make another approach; it was rather the danger of collision in the air if the instrument flying and radar guidance were faulty, especially in the final approach. We agreed on the mutual starting points, air speed, rate of descent etc., and we decided that the pilot of the leading aircraft would not use the hood but would nevertheless concentrate on instruments, then land visually from 50 feet. Thus he would be allowed two discretionary outside observations on his descent, to take evasive action should it be needed. The second aircraft was to follow the first at a ten-second interval; the first was to approach on the edge of the beam where the steady sector met the dash area, the second on the steady merging to dot line. This would not only test the skill of the radar operator, but would keep the tracks of the two aircraft apart until the last few yards of the approach, where the width of the steady sector was approximately the width of the runway. We tossed a coin for position; I was number two.

Communication with the Control Tower was not available by radio/telephone, so we decided we would not inform the Controller before the flight in case he objected; however, we had a word with the airman in his black-and-white signalling box at the downwind end of the runway, for his job was to flash a green or a red on his Aldis lamp to aircraft about to take off or land. In emergency, he would fire a red Verey pistol cartridge if there was a possibility of two aircraft on the runway at the same time, a likely cause of panic in the ivory Tower – a situation to avoid if at all possible!

We decided the best way to achieve a ten-second gap, or as near to it as possible, was for me to follow the first aircraft's take-off at that time interval, then to check the interval as first he, and then I, came level with the upwind end of the runway on the downwind leg of the circuit, and to follow him into the middle of the beam before we each migrated to the ordained position on the approach. All went well, and he was still rolling along the runway as I touched down. However, we had chosen the wrong day: the Controller on duty was not the best friend of pilots, and he opened a window to address us in phrases containing several unusual epithets, with not a word of congratulations.

A few days later, following another bout of patient exposition of the BABS system to pilots from USAAF squadrons, I was flying over the pleasantly undulating countryside between Perth and Crieff when I noticed a small grass airfield which appeared to be deserted, devoid of any aircraft, and boasting a scale-model 'control tower' with a small building which could have been a barn or a hangar for two Tiger Moths – at a squeeze! It was Findo Gask. There was no sign of life, and whatever its inadequacies as a reception area for anything larger than an Anson, it appeared eminently suitable for a plan which commended itself there and then.

I had not seen the young lady who was left to regret my invited intrusion into the physical training domain in which she was incarcerated, since that eventful visit, but I knew she was expecting to stay with her aunt and uncle who had a farm near Methven, on the road between Perth and Crieff. After landing, I telephoned for further news and found that she had arrived, whereupon we arranged a rendezvous at Findo Gask the next day. I had been detailed to take an Anson on an extended air test, and, for the record, I was rather unhappy with the performance of one engine, so, being in the vicinity of Findo Gask, I put down there. After landing from a precautionary approach, two figures appeared. One was the young lady in question, the other an airman who, surprisingly, appeared from the tower. I taxied up to him, and, as I wished to keep the engines running, beckoned him into the cabin.

"I'm told you have a radar beacon here which needs testing, but there seems to be no sign of one," I said, trying to give the impression of blaming him for this. The poor chap seemed nonplussed, but, being new to the Service and appreciating unexpected, if solitary, freedom he obviously decided not to risk his caretaker job by giving the wrong answer to a Flight Lieutenant.

"Oh", he replied.

"This is number nine F.T.S. isn't it?" I continued.

"Ah", he felt safe to answer "It was Sir, but it isn't now."

"Isn't the airfield in use at the moment, then?"

"No sir! I'm the only one on duty here today. Sid's got the day off; I'm off tomorrow."

I was grateful that Sid wasn't around to complicate the situation; he might not have been as accommodating as this airman appeared ready to be.

"I see," I continued "so I've had a wasted journey!" – again with mischievous inference.

No response.

"Do you have a landing log for me to sign?"

"A what sir?" – pause – "Er..no, sir!". His tone suggested he might as well have said "What on earth is that?"

I revved up the 'suspect' engine, holding the shuddering aircraft against the brake.

"Don't you think that engine is running a little rough?" I asked.

A mystified, doubtful look told me he was not an engine fitter, so another of my queries had been favourably answered.

"I'd better test it on a circuit and landing before I move on." He was already turning to leave when I shouted:

"Just a minute!" He turned back. "Do you know that young lady over there by that gate?" He looked, with evident surprise at the suggestion.

"Me, sir? No sir!" (Sir, what are you suggesting?)

"Just the place for a harem!" I joked, "I wonder if she would like a short flight?" I mused, "Might persuade her to join the WAAF. Why not pop over and ask her? Perhaps you would like to come up on a quick circuit as well?" – and I used my hand to demonstrate spine-chilling aerobatics. I chuckled, he gulped, and, being an airman but not a budding aviator, with a shake of his head and a rapid salute, he was out of the aircraft and across to the young lady by the gate.

I taxied slowly round, he held the door open for her, then shut it firmly with himself on the outside. She came through the cabin to sit beside me at the dual controls, we passed more than the time of day, and eventually taxied round to turn into wind for take-off. I held the Anson down so that after take-off we skimmed the far hedge to encourage the airman to believe he had taken the right decision, then we climbed as steeply as the dignity of an Anson allowed. She held the controls on the downwind leg after emulating the 'butterfly in the sky' routine, and when I took over as we turned cross-wind, she seemed rather concerned that we were going down on to such a small area of grass. However, as we came in low over the boundary, she admitted it seemed considerably larger, and we settled to a good three-pointer, rumbling across to the gate. The airman was still waiting; again he held the door open.

"Tell him that the engine seems O.K. now, so I'll be on my way, and thank him for his help," I suggested as she moved down the cabin. Before taxying round to the far side for take-off I looked back towards the gate; she was waving and he was saluting in barrack-square fashion. As a new recruit, he deserved a commendation for helping to maintain morale.

On the 15th May I was detailed to fly to Turnhouse aerodrome, near Edinburgh, to collect Lord Rosebery, who was mentioned anonymously in my briefing as the most important V.I.P. in Scotland. Anonymity apparently mattered little when I entered the Control Room to report, for as soon as I explained my orders he came across before the Controller could respond, and simply said:

"Rosebery. Who are you?" I saluted in reply, gave him my name, and discovered that I was to take him to Newmarket for the 1944 Wartime Derby. The race was to be run on the July Course on the 17th May, instead of at the traditional Epsom. He had entered 'Ocean Swell' for the race, to be ridden by Billy Nevett.

"Don't bother about that", he said, as I moved towards the Controller to give details of our flight. "He knows where we're going, as the crow flies. Let's move!".

Move we did! It was as if the excitement of the Race had already caught up with him; he gave the airman holding open the door of the Anson a fatherly pat on the head, and missed his footing as he stepped into the aircraft, so that one foot was still outside. Like a born equestrian, the airman cupped his hands together in the approved help-into-the-saddle manner, and carefully guided the foot to its proper place. On recovering, His Lordship turned to the airman with a "Well done, laddie!" then followed me up the cabin to the cockpit for an explanation of which instruments and controls did what.

We made the flight in beautiful sunshine, with visibility only slightly affected by a faint heat haze. First, the Southern Uplands of Scotland, then much of Eastern England, was spread out before us, and my passenger showed the interest in the countryside one would expect of a great patriot. He was sitting behind me in the seat normally occupied by the navigator.

On such flights across England, once the course set had proved satisfactory by checking the first few landmarks, it was customary to follow earth-bound activity rather than the map when visibility offered landmarks even twenty miles away which we itinerant flyers had come to know well. From time to time the eye would settle on the L.N.E.R. express hauled by a Gresley locomotive, the line of barges waiting to pass through a lock on a canal, a convoy of Army lorries, a familiar airfield where the squadrons were obviously re-equipping with Lancasters, the bustle of a street market in a small town, the number of new tractors which were displacing horse-drawn farm implements, a field of sheep being rounded up by a dog: England, this England! And at predetermined points one would look for proof that the course being flown was correct, then continue to enjoy the kaleidoscope on offer. Many villages and small towns were admired, but remained anonymous.

On this flight, as soon as we were on course, Lord Rosebery showed an interest worthy of a Baedeker. As we approached a town nestling in the hills of southern Scotland I heard a shout behind me – "Hawick!", pronounced as a Scotsman would. I nodded; it wasn't one of my landmarks, but a quick glance at my map confirmed it. We had hardly crossed Hadrian's Wall before there was a tap on my shoulder, a shout in my ear: "Where is that?" – and a finger pointing at the appropriate conundrum. Fortunately I knew it was Consett from the steel works there. My next landmark was Darlington, but before we reached it I replied to another question by, in all probability, giving one town the name of another 'off the top of my head'. From Darlington we had the choice of following the L.N.E.R. main line or the A 1 road to Peterborough, across areas such as the Vale of York, the Lincolnshire Wolds, then the Fens – areas where towns are small and villages smaller. In response to taps on the shoulder, questions, and pointing fingers, several habitations were re-named that day!

On the return journey I flew a course which took me around some of the airfields in southeast England, testing radar beacons. Aircraft were being assembled and prepared for the forthcoming invasion of the continent – broad white stripes alternating with black over the inner part of each wing on those aircraft which had a role to play in the ensuing battle. Unmarked aircraft would in future need special clearance to enter the airspace over the quart which had somehow been squeezed into the pint pot.

Two days later, on Derby Day, the radio news that evening announced the name of the Derby winner: it was Lord Rosebery's 'Ocean Swell'! I had a few drinks in celebration of his success and the slight pecuniary advantage a wager had brought me, and tried to avoid thinking of him viewing his many horses with his aide and asking: "What's the name of that one? And that? And...."

I was on leave when, on the 6th June 1944, we heard the announcement for which the country had long been waiting – the Allied landings on the beaches of Normandy which would lead to eventual victory. For a few weeks many of the pilots seconded to the BABS course at Leuchars were relatively inexperienced, with some not yet qualified on operational aircraft, a fact indicative of the need for maximum effort from experienced crews during the preparatory phase of air bombardment of German Army targets and logistical support.

When I returned from leave I found that a new course had arrived, and there were vacancies which had not been taken up, but the intake was normal thereafter; in fact, as the weather improved we were encouraged to 'push 'em through a.s.a.p.', presumably for squadrons to be in a position of maximum availability for operations during autumn and winter weather by using this, and other, technological aids.

After three weeks back in the old routine, on 27th June I was ordered to report to Headquarters, Coastal Command at Eastbury Park, Northwood, one of the outer northwest suburbs of London. I flew down to Northolt aerodrome, whence I was taken by staff car to H.Q., with instructions to report to Group Captain Nolan, the Senior Personnel Officer.

After a brief, pleasant introductory chat, he informed me that he had scrutinized my records and was offering me the post of Personal Assistant to Air Marshal

Baker. This was music to my ears, for the needs of the Service beyond the end of the war were emerging as a possible choice between leaving the R.A. F. or staying on, and such a posting would enhance one's prospects. The Air Marshal, I was told, needed an articulate, presentable officer who would pay attention to detail, and who could fly his personal Hudson aircraft anywhere at any time, and I was one of the most experienced Hudson pilots left! – He eulogised my Service Record with no mention of my gaffes, then went on to say it was a never-ending job, probably with no home leave as it was an overseas posting. The Air Marshal had been given command of the R.A F's recently formed Balkan Air Force.

"Do you have any problems that can't be put aside for, say, a couple of years? It's a job which won't allow worries at the back of one's mind."

Unfortunately, I had, though I was sorely tempted then to dismiss them and the responsibility involved: domestic matters which would need resolving in considerably less than two years. I gave him the details.

"However, I do count my blessings, Sir; I've been more fortunate than many, in fact than most of my friends and needs must, etc. .." – then I remembered the ending of that particular adage and continued hurriedly "Beg pardon Sir, I mean if it's necessary...."

"Don't concern yourself," he replied, "this isn't a posting by command" (obviously relishing the play on words) "we're just offering an opportunity to an appropriate officer, and I don't doubt someone will jump at the chance. You obviously can't."

I thanked him, then made a pensive car journey back to Northolt, and thence to Leuchars, by which time I was convinced I had done myself a bit of no good.

After another three weeks of the usual BABS routine with 1510 Flight, it was therefore all the more surprising to be ordered once more to present myself for interview at HQCC. Again I reported to Group Captain Nolan.

"There's more of a 'command' element about this one!" were his first meaningful-words after the usual introductory preamble, evidently pleased to continue the use of the pun. "You are to take a Staff appointment here at Headquarters, in the post of Air Two, which at present is held by the American golfer Charles Sweeny, one of the originals in the 'Eagle' Squadron. Your immediate boss will be Squadron Leader Powell, known as Air One. Can you report for duty on Monday next?"

I certainly could! My faith in Anglo-American co-operation received a boost when it was rumoured that Flt Lt Sweeny had a role elsewhere in helping the final 'play-off' achieve par for the course, for a Staff appointment at this stage, even after being obliged to turn down a plum job, would look just as good on my file as a

P.A. posting. It would also give me an insight into the workings of a Command Headquarters.

I took the Anson back to Leuchars at maximum cruising speed, seldom used before, and hurried through the routine of permanent departure. If I had believed an option on the posting existed without detrimental consequences, perhaps I would have sought to avoid it, for I had been very happy with Tubby Sunnucks and his cheerful outfit. During a final drink he said I may be moving on at the right time, and whether he had an inkling that the unit might be leaving so that Leuchars could revert to strike duties, I knew not, but within weeks 1510 had transferred to Blackpool.

CHAPTER 16

WINGS CLIPPED

By the time 1510 had moved, I was well into a routine of paperwork, mounting files of memoranda, and telephonic communication which kept my feet firmly under my desk. There were two welcome diversions which enabled the Squadron Leader and me to achieve an occasional release from the office: a responsibility for the smooth working of the Operations Room, and a link with the Communications Flight which was based at Northolt.

The Operations Board covered the whole of one wall in the large underground room, with an area reminiscent of the bridge of a ship opposite to it, from which the Controller and the Senior Officers conducted the operations of the day (and night!). The Board was in effect a large outline map of the Atlantic from the eastern seaboard of North America to Europe and the Mediterranean, including lines of latitude and longitude, and a numbered grid. The symbols representing various forces were moved to their appropriate positions by members of the W.A.A.F. climbing up stepladders to add or move a symbol, then descending to await the next order. In the midst of one of the most interesting periods of the war, there was an air of hushed efficiency as the symbols covered a panorama of activity by all our Forces. History, total but transient!

In the Atlantic, the position and strength of convoys, escorts, U-boats, aircraft, and engagements with the enemy; in the western end of the English Channel the patrols in support of the invasion forces, with a similar responsibility at the eastern end; the missions of Photo-Reconnaissance and Air-Sea Rescue aircraft; the changing pattern of the battles raging in Northern France, and the U.S. Army dash into Brittany; Bomber Command support as the Canadians struggled towards the Falaise Gap; and the surrender of the Germans defending the citadel at St Malo; the continued maritime transport of reinforcements across the Channel; and the developing attack against oil targets pursued by Bomber Command and the USAAF 8th Air Force – this was the expanding human conflict reduced to symbolic representation on a large black square.

The other diversion from desk duty was the Communications Flight at Northolt aerodrome which had a mixed inventory of single- and twin-engined light aircraft – a Percival Proctor, Mew Gulls, Oxfords, a De Havilland Domini – for use by H.Q.C.C. staff. The occasional flight taking a senior officer who preferred to be chauffeured on some mission, or delivering documents to various bases, provided an opportunity to handle a joystick instead of a pen.

A fleeting attraction of a different kind could be seen as I cycled from my billet in Northwood up the hill to the H.Q. at Eastbury Park on the 17th September. It was part of the air armada of tug-aircraft and gliders, on its way to Nijmegen and the ill-fated dropping zones of Arnhem, with the sound of hundreds of straining engines filling the bright morning sky. The new symbol appearing on the Ops Board was one of many changes which had moved southwards and eastwards since I first saw it on taking up my appointment. Not only had the battle for the bridges across the lower Rhine, and the rivers Maas and Waal, now been joined, but resistance by the enemy garrison in Brest had ended, and Boulogne was ready to fall to the Canadians after heavy bombing.

The sight of a German flying-bomb (V1) overhead a couple of nights later enlivened conversation in Northwood. I was walking down the road to my billet when the throbbing drone of a V1 broke the silence of a deserted street, and a jet of orange flame suddenly came into view at a height of about 300 feet. Flying bombs seldom penetrated to the northwest suburbs of London, and certainly this one had overshot its target, as open countryside lay beyond. Unless, across the Channel, the despatching crew had by some miracle targetted HQCC! Ridiculous! On immediate second thoughts this was impossible, as the V1 was a random-target terror-weapon lacking precision. It was an acknowledgement that air superiority in manned aircraft had irrevocably passed to the Allies. The target the V 1 reached depended entirely on the point at which the jet had used all its fuel, the engine stopped, the bomb fell to earth and exploded. The interval between engine failure and explosion was usually about ten long seconds.

I watched it pass above the street, the flame grew larger, the noise louder, it was overhead, then beyond, continuing its overshot journey. Silence – count of 10 – bang! This time, not somewhere over London, but somewhere beyond London. Intelligence soon had the answer to this resurgence of sporadic attack after the fixed V1 launching sites in northwest France had been overrun by the advancing Allied armies: flying-bombs were now being launched from Heinkel III aircraft flying from airfields in Holland, and the one which crossed Northwood was probably one of those, as were others to follow, since the incoming direction was now from the northeast rather than the southeast.

In the autumn and winter of 1944/45 V2 rockets, fired from areas around The Hague in Holland fell from the skies across southern England, particularly around London, and on any day as we sat at our desks working at some minor task as part of a grand strategy to end the war, we could expect to hear a loud explosion and occasionally feel a resultant tremor, as another terror weapon landed to try to thwart the Allied design. It was another great and fearful trial successfully overcome by the citizens of London until the last V2 fell, on 27th March, 1945.

From September 1944 onwards, the Operations Board had shown some remarkable changes in the continuing war against the U-boat menace. Those which were in French ports when the Allied Armies began to spread over France after the successful Normandy landings, were ordered to leave and make for Norway. It had become obvious to the German Command that they had failed in their efforts to interfere with the Allied landings, and they would be isolated if they continued to try to operate from those ports. They had to be redeployed, and during October it was seen that their revised role was to harass the traffic between Britain and the Continent, to help the beleaguered German armies. Operations against shipping in the Atlantic were down-graded to a secondary consideration, and U-boats were being sunk closer to our shores than had been the case since 1940. In those early days, U-boat forays around our coasts were offensive, the beginning of the effort to deny us resources; now they were defensive in effect, as part of the effort to avoid the unconditional surrender which the Allied leaders required. The symbols on the HQ Operations Board showed the reinforcement of Coastal Command aircraft to provide day and night patrols in the Southwest and Northwest Approaches, and offensive strikes against enemy shipping well into the Skagerrak and Kattegat areas of the Baltic Sea. In the last four months of 1944, the Command carried out over 9,000 sorties.

Throughout November and December, in poor flying weather, the line of Allied advance on the ground continued eastwards, but on the 17th December the Operations Board showed an ominous 'enemy arrow' pointing westward through the Allied line. It was the Ardennes offensive by the Germans, begun the previous day, the very same day that it had been reported that they were unable to carry out a major offensive operation! The 'bulge' appeared, and day by day grew, until, 60 miles through Belgium, it almost reached the border with France. It was a month later before the bulge could be removed from the Board.

My sixth December of the war ended in dismal weather outside, and a lack of fuel inside, my billet. Mrs Danvers, the landlady, had departed to spend Christmas at Pevensey Bay, and I discovered the coal-cellar was bare. Open fires were the only source of heating in the house, and I was very glad to be on duty during the festive season. George, my boss, took some leave, and I sat rather morosely at my desk and thought of another three personal friends who had not survived the year.

It was with mixed feelings that I had the good fortune to visit Pinewood Film Studios, the wartime base of the Crown Film Unit, to see the film "Coastal Command" which had been in the cinemas whilst I was in Iceland. Squadron Leader

Hodgkinson, now confirmed as a POW, Johnnie Lane (lost in Greenland) and I had done the flying for the Hudson sequences in the film, and the opportunity to see it on the screen came about through a Public Relations colleague on the Staff who had contacts at Pinewood. When I spoke to the girl who had been responsible for continuity in the making of the film, she arranged a private showing, and on arrival I was ushered into a small projection room with comfortable seating for about thirty viewers. By the time the film had run its one-and-a-quarter hours I felt rather embarrassed, as the Hudson sequence lasted for no more than two minutes, the result of about sixty hours flying time between the three of us, plus another ten hours if the opening formation of nine aircraft were included. That was evidently not unusual, and she thought the location director had done quite well to obtain good continuity flow.

There were three or four similar projection rooms in which films were being screened, each viewed by a handful of itinerant onlookers who appeared to be either trainee directors or standby technicians passing a waiting hour. During a guided tour of the C.F.U. Section of the studios where various instructional films were being made, there was a particularly appropriate one concerning the latest type of airborne rescue boat with which the ASR Squadrons were being re-equipped. Back in the Command Operations Room there was evidence enough that it would be well used.

Two flights I made at this time illustrated the vastly changed fortunes of war. As I approached Thorney Island, on the south coast near Portsmouth, the devastation caused by the heavy bombing was still apparent amongst the buildings where, as in other parts of the country, complete obliteration was only avoided by the courage and skill of the heroic Few. Within days, I took a Percival Gull in poor visibility down to Hawkinge, near Folkestone in Kent – thankful for the long straight stretch of the Southern Railway line between Redhill and Ashford – and as I taxied in towards the Control Tower a Corporal of the RAF Regiment emerged to check my credentials. I was at an airfield which was very much in the front-line against German bombers in 1940; now it was used as a Command link with the Allied continental offensive.

The first occasion on which I had pushed my bicycle up the hill from Northwood to the HQ at Eastbury Park in the summer of 1944 had been the forerunner of many hot and sticky days. At the turn of the year, it was still a task likely to cause a rise in body temperature, but only because of the need for protective clothing against the snow. On such a day, in the early morning when there was an absence of other traffic, my cycle wheels ploughed a lone furrow and my shoes squelched alongside them in the soft snow. On my return, long after darkness had fallen, the traffic had compacted the snow on the road into a covering as slippery as a skating rink, as I found to my cost shortly after turning into the road leading down to the town. The bike was drawn from beneath me by an underling of Jack Frost, and I slid down the hill on my backside vainly trying to regain my feet, whilst my steed followed obediently behind.

I came to a halt in front of an elderly Group Captain whose feet had suffered the indignity of providing a buffer for my bicycle. He gave an immediate impression of hating the weather, its effect on the route of his daily constitutional, all bicycles, and all junior officers. The moonlight on his face didn't improve it.

"If you must do that, young man, why not try a toboggan, preferably somewhere in Switzerland?"

I knew by now from past experience that a senior officer addressing me as "young man" did not bode well; was meant in fact to be disparaging.

"Yes Sir,....." I began, as I made a tricycle movement of recovering, pointing to the bicycle, and starting a salute.

"Name?"

"Flight Lieutenant Rayner, Sir. I was...."

"I can see you're a Flight Lieutenant, man! Look at me when you're addressing me!", he commanded.

I managed a fulsome salute. "Sir!".

"Hat!", he replied in disgust.

Horror of horrors, I had saluted without wearing a hat.

Although not an offence as far as I knew, it was obvious that to the Group Captain it was a meaningless gesture, the sort of thing that American Servicemen might do, but we definitely did not!

"Sorry, Sir!", I said, then retrieved my hat, put it on, saluted again, picked up my bike, whilst he glared at me and showed his own lack of etiquette by not returning the salute.

"Remember"– parting words – "uniform incomplete without hat!", and he strode away as best he could up the slippery hill.

After brushing myself down, I checked my bike, straightened the handlebars and decided that discretion was the better part of valour, therefore I would walk. I looked up the hill and saw that the Group Captain was about thirty yards away. Suddenly a snowball flew out from the side of the road, knocking the Group Captain's hat off his head. With fist raised he turned to look for a sign of the culprit then realised that I was watching down below. I came to attention and gave a smart salute, and it seemed to me that his right arm twitched a little. As I jumped on my bike, having decided it was worth the risk of another tumble to get away from the scene of the crime as quickly as possible, he was bending down to retrieve the important item of uniform. Although a distant view can deceive, the expression on his face did not seem to be a pleasant one.

As we moved further into 1945 it became obvious that it was now possible to give the war in the Far East a higher priority, and as a consequence I was a small cog in the movement of "Refors" flying boats to the Indian Ocean and points east. These were Sunderlands and Catalinas destined as reinforcements to existing squadrons, or to equip new squadrons as the Groups out there expanded. Various documents regarding this movement reached my desk for processing, and were then passed on to other departments. It seemed to generate much paperwork, which led me to wonder if the Japanese had adopted similar time-consuming methods in equipping their original overwhelming offensive. The day of the time-and-motion study had not yet dawned in the Service.

George, my Air One, had quite an interest in this aspect of the Far East campaign now being mounted, as he had been a Flight Commander on a Catalina squadron, and could expect promotion to Wing Commander at the end of his year's stint in the Staff post. He could see that if he was to be Commanding Officer of a Squadron, by the time that came along the war in Europe would probably be over, so it would mean at least a couple of years in the Far East, and he was engaged to be married before that happened. We agreed that neither he nor I was a natural 'desk-driver' – we preferred to be flying – but in his case he had made the RAF his career before the war, had risen through the ranks, and wished to continue after hostilities ceased. For my part, the activities of the strike squadrons shown on the Ops Board had revived my interest in joining them, but when I mentioned this to George he advised me to sit tight because I could expect to take over his job when he left.

By February 1945 the dispositions on the great wall map suggested that victory in Europe would not be long delayed. Belgium had been entirely freed of German forces, the offensive towards Nijmegen and the Rhine was moving forward relentlessly, and I, like many others, began to wonder what the consequences of a cessation of hostilities in Europe would be. Already, units were being prepared for transfer to the Far East, and with declining rates of loss would need little reinforcement of personnel. Paperwork concerning redundancies was even less interesting than that concerned with reinforcements, and I guessed that unless I made an attempt to return to a flying post now, it would be more difficult later.

At my interview with the personnel people, I renewed my plea for a posting to a Beaufighter or Mosquito strike squadron, but the request was given short shrift, since I had completed two operational tours and many pilots had not yet finished one. Contrary to the casualty rate among pilots which had been forecast, the percentage of losses in the later years of the war had been below the estimate, and a situation was arising in which there was a surplus. "If there is an increase in the casualty rate or if those on ops are not doing their stuff, there may be a chance later" was all I could get, and held out little hope in view of the diminishing German opposition.

There were still vacancies, I was told, on courses in Flying Training Command leading to "Qualified Flying Instructor" status. When I mentioned that I had completed about 700 hours instructional flying, presumably having been 'qualified' to do so, I was reminded of two things – firstly, I could be regarded as a qualified operational-flying instructor, which was different to a QFI, because secondly, what I would learn on a QFI course would qualify me as an instructor on any type of Service aircraft after familiarisation, whereas as an operational-instructor I was only qualified on the type of aircraft on which I had been operational. Q.E.D! Notwithstanding the evidence that I was entering a part of the RAF where, at least at that time, words spoke louder than actions, if this was the only way to return to regular flying, it would have to suffice. So far as I could tell, I was in every way the junior in the cloistered but effective administrative temple where a head lacking at least a few grey hairs was an unusual sight. Even the thought of probable promotion were I to be given George's job and with it the uninspiring paperwork, did not diminish my desire to 'drive an aircraft' again rather than a 'desk', and 'carefree youth' would take the blame if my prospects had been damaged.

I had a few days to initiate my successor into the office routine, and as he was not aircrew but from an administrative background, I convinced myself I was going at the right time if the work was to move in that direction rather than to continue a tenuous connection with aircraft in their proper medium. This conviction faltered a little a few months later when I discovered he had been promoted to Squadron Leader, but then I remembered that he was an earthbound one!

When I visited the Operations Room for the last time there was an all-pervading atmosphere of optimism, as reports of success on land, sea, and in the air filtered through; I noticed that the Rhine had been reached at Millingen, and in the revived U-boat campaign in the Western Approaches, many more U-boats were being sunk than ships lost.

No. 78 F.I. COURSE (7 F.I.S.) UPAVON, February–May, 1945

Back Row: *F/Sgt Mowberry. F/Sgt W. Bucklow. Sgt G. de Looze. F/Lt B. Dix. F/O W. Wooden. Sgt C.R. Bartlett. Sgt C.O. Birch. Sgt P.T. Lister. F/Lt A.W. Culfe.*

Middle Row: *F/Lt A. Hart. F/O G. Sim. F/O A. Fernie. F/O L.F. Swallow. F/O G.H. Bainbridge. F/Lt J.S. Brister. F/Lt A.K. Ingle,* AFC. *S/Lt R.G. Whittle,* RN. *S/Lt A.W. Sabey,* DSO, RN. *S/Lt (A.) R. H. Clarke,* RN.

Sitting: *F/O K. Johannesson. F/O H.G. Perry. F/O R.H. Burgess. S/Ldr G.W. Couzens. S/Ldr E.J.B. Langhorne. S/Ldr A. Scott. G/Capt F.A.C. Briton,* DFC. *F/Lt F.A.C. Burditt. W/C. D. Parker,* DFC. *S/Ldr T. Walls. S/Ldr Cubitt. F/Lt T. Rayner. F/O A.A. Pritchard.*

CHAPTER 17

FULL CIRCLE

The day was a harbinger of Spring in February 1945 when I reported to No 7 Flying Instructors' School – wartime equivalent of the Central Flying School – to join No 78 Flying Instructors' Course at RAF Upavon on Salisbury Plain. The station had been in constant use by the RAF since the First World War. The buildings were mostly of stone, solidly attractive, with ivy and other climbing plants adorning the walls of the Mess. There were two hangars which appeared to date from the earlier conflict, with rounded roofs instead of the saw-tooth pattern common on the larger 1930s type; later buildings were something of an anomaly, but it was altogether a gentler-looking station than the operational ones.

It soon became apparent that there was a stricter regime of instructional procedure than that by which we endowed our pupils with our experience and wisdom in operational training. At Operational Training Unit there had been a basic schedule to follow and a basic form of patter appropriate to the aircraft, on to which the instructor grafted his most important contribution , his rapport. If one approach to a pupil's problem had not succeeded we tried another.

The closely-defined stages, and the means of successfully negotiating them which the QFI course involved appeared to restrict such freedom of action. On the other hand, it was soon obvious from both lecture and demonstration, that the Course was designed to be applicable, with appropriate modification, to all aircraft. The limitations of the Oxford aircraft which were in use on the course made some of the manoeuvres which the syllabus covered an invitation to suicide if attempted; we achieved a high success rate in carrying them out theoretically!

On many of the exercises, we were detailed to fly in pairs, one to 'instruct' the other in time-honoured fashion, paying particular attention to the prescribed patter, the spoken counterpart of remembering to 'dot the i's and cross the t's', and on many such occasions my co-pilot was Squadron Leader Tom Walls, son of the well-known farceur Tom Walls senior, who, with Ralph Lynn and Robertson Hare, had made the pre-war Aldwych farces so popular. Sdn Ldr Walls was more an archaeologist than an actor, and Salisbury Plain seen from the air was such a person's paradise. We would start the exercise as detailed, but to the practised eye there was so much of interest down below that some historic site would inevitably appear, and we would examine it from different angles and heights. There was a new world below for me and I was an enthusiastic participant in the search for pre-history; I found the accompanying explanations so interesting, as even well-known landmarks such as Stonehenge were given an aura of ancient mystery as my ignorance was exposed. We justified this ancillary interest by considering ourselves to be two of the most experienced pilots on the course!

Tom was able to deduce the real implications of a few slightly different shades in the texture of the soil in a field, and in that respect we were viewing this archaeological panorama at an opportune time of year. Although green shoots were appearing in the huge fields where pasture had been turned to arable to help fill the wartime bread-basket, they were still small enough for the pattern to be more of soil than cereal, and even in meadows which would later be cut for hay, the grass was still dormant.

Whether my enthusiasm acted as 'carte blanche' for our surveys I know not, but there was tacit acceptance that flights together would include a 'history lesson'. In addition to discoveries which other eyes may not see, I was treated to explanatory visits looking for the outlines of prehistoric earthworks known as Vespasian's Camp, west of Amebury; the 600ft Codford Circle; Bratton Castle, an Iron Age hill fort near the highest point on the Plain; Yarnbury Castle, ancient earthworks just west of Winterbourne Stoke, at its southern edge; and the Neolithic earthwork, older than Stonehenge, at Woodhenge, where it was possible to see the six concentric rings of holes where wooden poles had formed a shape similar to Stonehenge before that monument was constructed.

On occasions we ventured north to the Marlborough Downs, there to see in its proper perspective the massive sarsen stones of the Avebury Circle, the most important early Bronze Age monument in Europe, and the huge conelike flat-topped hill of Silbury, 130ft high and 600ft round the base, thought to have been built about the same time as Stonehenge. From the air, it was easy to understand why the attractive town of Marlborough claims to have the widest main street in the country, and on one flight through the area we passed over Savernake Forest, in which great oaks and beeches opened on to green glades, and where the Grand Avenue is four miles long, with a canopy reminiscent of a cathedral. I determined to enjoy its pleasures on foot.

On my first succeeding day off, therefore, I ventured with a friend along the forest paths. After finding the Grand Avenue with its verdant borders and pristine boughs bursting to a green haze, we chanced along a side-path and came upon a number of deserted huts. Peering inside, it was soon obvious that the recent inhabitants had been members of the US Army – mementoes were strewn around in abundance, ranging from lanyards to steel helmets, from holsters to puttees, odd boots, scraps of paper, all in no sense of order, but cast-offs of either surplus equipment or vestiges of a hurried exit as before a Vesuvius. The leftovers in another hut suggested it had been a typing-pool: five tables, each with a typewriter remaining on it, trays, shelves of typing paper and other stationery – one almost expected a trim, nattily-uniformed typist to enter, sit at one of the desks, and begin typing Orders of the Day!

Equipment, yes; but not a sign of personnel. More investigation suggested that the Forest had served as an arms dump, for we found several empty rifle boxes and ammunition containers, the contents of which were by this time probably in use across the Channel against the foe.

A couple of weeks later, the news that there had been a loud explosion at Savernake was of no surprise when I remembered the condition of the deserted camp, although I wondered whether it had 'died' from natural causes, or by the hand of some alien intruder who had arrived too late to destroy the stores it once contained. I hoped the damage to the beautiful area would be minimal, for I had been sufficiently interested after my visit to learn more of its important history. The Forest covered more than 4,000 acres, had been in the Earl of Cardigan's family since the year after the Battle of Hastings, the Grand Avenue was by Capability Brown, and Henry VIII first met Jane Seymour when hunting there. What chance would a relatively minor explosion have of blowing all that away!

The trips with Tom Walls gave added interest to flights which were otherwise mundane and repetitive. The differences between the type of instructional technique expected, and that which had been approved at OTU, seemed almost non-existent, in spite of the stress put on such differences, and again I had cause to wonder 'if the left-hand knew what the right hand was doing?' I was annoyed with myself to find my enthusiasm declining, and whereas 'Above average' assessments in my Log Book for both operational and instructional flying had been a source of satisfaction, the inference was that there was now no further opportunity to put that experience to better use.

Two events during night-flying caused some excitement. I was flying solo on a westerly course towards an horizon where the clouds were bathed in light. No flares, no runway floodlights, nor searchlight belt, had ever produced the wide illumination now reflected under the low clouds, which grew yet brighter as I approached. I checked my position and realised I was heading towards Bristol. What calamity had overtaken the city – had a salvo of V 2 rockets penetrated so far? Quite suddenly, I could see over the ridge of a hill into the valley below, and I realised it was the city of Bath; all the street lamps were on, and in buildings everywhere lights were blazing forth. The entire population seemed to be indulging in the most brilliant illuminated display I had ever seen from the air.

Blackout regulations had been modified in the latter part of 1944, and in the Spring of 1945 were completely relaxed, but I had neither flown at night nor visited a town since the lifting of the ban. A vague recollection of a radio announcement was inadequate preparation for the thousand sources of light which lit the urban panorama. Bath and Bristol may prefer to be separate entities in daytime, but on this night, seen from the air, they were joined by chains of light strong enough to almost submerge the narrow beams of the traffic underneath. I circled round these beacons of fortitude repaid, certain in the knowledge that the citizens below were enjoying the extravaganza as much as I was.

A short time later, when again night-flying, three members of the course and I were in an aircraft with an instructor who was intent on saving time during his detail. Under his supervision we were to practise homing on the Lorenz beam, and to avoid landing after each exercise to pick up the next pilot, we were to change from one to the other whilst airborne.

During the last approach along the beam, the three of us in the cabin became aware of an agitated conversation between Don, the pilot at the controls in the left-hand seat, and the instructor to his right, which eventually led to the pair of them changing seats, with the instructor now emphatically in charge. He looked anxiously ahead, and with equal determination he peered to the side, then opened the throttles and put the aircraft into a climbing attitude. This was unexpected, as we had each completed the exercise, and were ready to return to base for a relatively early night, which was our understanding of the intention of the instructor, by virtue of his arrangement of the detail. It had been rumoured that his wife objected to being left alone at night.

From his unwelcome vantage point in the right-hand seat, Don turned to look down the cabin, and whilst the flight instruments captivated the instructor's attention, he passed an uncertain message to us by shaking his head and pointing downwards with his index finger. I went forward for clarification.

"Upavon seems to be covered in mist or low cloud which is rolling across the Plain" he shouted, then, carefully placing the words in my ear so that the instructor remained ignorant of them – "I don't think he's very happy about it!"

"Surely he'll try to go down on the beam?" I replied.

Don pointed to the altimeter; we were still climbing, though the pilot could have been unaware of it, as his gaze appeared to be fixed on the outer darkness.

I went back to the other two. Part of the course had consisted of Lorenz blind-approach training, and we assumed that each instructor would have taken the trouble to be at least as familiar with, and confident in, beam approaches as we were. Furthermore, ours was the only aircraft airborne from Upavon during that detail, so the risk of collision during an attempted approach was slight. But there was still no sign of imminent descent on an appropriate heading to reach the beam.

After another ten minutes of apparent indecision, I ventured forward and joined the instructor in surveying the dark curtain outside. Then I turned to him and attempted a smile.

COASTAL COMMAND PILOT

"What an opportunity to show how much I've learned from this course!" I said, tongue in cheek, "I'd like to have a go at getting down on the beam!" No reply.

"I'm qualified on both BABS and Lorenz," I added as an afterthought, in case he hadn't perused my log book.

He gave me a look which showed he had less difficulty in putting me down than the aircraft, and waved me away. I joined the others in the cabin, undecided as to whether Don had the advantage in his overview of action at the controls, against our mere trepidation awaiting the outcome of that action.

Eventually, the aircraft began to descend, and from the manoeuvres which followed we knew we had joined the circuit of some airfield for a visual approach and landing. Had it been a beam approach it would have been along a more direct line. On the downwind leg, through the cabin window, we could see runway lights and the red identification beacon flashing recognition letters in Morse Code.

"RAF Hullavington!" – and there, in some embarrassment and straitened circumstances, we were to spend the night. The instructor telephoned his wife, and was thereafter ill at ease; we assumed he suffered a sadistic inclination in preferring the displeasure of his wife to the pleasure of a satisfactory beam approach and landing.

When we returned to base the next morning, we found that a visiting aircraft had achieved one there the previous evening. A generous view of the eventful night could suppose that the instructor wanted to avoid the possible gaffe of losing five pilots in one aircraft crash!

The battles on the continent were moving rapidly to a climax, and each radio news bulletin offered further evidence of German collapse. On the 30th April, Hitler and his wife Eva Braun, whom he had married the previous day, committed suicide in Hitler's bunker. On 2nd May, Dönitz was proclaimed second Feuhrer of the Reich; Goebbels and his wife poisoned their six children, then took their own lives. On 3rd May, the British XII Corps ended their advance by occupying Hamburg, and Soviet forces reached the Elbe west of Berlin. The German representatives Admiral Freideburg and General Jodl signed unconditional surrender terms on the 7th May, and the 8th was celebrated by the Allies as V.E.Day.

The Celebrations in the Mess were curiously muted, as if there were many who felt some concern about what would happen next. There were still several pilots who had not yet been on operations, and the idea of an initiation which involved flying from a jungle airstrip on the other side of the world had little appeal, apart from one or two for whom a readiness to volunteer would have rapid results.

I joined a trio who had decided to celebrate in Devizes. The town and surrounding countryside had been host to the American Army, and it seemed as if every G.I. in it had jumped into his truck, car, jeep, or available machine in a race to lead the hunt for the few members of the opposite sex left in the area. We saw one jeep parked on top of another, from the aerial of which flapped the daintiest example of a lady's under-apparel; a large recovery vehicle with a small armoured-car on it; and a large staff car with four G.I's on the roof attempting a vocal accompaniment to a swaying guitar player. Most of the merrymakers had a bottle of rum in one hand, and a 'coke' in the other, taking alternate swigs from each. We attempted to move amid the throng to a pub, but before we had squeezed through a few yards, hindered by elbows moving up and down, large feet, and a heavy alcoholic vapour potent enough to ignite given a stray match, a large bottle of rum was thrust into my hand. Memory fails to indicate what happened after we effectively disposed of it; fortunately, flying was cancelled the next day.

By the end of May, the members of Course No 78 were deemed to be Qualified Flying Instructors to Central Flying School standards, and we were dispersed to various units. It was a pleasant and quite unexpected coincidence to find that I was posted to Little Rissington, where I had gained my 'wings', and which was now designated No 6 (Pilot) Advanced Flying Unit.

Full circle!

Inevitably there had been many changes since early August 1940, when with Tom Mycock I had made my last landing in an Anson on a grass airfield whilst under training. Now there were concrete runways, and Oxford aircraft using them. The pilots who were to be the objects of our instruction had qualified at Flying Training Schools overseas, and on their return to U.K. many had not flown for up to three months, so a better designation might have been simply 'Refresher Course'.

The unit was commanded by Wing Commander Thompson who, on 27th August 1941, had forced U-boat U 570 to surrender, after attacking it in a Hudson of 269 Squadron. On a generous interpretation, the station had a more relaxed atmosphere than any I had been on, so far as flying training was concerned, but there were unmistakeable signs of a hierarchical desire to return to peacetime routine. "Dining-in Night" notices appeared on the Mess Notice Board, events which required living-out officers to attend with their ladies, when Mess funds would provide appetising supplements to the meagre rations. Occasionally, the need for a parade would be invented, apparently to counter the spreading ennui. With the end of the war in Europe, and the Japanese now on the defensive in the Far East, the transfer of resources in men and materials would take several weeks, and the pilot surplus in units such as ours would grow. Indeed, to the extent that in some cases pilots who had satisfactorily completed the course were posted almost immediately to non-flying duties. Administration was taking off, aviation was on prolonged descent! It seemed increasingly likely that the Americans would bomb the Japanese into submission: their Superfortresses ranged far and wide, and on 10th July 1,022 'planes bombed Tokyo. Was it going to be over before these pilots reached the war zone?

I had been fortunate in having the option of accommodation out of camp; I was glad I took it. On several previous stations the Mess was the place to be, but here was a different atmosphere which provided little buoyancy for an old Thornaby Bag! My alternative was the Merrymouth Inn, close to the airfield, where I had a cosy little room; a tall, narrow hostelry in stained Cotswold stone on the road between Burford and Stow-on-the-Wold. Ken Strong, the landlord, also farmed the few score surrounding acres, some of which reached up to the boundary of the airfield.

In the latter part of July, when the sound of aircraft was subdued and the clatter of reaper-binders could be heard in adjoining harvest fields, the uncertain weather created a greater sense of urgency among agriculturalists than aviators. Each succeeding wartime harvest had become more critical for the 'bread-basket' of the country, and every acre of wheat was important. This, I felt, justified my preference for lending a hand on the land whenever the flying detail allowed. If I flew in the morning and had little to do after lunch, I would slip out by the sidegate and join Ken in arranging the freshly-reaped sheaves into stooks, or shaking the raindrops out after a shower, and rearranging them to dry.

On a day of shower-and-sunshine, as my pupil-pilot was on the final approach before lunch, I saw Ken driving his tractor into the field and could imagine his frustration at finding the sheaves still not fit for carting and stacking, so I had a quick lunch and joined him. We were turning the stooks to dry for the third time that week, and the urgency of the task allowed a couple of hours to pass before I realised I had missed my next flight. I hurried back to the locker room and grabbed my parachute.

"C.O. wants to see you!" a colleague announced, with a notable lack of concern.

I dumped my 'chute, put on my hat, and on entering the C.O's office gave him the smartest salute he had seen for many a day. My sense of dereliction of duty seemed to permeate my explanation, but the C.O. was in a generous mood, and evidently expected me to be also!

"I cannot disagree that the harvest is very important, but I didn't know that our unit was one of those now encouraged to supply volunteer farm-workers; we must be careful we don't do the Land Army girls out of a job!" he said, then

"Did I hear someone say that the Merrymouth purveys excellent scrumpy? Perhaps if there were one or two flagons in the Mess, we could acquire a taste for it!"

Fair exchange!

The pilot-in-waiting accepted my apology with the good grace best known to NCOs and after completing the flying detail, I hurried back to the Merrymouth for a stint behind the small, homely bar which the Inn boasted, for Mr and Mrs Strong had a rare social engagement that evening.

I had been pulling pints and serving scrumpy for about an hour when I realised there were stray horses loose in the adjoining yard, so with a word to one of the regulars who was familiar with both sides of the bar, I went to investigate. I saw a pair of hunters nibbling at the haystack across the yard, and in their epicurean search for tit-bits they had so damaged one corner that it was in imminent danger of collapse. Lacking equine expertise, my reaction was to give a mighty yell, whereupon in one sweeping movement they turned in surprise – wisps of hay still hanging from motionless jowls – they knew they were trespassing, and in a couple of strides were galloping across the road and into the lane on the opposite side.

My aim in following them – at least for a hundred breathless yards – was in the hope that they might lead me to their owner or perhaps the field from which they had strayed. The joys of their freedom had evidently not been exhausted! They had reached the long drive of a superior private hotel, into which they turned at full gallop, leaving me feeling that it was perhaps as well that I was some distance behind! I stopped, transfixed at my vantage point amid the hedgerow trees, as an elderly gentleman came through the open door of the hotel and turned to three people emerging behind him. He was obviously surprised at their gesticulations as they beat a hasty retreat back inside. I could only assume that his hearing was defective, for by this time the two galloping steeds were almost upon him. When he did turn it would not be too fanciful to suppose that he could feel the hot breath from their flaring nostrils, and his collapse, therefore, was not unexpected. Fortunately, a uniformed steward had reached the doorway in time to catch him as he fell, and with this evidence of their misdemeanour directly before them, the horses saw the error of their ways, and changed to a lower gear. At a stately trot they diverged, as did the drive; one went to the right, the other to the left, and they disappeared behind the hotel. The parting whinny of one of them sounded more like "See you at the servants' entrance!" Then I noticed the sign on the hotel board: "Facilities for Riding", and gave myself a metaphorical pat on the back.

I also disappeared and quickly transferred to my place behind the bar, trying to give the impression that I had been busy there all night. I was assisted by the feeling of exhaustion which followed a day of flying, stooking, being 'carpetted', more flying, equine pursuits, and bartending! Busy war!

As the days passed, the need for pilots diminished even further as the successes in the Far East increased, and my interest in the land grew as that in the air was restricted. On the 6th August, the first atomic bomb was dropped on Hiroshima, and the second on Nagasaki on the 8th.

COASTAL COMMAND PILOT

Six days later, the Allies announced the unconditional surrender of Japan, and VJ Day was celebrated on the 15th August 1945.

Six years previously, my Log Book showed just one hour's flying time; it now recorded well over 2,000. In the context of a wartime era, those years flew by, but the change from boyish exuberance to adult perception of reality seemed to have taken much longer. I had enjoyed working with Ken Strong, so my immediate intention was to respond to the national call to 'Lend a hand on the land', supposing that farming offered more satisfaction, at that time, than military flying – or the lack of it!

But when demobilisation leave made the break final at the end of January 1946, the lines I found in the Mess at Fair Oaks aerodrome in January 1940 –

"HOW CAN THEY KNOW THE JOY TO BE ALIVE
WHO HAVE NOT FLOWN?"

– engendered a belief that, some day, there would yet again be flying controls and instruments waiting between uplifting wings to make

"THE VERY SKY ONE'S OWN!"

1946 – down to earth on two wheels!

HUDSON COCKPIT:

1) Clock. 2) Artificial horizon. 3) Fuel pressure gauges. 4) Turn and bank indicator. 5) Synchroscope. 6) Rate-of-climb indicator. 7) Propeller controls.
8) Carburettor heat controls. 9) Supercharger controls (Marks III and V only) / Oil cooler control (Marks I, II and IV only). 10) Engine-speed indicators.
11) Gun loading handles. 12) Throttle levers. 13) Feathering buttons. 14) Boost pressure gauges. 15) Sperry control panel. 16) Fuel-air ratio gauge. 17)
Cylinder temperature gauge. 18) Air temperature indicator. 19) Cylinder temperature gauge. 20/21) Fuel contents gauges. 22) Gun firing pressure
gauge. 23) Aerofoil de-icing gauge. 24) Tail-wheel lock. 25) Bomb doors control. 26) Signal pistol cartridge rack. 27) Auto-pilot pressure gauge. 28)
Mixture controls. 29) Gyro-pilot lever. 30) Engine selector cock. 31) Cowling gills switches. 32) Flap lever. 33) Ignition switches. 34) Intercom panel.
35) Rudder trim tab. 36) Electric control panel. 37) Fuel hand pump (replaced by electric pump switch on Mark VI). 38) Brake handle. 39) Aileron trim
tab. 40) Fuel tank selector cock. 41) Elevator trim tab. 42) Undercarriage lever. 43) Identification lights switch. 44) Signalling switch box. 45) Flap
position indicator. 46) Oil cooler indicator. 47) Undercarriage indicator. 48) Oil cooler switches. 49) Compass. 50) Fuel pressure warning lights. 51)
Hyd. services pressure gauge. 52) Oil cooler indicator. 53) Hyd. pump pressure gauges. 54) Oil temperature gauges. 55) Turn and bank selector valve.
56) Altimeter valve. 57) Oil pressure gauges. 58) Vacuum pressure gauge. 58) Gun button. 60) Sensitive altimeter. 61) Bomb release button. 62) Check
altimeter or beam approach indicator. 63) Airspeed indicator. 64) Landing lamps switches. 65) Formation lights switch. 66) Navigation lights switch. 67)
Electric panel light switch. 68) Bomb compartment lights switch. 69) Cockpit lights switch. 70) Cabin lights switch. 71) Pressure-head heater switch. 72)
Generator master switches. 73) Dimmer-engine instruments. 74) Dimmer-flying instruments. 75) Fuel gauge selector cock. 76) Oxygen regulator. 77)
Propeller de-icing indicator. 77a) Pressure-head indicator light. 78) Volts/amps meters. 79) Electric master switch. 80) Tunnel gun indicator. 81) Bomb
master switch. 82) Bomb doors indicators. 83) Dimmer for cockpit lights. 84) Propeller de-icing rheostat. 85) Booster-coil button. 86) Starter button. 87)
Starter change-over switches. 88) Beam approach controls. 89) Bomb jettison control. 90) Forced landing flares controls. 91) Hyd. hand pump. 92) Fire
extinguisher control. 93) Aerofoil de-icing control. 94) Fuel priming pump. 95) Oil dilution buttons. 96) Hyd. emergency by-pass. 97) Fuel jettison
control.

Also published by Woodfield...

The following titles are all available in our unique high-quality softback format

RAF HUMOUR

Bawdy Ballads & Dirty Ditties of the RAF – A huge collection of the bawdy songs and rude recitations beloved by RAF personnel in WW2. Certain to amuse any RAF veteran. Uncensored – so strictly adults only! *"Not for the frail, the fraightfully posh or proper gels – but great fun for everyone else!"* **£9.95**

Upside Down Nothing on the Clock – Dozens of jokes and anecdotes contributed by RAF personnel from AC2s to the top brass... still one of our best sellers. *"Highly enjoyable."* **£6.00**

Upside Down Again! Our second great collection of RAF jokes, funny stories and anecdotes – a great gift for those with a high-flying sense of humour! *"Very funny indeed."* **£6.00**

Was It Like This For You? A feast of humorous reminiscences & cartoons depicting the more comical aspects of life in the RAF. *"Will bring back many happy memories. Highly recommended."* **£6.00**

MILITARY MEMOIRS & HISTORIES – THE POST-WAR PERIOD

I Have Control... by **Edward Cartner** A former RAF Parachute instructor humorously recalls the many mishaps, blunders and faux-pas of his military career. *Superb writing; very amusing indeed.* **£9.95**

Korea: We Lived They Died by **Alan Carter** Former soldier with Duke of Wellington's Regt reveals the appalling truth of front-line life for British troops in this now forgotten war. *Very funny in places too.* **£9.95**

Meteor Eject! by **Nick Carter** Former 257 Sqn pilot [1950s] recalls the early days of RAF jets and his many adventures flying Meteors, including one very lucky escape via a Mk.2 Martin-Baker ejector seat... **£9.95**

Pluck Under Fire by **John Pluck** Eventful Korean War experiences with the Middlesex Regiment **£9.95**

Return to Gan by **Michael Butler** Light-hearted account of life at RAF Gan in 1960 and the founding of 'Radio Gan'. *Will delight those who also served at this remote RAF outpost in the Indian Ocean.* **£12.00**

Tread Lightly into Danger by **Anthony Charlwood** A bomb-disposal expert's experiences in some of the world's most dangerous hotspots (Kuwait, Iraq, Lebanon, Somalia, etc) over the last 30 years. **£9.95**

The Spice of Flight by **Richard Pike** Former RAF pilot of Lightnings, Phantoms and later helicopters with 56, 43(F) & 19 Sqns delivers a fascinating account of RAF flying in the 60s & 70s. **£9.95**

Flying the Waves by **Richard Pike** The author's eventful second career as a commercial helicpter pilot involved him in many Coastguard Air/Sea Rescue operations in the Shetlands and North Sea. **£9.95**

MILITARY MEMOIRS & HISTORIES – WORLD WAR 1 & 2

2297: A POWs Story by **John Lawrence** Taken prisoner at Dunkirk, the author endured 5 years as a POW at Lamsdorf, Jagendorf, Posen and elsewhere. Very interesting & delightfully illustrated. **£6.00**

A Bird Over Berlin by **Tony Bird DFC** Lancaster pilot with 61 Sqn tells a remarkable tale of survival against all the odds during raids on the German capital. *"An almost miraculous sequence of events."* **£9.95**

A Journey from Blandford by **B.A. Jones.** The wartime exploits of this motorcycle dispatch rider/MT driver began at Blandford Camp but involved Dunkirk, the Middle East, D-Day and beyond... **£9.95**

A Lighter Shade of Pale Blue by **Reg O'Neil** A former Radar Operator recalls his WW2 service in Malta and Italy with 16004 AMES a front-line mobile radar unit. *'Interesting, informative and amusing.'* **£9.95**

A Shillingsworth of Promises by **Fred Hitchcock.** Delightfully funny and ribald memoirs of an erk during the wartime years and beyond in UK and Egypt. A very entertaining read. **£9.95**

Beaufighters BOAC & Me by **Sam Wright** – WW2 Beaufighter navigator served full tour with 254 Sqn and was later seconded to BOAC on overseas routes. *'Captures the spirit of the mighty Beaufighter'* **£9.95**

Coastal Command Pilot by **Ted Rayner.** Former Hudson pilot's outstanding account of WW2 Coastal Command operations from Thornaby, St Eval, Wick, Iceland and Greenland. **£8.00**

Cyril Wild: The Tall Man Who Never Slept by **James Bradley.** Biography of a remarkable Japanese-speaking British Army officer who helped many POWs survive on the infamous Burma railway. **£9.95**

Desert War Diary by **John Walton** Diary and photos recording the activities of the Hurricanes and personnel of 213 Squadron during WW2 in Cyprus and Egypt. *"Informative and entertaining."* **£9.95**

From Fiji to Balkan Skies by **Dennis McCaig** Spitfire/Mustang pilot recalls eventful WW2 operations over the Adriatic/Balkans with 249 Sqn in 43/44. *'A rip-roaring real-life adventure, splendidly written.'* **£9.95**

From Horses to Chieftains by **Richard Napier** An Army career from Egypt in 1935 with 8th Hussars through WW2 with 7th Armoured division (Desert Rats) and on to the 1960s is entertainingly remembered. **£9.95**

Get Some In! by **Mervyn Base** The life & times of a WW2 RAF Bomb Disposal expert **£9.95**

Just a Survivor by **Phil Potts** Former Lancaster navigator with 103 Sqn tells his remarkable tale of survival against the odds in the air and as a POW. *'An enlightening and highly agreeable account.'* **£9.95**

Memoirs of a 'Goldfish' by **Jim Burtt-Smith** The eventful wartime memoirs of a former 115 Sqn Wellington pilot, now president of the Goldfish Club, for aviators who have force-landed into water. **£9.95**

No Brylcreem, No Medals by **Jack Hambleton** – RAF MT driver's splendid account of his wartime escapades in England, Shetlands & Middle East blends comic/tragic aspects of war in uniquely entertaining way. **£8.00**

Nobody's Hero by **Bernard Hart-Hallam.** An RAF SP's extraordinary adventures with 2TAF Security Section on D-Day and beyond in France, Belgium & Germany. *"Unique and frequently surprising."* **£9.95**

Once a Cameron Highlander by **Robert Burns** Biog of Robert Burns, a Battle of the Somme veteran who lived to be 104 and became the oldest surviving Cameron Highlander. A fascinating account of his WW1 experiences, his later life in show business and his celebrity status as a centenarian. **£9.95**

Operation Pharos by **Ken Rosam** The story of the Cocos Keeling islands and of operations from the RAF's secret bomber base/staging post there during WW2. *'A fascinating slice of RAF history.'* **£9.95**

Over Hell & High Water by **Les Parsons** This WW2 navigator survived 31 ops on Lancasters with 622 Sqn, then flew Liberators in Far East with 99 Sqn. An exceptional tale of 'double jeopardy'. **£9.95**

Pacifist to Glider Pilot by **Alec Waldron** This son of Plymouth Brethren parents renounced pacifism and went on to pilot gliders at both Sicily & Arnhem. *Excellent photos.* **£9.95**

Pathfinder Force Balkans by **Geoff Curtis** Pathfinder F/Engineer saw action over Germany & Italy before baling out over Hungary. POW in Komarno, Stalags 17a & 17b. Amazing catalogue of adventures. **£9.95**

Per Ardua Pro Patria by **Dennis Wiltshire** Humour and tragedy are interwoven in these unassuming autobiographical observations of a former Lancaster Flight Engineer who later worked for NASA. **£9.95**

Ploughs, Planes & Palliasses by **Percy Carruthers** Entertaining recollections of an RAF pilot who flew Baltimores in Egypt with 223 Squadron and was later a POW at Stalag Luft 1 & 6. **£9.95**

RAF/UXB The Story of RAF Bomb Disposal Stories contributed by wartime RAF BD veterans that will surprise and educate the uninitiated. *"Amazing stories of very brave men."* **£9.95**

Railway to Runway by **Leslie Harris** Wartime diary & letters of a Halifax Observer – later killed in action with 76 Sqn in 1943 – capture the spirit of the wartime RAF as recorded by a 19 year old airman. **£9.95**

The RAF & Me by **Gordon Frost** Stirling navigator recalls ops with 570 Sqn from RAF Harwell, including 'Market-Garden' 'Varsity' and others. *'A salute to the mighty Stirling and its valiant crews.'* **£9.95**

Training for Triumph by **Tom Docherty** This encyclopaedic work contains details about every training facility operated by the RAF during World War 2. *'An impressive achievement.'* **£12.00**

Un Grand Bordel by **Norman Lee** & **Geoffrey French** – WW2 tail gunner's fascinating account of his adventures with the French Secret Army after being shot down is both funny and highly eventful. **£9.95**

UXB Vol 2 More unusual and gripping tales of bomb disposal in WW2 and after. **£9.95**

While Others Slept by **Eric Woods** The story of Bomber Command's early years WW2 by a Hampden navigator who completed a tour with 144 Squadron. *'Full of valuable historical detail.'* **£9.95**

WOMEN in WORLD WAR TWO

A WAAF at War by **Diana Lindo** Former MT driver's charming evocation of life in the WAAF will bring back happy memories to all those who also served in World War 2. *"Nostalgic and good-natured."* **£9.95**

Corduroy Days by **Josephine Duggan-Rees** Ex-Land Girl's warm-hearted and amusing recollections of wartime years spent on farms in the New Forest area. *"Funny, nostalgic and very well written."* **£9.95**

Ernie by **Celia Savage** A daughter's quest to discover the truth about the death of her RAF father, a Halifax navigator with 149 Sqn who died in WW2 when she was just 6 years old. **£9.95**

Lambs in Blue by **Rebecca Barnett.** Revealing account of the wartime lives and loves of a group of WAAFs posted to the tropical paradise of Ceylon. *"A highly congenial WW2 chronicle."* **£9.95**

Radar Days by **Gwen Arnold** Delightful evocation of life in the wartime WAAF by a former Radar Operator at Bawdsey Manor RDF Station, Suffolk. *"Amusing, charming and affectionate."* **£9.95**

Searching in the Dark by **Peggy Butler** The amusing diary of a former WAAF radar operator 1942-1946 written when she was 19 yrs old and serving at Bawdsey Manor RDF station in Suffolk **£9.95**

MEMOIRS & HISTORIES – NON-MILITARY

20th CenturyFarmers Boy by **Nick Adames** – A Sussex farmer looks back on a century of rural change and what it has meant to his own family and the county they have farmed in for 400 years.   **£9.95**

Call an Ambulance! by **Alan Crosskill** – A former ambulance driver recalls a number of light-hearted episodes from his eventful career in the 1960s/70s. Very entertaining.   **£9.95**

Harry – An Evacuee's Story by **Harry Collins**. The misadventures of a young lad evacuated from his home in Stockport UK to Canada in WW2.   **£9.95**

Just Visiting... by **Molly Corbally**. A charming, nostalgic and funny book by a former Health Visitor, who brilliantly depicts the colourful characters and entertaining incidents from her long career – from the 1940s to the 1970s – in the rural villages near Kenilworth in the West Midlands.   **£9.95**

Occupation Nurse by **Peter & Mary Birchenall**. This book records, in their own words, the unique achievement of a group of untrained young nurses who, under extremely difficult circumstances, provided health care at the Channel Island of Guernsey's only hospital during the German occupation of 1940-45.   **£9.95**

FICTION

A Trace of Calcium by **David Barnett** – A commuter comes to the aid of a young woman in trouble, becomes implicated in murder and must use all his resources to clear his name.   **£9.95**

Double Time by **David Barnett** – A light-hearted time-travel fantasy in which a bookmaker tries to use a time machine to make his fortune and improve his love-life with hilarious consequences.   **£9.95**

Last Sunset by **AA Painter** A nautical thriller set in the world of international yachting. A middle aged yachtsman becomes accidentally embroiled with smugglers, pirates and a very sexy young lady...   **£9.95**

Retribution by **Mike Jupp** A very funny comedy/fantasy novel for adults and older children, featuring bizarre goings-on in a quiet English seaside town. Brilliantly illustrated.   **£9.95**

The Cherkassy Incident by **Hunter Carlyle** A tense international thriller featuring a terrorist plot to steal nuclear missiles from a sunken Russian nuclear submarine.   **£9.95**

MISCELLANEOUS SUBJECTS

Just a Butcher's Boy by **Christopher Bolton** Charming account of small town life in the 1950s in the rural Leiston, Suffolk and idyllic summers spent with grandparents who owned the local butcher's shop.   **£5.95**

Impress of Eternity by **Paul McNamee** A personal investigation into the authenticity of the Turin Shroud. A former shcoolmaster examines the evidence and comes to a startling conclusion.   **£5.95**

Making a Successful Best Man's Speech An indispensable aid to anyone who feels nervous about making a wedding speech. Tells you what to say and how to remember it.   **£5.95**

Near & Yet So Far by **Audrey Truswell** The founder of an animal rescue charity tells charming and heart-warming tales of the rescue and rehabilitation of many four-legged friends in need.   **£9.95**

Reputedly Haunted Inns of the Chilterns & Thames Valley by **Roger Long** – A light hearted look at pubs & the paranormal in the Heart of England   **£5.95**

A Selection of London's Most Interesting Pubs by **David Gammell** – A personal selection of London's most unusual and historic hostelries with instructions how to find them.   **£5.95**

Unknown to History and Fame by **Brenda Dixon** – Charming portrait of Victorian life in the West Sussex village of Walberton via the writings of Charles Ayling, a resident of the village, whose reports on local events were a popular feature in *The West Sussex Gazette* over many years during the Victorian era.   **£9.95**

Woodfield books are available direct from the publishers by mail order as well as via all usual retail channels...

Telephone your orders to (**+44** if outside UK) **01243** 821234

Fax orders your to (**+44** if outside UK) **01243** 821757

All major credit cards accepted.

Visit our website for full details of all our titles – instant online ordering is also available at **www.woodfieldpublishing.com**

Woodfield Publishing

BABSHAM LANE ~ BOGNOR REGIS
WEST SUSSEX ~ ENGLAND
PO21 5EL

www.woodfieldpublishing.com